Late in the Day

LATE IN THE DAY

A NOVEL BY BRETT SHAPIRO

atmosphere press

© 2022 Brett Shapiro

Published by Atmosphere Press

Cover design by Senhor Tocas

No part of this book may be reproduced without permission from the author except in brief quotations and in reviews. This is a work of fiction, and any resemblance to real places, persons, or events is entirely coincidental.

Atmospherepress.com

...What makes the engine go?
Desire, desire, desire.
The longing for the dance
stirs in the buried life.
One season only,
and it's done.
So let the battered old willow
thrash against the windowpanes
and the house timbers creak.
Darling, do you remember
the man you married? Touch me,
remind me who I am.

    From "Touch Me" - Stanley Kunitz 1990

1

Hank Bauer looked at his rotary watch. Forty-five seconds and time to check the pizza. He was hopeful that this time the cheese would be bubbling but not yet brown, and laced with rivulets of orange drippings that oozed from the disks of pepperoni distributed to offer four to five disks per slice. What he wasn't sure about, however, was the crust. Tricky business, that. He wanted its edges to bubble and, as they cooled, to form crispy air pockets. Marilyn, his wife, used yeast to produce that effect, but he couldn't remember whether it was a special kind or a special brand, or both. She was full of such expertise, which always struck him as being exclusive privileges of her domain—the house and the two children—just as he had his expertise in providing for them away from the house for eight hours each day at the aerospace company. She didn't know a stitch about thermodynamics, and he was clueless about bubbling pizza dough. He was trying.

Where was she when he needed her? He knew where she was. It was a place that he had heard about from the time he was a child, an exotic place, a beautiful place, a safe place, or so he had been told year after year, sermon after sermon. He too dreamed of going there one day. They'd gone to the top of the Eiffel Tower together (before their two boys were born), to the bottom of the Grand Canyon (when the boys were no higher than their waist). They'd almost made it to the Great Wall of China (when the boys were old enough to manage on their own) but the tour was canceled several weeks before departure because not enough people had signed up. This place was a place where, it had been determined (perhaps pre-determined, he thought), she needed to "go it" alone. At least for now. He missed her. He knew that she had to be enjoying herself there and thinking about him as much as he thought about her—because she deserved to be thought about but also because he missed her. And so a portion of happiness was mixed in with the larger sadness of missing her to produce a sense of contentment and patience. He trusted that ultimately, and before long, he would join her there, for a kind of second honeymoon, but instead of the majesty and the fury of Niagara Falls (so apt a place for those about to consummate their vows in a physical act that, as good Christians, was officially and finally permissible) they would be in a softer, safer and eternal place which many, like he, called Heaven.

He switched on the oven light and bent over, pushing his red and white checkered apron to the side so that it didn't block the view inside the oven window. Sure enough, the crust was puffed up but not bubbling on its edges. And it wouldn't bubble, because there was no more time to leave it in the oven: The pizza was ready and had to be pulled out before bits of crust, cheese and pepperoni started to burn. He grabbed the two green oven mitts that he had placed on the walnut-look Formica counter, slowly extracted the round aluminum pizza tray from the middle rack, and placed it on the stove, where the bubblings and swellings subsided as the fragrance of oregano, cheese, dough and pepperoni filled the air of the small, functional kitchen.

I'll perfect the crust one day, he thought, as he dabbed the entire surface of the pizza with three layers of paper towel in order to remove the excess grease. His doctor had recently told him that his cholesterol was too high. Nothing serious, but slightly out of range. How he missed Marilyn, even after three years. Still, at seventy-three years old, death could wait. How often, sermon after sermon, he'd heard that death marked the beginning of an eternity of peace and serenity, for those who deserved it. How often, especially during adolescence, had he scoffed at what he then considered a lame idea, wanting nothing more than to slip out from the church and tear into the surrounding fields as he undid the Windsor knot of his necktie and screamed forbidden expressions: "God dammit!", "Jesus Christ!", "Holy crap!". He didn't cut loose. Week after week, year after year, he sat in the same pew, between his mother and father; and slowly the lame idea entered into his blood and soul like a life-sustaining infusion. Marilyn was the first and only woman he'd kissed, embraced, explored, penetrated. And now he felt lonely, desolate at times, but always patient.

Hank looked younger than his years. He was graced with a slender build from the time he was a child growing up outside of Cleveland, and he managed without any exertion to maintain upright shoulders and back, firm legs, a springy gait and a head of light brown hair—white only at the close-cropped sideburns and further up around the temples—that showed general signs of thinning but not of etching an explicit bald patch. The skin on his face had taken on a healthy tan from the twenty years since he, Marilyn and their two boys moved from their 4/3 split-level in a Cleveland suburb to a 3/2 ranch in Atlantique, a working-class town in Florida not far from the beach, where the sun's rays were to be guarded against even in winter. Lines had accrued on his face, perhaps because of the sun, perhaps a matter of genes. They weren't deep, but they were many and could have been interpreted as a fatigue that comes with age had it not been for his blue-gray eyes (more blue than gray), whose glimmer and expression of wonderment at things both large and small suggested someone who was far from growing weary of carrying out his days of living. He took little note of the way the passing of time inscribed itself on his body. It wasn't a necessary reminder. His dead wife was enough. He missed the anchor of her so terribly that it made his eyes well up, even in moments like this one—placing the pizza on the stove top to cool, resigning himself to the fact that the edges of the crust would once again not have bubbles and asking himself what Marilyn's secret was.

It was absurdly early in the morning. In fact, it could still be considered night: four o'clock. He decided that the pizza experiment was to be conducted at this hour, before he headed to the beach for his sunrise walk and two or three hours of fishing and returned home for the weekly Skype call from his son Matthew and the grandchildren, who would make a cameo appearance and compete to hog the screen and brag about their antics of the week. He wouldn't dream of missing that. He was a family man, and those few minutes gave him a respite from a certain weight he carried around, although the weight doubled down as soon as the "end call" key was pushed and his family disappeared. It annoyed him that his younger son, Jonathan, insisted on not having a regular time and day to call. "Dad, let's get in touch when we have something we want to share," Jonathan said.

When the cheese on the pizza looked cooled and firm enough to be cut without messy strings dangling from the knife, he set to work making the traditional eight slices: two to be left on the tray and spatula-ed later onto a plate for lunch, two to be placed in the fridge for dinner or tomorrow's lunch, and the remaining four to be placed in two zip-lock bags of two each and stored in the freezer for another time. He checked his white t-shirt: not a single stain. He was disappointed. If his fingers made some blotch of cheese or pepperoni on the white all-cotton fabric, he could have taken off the t-shirt and thrown it in the washing machine, which needed only one or two more items to justify his running the cycle, thus relieving him of trying to figure out how to consume a bite of another flavorless day.

He grabbed his rod from the garage and left the house through the front door. He kept the door unlocked, which he did whenever he left home on foot, since he kept his 2009 silver Honda Accord in the driveway to suggest that someone was at home. Who would break into an occupied home? And who would break into an old car? He'd thought about trading it in for a new one, as he did every eight to ten years when he and Marilyn were busy raising their children and taking road trips for their vacations. But such times were gone. He used the car to run local errands, and it still ran like a dream. He couldn't imagine packing it with ice chests and tents to drive thousands of miles to see a canyon or a waterfall. Yes, those times were gone.

The neighborhood was a safe one, not like the older beachside neighborhoods of Atlantique whose residents had picked up bungalows for a song back in the day so they could spend their days surfing and have a shelter to return to, without paying attention to the upkeep that would be required when their roof started to leak or their windows spawned hairline cracks from seasons of hurricanes. The residents of those neighborhoods got by with word-of-mouth yard work, car repair, plumbing emergencies. Many ended up dealing drugs. It didn't matter much to them, as long as they could hit the beach at a few minutes' notice when the waves were right. In those neighborhoods, police cars patrolled regularly, but not enough to prevent regular incidents of domestic violence, homicide and an occasional murder. Hank's neighborhood was in the newer part of Atlantique, filled with widows, widowers and other retirees, most of whom had relocated from colder climates to enjoy life in 55+ apartment and townhouse complexes spread out among ample and manicured lawns that were well lit at night. "We'll be happy here," he told Marilyn.

"We're already happy, praise be He," she said. "We'll be safe here."

Walking down his driveway, he thought about catching a pompano, about Marilyn and the boys, and about Jesus. He enjoyed the ritual of fishing: the preparation of the rods, the casting, and especially the waiting and watching for the pull on the line. The sequence didn't require so much concentration that he couldn't daydream, but not too little that his daydreams pushed their way into dark places. It was a good way for him to pass the time; or rather, as he decided shortly after his wife's death, for the infinite continuum of time to pass through him. In addition, he might run into one or more of the other regular fishers and strike up a conversation, about baits and weights and the like. He enjoyed that.

When he arrived at the beach, he could tell that it wasn't a good day for fishing. A thick layer of brown seaweed was floating along a band of ocean closest to where it breaks on the sand; there wasn't a fisher in sight, let alone his buddy Cap'n Tommy. Disappointed, he left his gear at the beach entrance and walked along the shoreline, gazing out toward the horizon as he softly sang one of his favorite verses from *Song of Solomon:*

"...Rise up, my love, my fair one, and come away. For, lo, the winter is past, the rain is over and gone; the flowers appear on the earth; the time of the singing bird is come, and the voice of the turtle is heard in our land; the fig tree puts forth her green figs, and the vines in blossom give their scent. Arise, my love, my fair one, and come away. O my dove, who art in the

clefts of the rock, in the secret places of the cliff, let me see thy countenance, let me hear thy voice..."

After he finished the verse, he thought about the man on his favorite radio program who spoke about how he'd come back to God and how the man said there were three things: nature, classical music, and romantic love. Hank didn't remember the order in which the man named these three things (or whether there was any particular order), and he didn't remember much of what the man said afterward. He remembered what he thought about after the man finished speaking. It had to do with overwhelming powers—of things greater than the entirety of humankind, of creative acts of individuals, and of connections between two people. At the same time, it had to do with humility. And it had to do with the terrible feeling of being grateful but with no one to thank, and to be awed but with nothing to worship.

"Good morning!"

He turned to his right. A middle-aged woman waved to him. He could see her smile and feel her ease as she stood ankle-deep in the water, fancy camera strung over her shoulder, long gray hair let loose to ride the breeze. Behind her and the dunes was a house that had been uninhabited and in disrepair since he didn't remember when. A long time. He ventured a smile, but one that was too tentative for her to be able to notice from the distance. Then he waved back to her and continued on his way.

2

Seth Erlich lifted his head from the two pillows underneath it, cracked open one eye and peered at the illuminated digital clock on the night table: four-fifty-nine in the morning, just enough time to reach over and flick the alarm button off before the soft but persistent buzzing began at five. Although he always set his alarm, he couldn't remember when, if ever, it had gone off to wake him up, and this fact continued to please him. It suggested an enthusiasm for another day, empty or full as it might end up being, and a genuine desire to watch the natural world slowly awaken before the hubbub of human enterprise set in and broke the spell. Seth became a morning person when he moved out of his parents' house in the suburbs of Pittsburgh (where his mother would lure him to wakefulness with the promise of eggs and bacon or, even better, pancakes before pushing him off to catch the school bus) to go to college. In the decades between the suburbs of Pittsburgh and this quiet beachside community, he lived in some of the larger cities of the globe—New York, Paris, Jerusalem—and assumed that his involuntary early rising had more to do with urban noise and its insistence on progress and ambition ("Get going! You're behind! You're missing out!

Others are ahead of you!") than with the appeal of simple sunrise beach walks with his black lab, Winston. He changed his mind. He simply looked forward to the day, whatever it might bring, and always had.

He reached over in the dark to feel his way to the alarm button and switch it off, and saw in the darkness the outlines of the large lithograph of Manhattan he mounted on the wall. How did I end up in Florida, he thought, the last place on earth where I would have imagined that I would have ended up? It was more of a light refrain than a serious consideration, since, when all was said and done, the question didn't provoke him. Winston slowly rose from his side of the bed as soon as Seth reached for the clock. He jumped off, tail wagging. Seth rose too and peeled off his pajama top, having abandoned pajama bottoms in his twenties. Winston knew the routine: the plumping of the pillows signified that the mesh harness would soon be positioned around his neck and strapped around his torso, the retractable leash hooked onto the harness, and off they would go for two hours at the beach.

"Soon, *mein shayneh hindt*." As Seth was smoothing out the top sheet with his right hand, he felt a damp blotch on the fitted sheet and remembered that he had sex a few hours ago, of the type that he considered the ideal encounter: quick, to the point, uncomplicated by conversation. He didn't know the man's name and didn't really care. At the age of sixty-three, he still couldn't get enough of attractive men showing up at his house to strip down and release their animal instincts and scents with him and because of him. It didn't happen often. Most of the men on the hook-up site were either rent boys or closeted married men who satisfied themselves with a hot chat and a fantasy. It also didn't happen often, he knew, because he was sixty-three, hardly the first-tier object of desire for a hook-up. But it did happen enough to make him feel that he was still in play, although he also felt that the supply would soon be running low, and then out.

More often than not, when he closed the screen door after saying good-bye to an encounter and watched him walk down the driveway to get into his car, his thoughts turned to Yoni, his partner of twenty-five years and the reason he stayed on in Israel for the first twenty of them before they moved to New York, where the relationship began to fray. Moments of thinking about Yoni happened less and less as each day went by. There were even strings of days when he realized that he hadn't thought about Yoni at all and came to understand with relief and with sadness that yet another intensity in his life, one of the longest of them, was losing its bumps and ridges. At sixty-three, how many bumps and ridges did he want to have persist? He was good-looking enough. He stood at six-foot-one, weighed one-hundred and sixty-five pounds, although his six-pack had long since vanished, kept his dirty-blond hair buzzed down to his nicely shaped skull, had white teeth, and young hands and skin. He loved to play the "How old do you think I am" game at some point during those encounters where some conversation happened to leak out, eagerly awaiting the usual underestimation of his age. It gave him hope. At the same time, he thought: such silliness.

Winston rested his chin on the mattress, staring at his master with patient and unflinching devotion. Seth patted him on the head, "Getting there, *bubelah*. Almost, ole' buddy."

He went down the dark corridor to the kitchen, where he pushed the stainless-steel button to start the coffee brewing in the Mr. Coffee that he set up the night before. He then proceeded to the desk in his living room to turn on the computer. As coffee and computer were humming to wakefulness, he went into the bathroom to pee, splash cold water on his face and neck, and shave those parts of his face above and below his white moustache and goatee that he liked to keep unstubbled. By the time he finished shaving and drying his face, the coffee and computer were ready for the day ahead—an act of perfectly timed choreography that gave him no end of satisfaction. Winston lay by the front door, waiting for the wee bit of time that his master needed to have elapse before the two of them would walk down the street and head to the beach, where Seth would unleash him and let him run freely, although the dog never strayed more than a few feet from his master, and even then without first turning his head around to look at the distance that he created and to glean the approval that Seth indicated by widening his blue eyes and saying, "T'sokay!"

The dog and the sporadic sexual encounters carried Seth through the demands and the tedium of the day, day by day. He didn't miss Yoni, but he missed the habit of Yoni and their proudly unremarkable ability to carry on like any couple that carries on long enough to enable their disturbances, private and relational, petty and otherwise, to take root and push through, above and below the surface. He wanted to carry on. He did. But his desire to not carry on was greater, and in the end it won. He resigned himself to this victory with a sense of defeat and doubt. Should I have tried harder? And what exactly should I have tried harder at?

Winston was circling by the front door. Sips of coffee had been drunk. The requisite few minutes had been spent in front of the computer to take stock of incoming emails. The time was approaching. His tail was on the ready to rise and shine.

"Get over here, you. Harness time."

Winston's long black tail arced upward and began to wag furiously. His bladder was full, his nose was aching to smell all that there was to smell outside under the still-dark sky, his master by his side.

"Let's go to the beach, you schmoo!" Winston lowered his head to accept the harness around his neck, as if it were some medallion being bestowed upon him for heroic deeds. Seth patted him on the head, and off they went. Seth kept pace with the dog so that the leash didn't pull. He believed in giving Winston a sense of freedom, even if it meant stopping for an entire minute as Winston's nose, which he referred to as "the black olive," fixated on a leaf or a blade of grass before determining whether it warranted a leg-lift and trickle. Winston could lead the way. The destination was clear to both, and there was no hurry. It was only 5:30 in the morning.

    Seth considered many times shaving off his goatee and moustache. Part of him thought that removing all the white from his face would make him look younger, but he also thought that the trim facial hair made him look rugged and sexy. Besides, the moustache retained the smell of sex hours after he and the strange man who ended up in his bed had put their clothes back on, walked to the front door, exchanged a curt "Thanks" or "Let's get together again" and returned to their life. It was that smell on his moustache that made him recall that he'd had sex just a few hours ago. He didn't remember the details. He'd downed two shots of tequila before the unknown guest arrived, just in case the chemical reaction wasn't strong enough; the after-smell on his moustache was good, and he felt good. "Let's go, buddy!"

    As they walked to the beach, two residential blocks away, he took his ritualistic ten deep breaths, pushing his lungs to their maximum limit of expansion and compression, and feeling with each set of deep-breathing a loosening up of his body, especially his back and shoulders, which he tended to keep unnaturally upright in his crusade to ward off the sloped-back and stooped-shoulder syndromes of most men in their sixties. At this hour, the streets were dark and deserted. No one was there to witness his youthful frame reveal its years as he let his muscles relax. And no one was there to share with him the slow creep of loneliness that spread like a mild ache as, with each unnatural breath, he let his body and mind revert to their natural contours. Loneliness, like his Jewishness, was always there. While neither ruled over him, they accompanied him everywhere, like his blue eyes and long lashes. He grappled with his loneliness from time to time, like when he had casual sex and felt guilty afterward; and with his Jewishness, like when, as a child, he begged his mother to buy the cupcakes with blue icing and she scoffed at him, saying, "*Feh. Goyishe dreck*," while he marveled at their brilliant colors and felt that his mother and the Jewishness in his life were unfair. All in all, he was unperturbed by the history of his Jewishness and the condition of his loneliness. They were facts of his being and he learned to use them to his advantage. His loneliness carved out pathways to thoughts and things that he felt were important; his Jewishness made him feel special, privileged and, dare he say, among the chosen.

Not always, however. Arriving at the beach after he completed his deep-breathing and the musky scent on his moustache was barely discernable, he felt the mild ache again. Still, he thought as he looked at the seascape in front of him and its promise of a technicolor sky, his "to do" list was sufficient for the day to be gotten through with a nominal sense of accomplishment. Life was good. When his feet touched upon the sand, he unhooked Winston's leash, removed his flip-flops and tucked them into the deep side-pockets of his twenty-nine-inch waist cargo shorts. The dog dashed off in a frenzied tail-wagging dervish toward the thin band of seaweed bordering the shoreline and started sniffing and clawing at the small puncture holes made in the sand by the crabs. The sky was beginning to lighten, and he saw a few cumulus clouds at the point on the horizon where the sun would poke out at any moment. From the look of things—the right kinds of cloud formations in the right positions above the seascape—there would soon be an explosion of pinks, oranges and yellows overhead to proclaim another cycle. The woman with the camera was there as well, in the distance, in front of the abandoned house. How lovely it would be if someone bought it and fixed it up, he thought, as he watched the woman feel her way through her large army-green case strapped over her shoulder to extract the proper lens, without needing to shift her gaze from the evolving tableau in front of and above her. Here was someone who knew what she was doing. She would capture the dawn of another day. He slowed his pace so as not to intrude upon the awe or religion that summoned her each morning to that spot. Winston was tormenting a sand crab that poked out from a hole. One day, Seth thought, I'll approach her, say hi, and see what happens. Not today, though.

3

Honey Cavanaugh grabbed her key chain off the foyer table and the camera strap looped around a hook above it. Underneath the table near the floor molding was a night-light, the only illumination in the house at an hour like this. She convinced Glen to put one there, to guide her through the waning of the night and the dawn of a new day. She was an early riser and didn't want to stumble when she woke up in the dark and, after slapping on some clothes, headed down the hallway to get the keys and camera. Once she stepped outside the house, the faint light coming from the east would be enough for her to find her way. Each day of each season, she had to adjust her timing incrementally to get it just right. She knew how to time certain things.

How nice it would be if Glen came with her once, she thought as she crossed the threshold and closed the front door behind her, pausing to hear the clicking sound of the latch to signal that the door wasn't ajar. She didn't lock the door with a key. When her husband was in the house, she didn't feel the need to, even if he was asleep or playing his video games or doing who knows what else in the back room. If he came with her, just once, they could stroll along the beach and watch the sun come up together. Maybe one of them would go so far as to extend a hand to clasp the hand of the other as they went about being together, in the way they'd joined hands everywhere in the first years of their marriage. She longed to hold his hand again. It would be dry and scaly, and she'd have to ignore the calluses where his plumped fingers met his palm. Even so, she thought, the interlacing of their fingers might rekindle an intimacy and passion that once seemed inextinguishable. Such a long time ago, that was. About the time when Glen's snoring became so disruptive they agreed to sleep in separate bedrooms every other day, then during the entire work week, then always. That's how the glue of intimacy dries out, she thought as she stood on the front porch cupping the camera with one hand so that it wouldn't knock against the side of her ample breast. When was the last time they held hands? She couldn't recall. And kissed? Bah! After forty years of marriage and more than thirty of raising children, the most he could muster was the occasional peck on her cheek or forehead when they found themselves bumping into each other in the house as they went about their business. She felt slighted by those pecks. They required so little of him and satisfied even less in her. "That's it?" she asked herself each time his mouth poked against her cheek or forehead like a chicken scavenging for seeds, and she understood, once again, that these kisses of his were the gestures of an indifferent coward, not an ardent lover. They weren't intended to arouse her carnal desires and draw them into each other, but simply to placate her so that they could maintain their distance. "Lip service," she said out loud as she reached the end of the driveway and turned left, toward the ocean.

    She didn't set an alarm clock before she got into bed. She wasn't the type to roll over in the thick of the darkness in hopes of drifting off for just a while longer. She looked forward to being awake. She preferred the things that happened when her eyes were open, even if sometimes they weren't so pleasant. The prospect of waking up excited her every time her body began to pull her out of her deep slumber and cause her to lift an eyelid, shift her arms and legs, fluff up the pillows, uncover herself, and rise to face the day. In the days when she and her husband shared the bed, he turned away from her after the sex was over, or when he wasn't in the mood for sex. The turning created a slender strip of space between them. He felt so far away and she had trouble falling asleep, undecided between inching her way toward him or lying there waiting for him to turn around and touch her, if only for an instant. When he gained all that weight, his body had an unpleasant smell at night, metallic and gamey. Still, she wished that he would shift over to her side from time to time, if only to let her know that he wanted her. But he didn't. She wished his eyes would meet hers whenever he gave her those insufferable pecks on the cheek. But they didn't.

When they started sleeping apart because of Glen's snoring, he bought her a camera, a Polaroid Instamatic. "What's the occasion?" she asked after she'd removed the gift box lid.

"As if I'd forget," he said. "Happy birthday."

He intercepted as she reached into the box and worked the camera out from the lavender-colored tissue. He held it up to his face. "Hold still," he told her. He focused long and hard on her. She wasn't used to it. It felt uncomfortable, but after a few clicks she loosened up and began shifting her pose. At one point she fluffed her hair; at another, she pushed up the underside of her bra. He too repositioned the camera at different angles and clicked away as he fixed on her through the lens. He continued in this way for what seemed to her like a delicious eternity.

"There you go," he said as he handed the camera to her. "See how easy it is?" He gave her a peck on the cheek. His lips were pursed, rough and dry.

The next morning, she took the camera to the film-developing department of the pharmacy down the street. The film counter was at the end of the Pain Relief aisle. She placed her camera on the counter. "How long will it take?" she asked the clerk.

He opened the back of the camera and looked at her quizzically. "I'd say about forever, and maybe then some."

"What do you mean?"

He picked up the open camera and turned its back toward her. "Ma'am, there's no film inside."

* * * *

She loved the camera. She loved taking pictures of random arrangements of objects on the beach that she came upon when she happened to look down at the sand: a shell sticking out from under an abandoned flip-flop; a strand of sargassum seaweed braided with washed-up nylon fishing line; an empty egg of a turtle hatchling resting on a forgotten half-full bottle of Banana Boat sunscreen. She snapped away with fervor at these incongruities of coupling. She didn't take pictures of Glen. She tried once. It made her feel uncomfortable and sad to have to look at him so long and hard through the lens while he just stood there putting up with it until she said, "Got it, thanks," and he could resume going about his business.

When the children were born and she was running on empty by dinner time, she still woke up early. The notion of catching up on sleep didn't make much sense to her. "How can you recover something that is already gone?" she asked herself at those moments of the day when her body was craving repose but her mind was still buzzing away with all that needed to be done. For her, that hour or two in the morning, so brimming over with stillness and quiet, was invigorating, however much fatigue resulted as the day wore on, especially with two toddlers underfoot.

The children adored having their picture taken, especially when they made a grand entrance in the living room all dressed up in a composite of Mommy and Daddy's apparel that they'd pulled out of drawers and closets. Honey had albums filled with photos of Cal and Aurora. Her favorite was the one of Cal lost in her blue cocktail dress and Aurora squeezed into one leg of a pair of Glen's boxers. Both of them had drawn gaucho-style mustaches above their upper lip. From the color, she knew they'd used her eyebrow pencil. Honey couldn't help but think, "What are they after with this premeditated cuteness?" She snapped away nonetheless, knowing that the day would come when they would no longer play dress-up and wait to have their picture taken; that the day would come when instead they would invent any reason to roll their eyes at her with an arrogance meant to hurt that was a specialty of adolescents, as if to say, "What do you know about anything? You're a fool. You embarrass me." She knew they wouldn't mean it. They couldn't. She understood. She was young once. When the day came, and repeated itself for years, she did understand. But the hurt devastated her every time.

She slipped her key chain into her pocket and set off, looking into the sky as soon as she heard the front-door latch click. The stars were out in full force. "No chance of rain this morning," she whispered. She had nothing against rain, except when she was walking in the dark and had no way of predicting how the rain would progress, and for how long. But this morning the coast was clear. "Full steam ahead to the beach," she thought. "Free and easy." She made a beeline for her choice piece of driftwood, stopping only to read the billboard on the side of the road: "Welcome to Atlantique". She laughed. "What's with the 'que'?" The three letters jumped at her whenever she waited at the crosswalk. She picked up her camera and took a picture of the billboard. The light wasn't ideal and there was no particular sense of composition or incongruity to what she observed through the lens, but she took a picture anyway. "Let's see how it turns out," she thought as she waited for the light to change and wondered whether those two men would be at the beach again. "They seem nice enough," she said to herself. "Definitely not the homeless type."

4

Atlantique marked the midpoint between Cape Canaveral and Palm Beach. It was a laid-back beach town off the radar to vacationers, except those who came to visit a family member or friend, especially in winter. A high-rise condo popped up here and there on the beach, as did a low-rise motel, but for the most part the beaches offered no amenities except sand and ocean. The downtown area organized street fairs that spawned the same food and beer trucks and smattering of local musicians. The public-beach-access parking lots set up art festivals, where the locals exhibited objects made of shells and driftwood, or paintings of seascapes in violent colors. Atlantique was a sleepy town with the sleepy ambition to remain so. Mood-lifting weather, good surf, local hangouts with names like Bunky's and Ichabod's, seafood shanties that offered the catch of the day fried in questionable oil and served in plastic lattice-work baskets. Those who lived here aspired to nothing more, and those few who may have had aspirations when they moved here quickly understood that their aspirations would need to be tempered in exchange for the balmy air, abundant sunshine and endless stretches of sand and sea. The torpor of the tropics.

* * * *

"What do you think, Marilyn?"

"It's like a dream."

When Hank's engineering firm offered him the transfer, there was little to discuss. He and Marilyn rejoiced at the prospect and amended their daily prayer at dinner to include a divine thanks for being blessed with such a golden, sun-drenched opportunity. They also understood it to mean leaving the aunts and uncles and cousins who were part of the fabric of their daily life. "They'll come and visit," Hank told her. "Our friends will too. We have room. There's the beach. Disney World is only an hour away. It's still warm in December. They'll come."

Of the four three-bedroom homes they shortlisted, they chose the one that had a homeowners' association and community pool.

"It might be a little cramped," Hank said.

"I like the sense of community," Marilyn replied. "Look how beautifully the common spaces are maintained. That says something. We can make do with less space. The boys will be outdoors more." The company arranged to have their belongings transported. Everything fit easily.

"How about that," Hank said as they finished walking through the furnished house. "Everything fits."

Marilyn scrutinized the bulky mahogany dining room set that she'd inherited from her mother, who'd inherited it from her grandmother. How dark and heavy, she thought. Like the rest of the furniture. But it would work for now. As a matter of fact, it would still work years from now when their second boy would head off to university, visiting them frequently but never again living at home since that's how things went these days.

They finished their inspection on the "lanai," a word

they'd never come across before looking at real estate in Florida. The ample, screened-in space had mint-green cement flooring and unpainted brick planters at each corner. They had no outdoor furniture in Cleveland, except for two chaise lounges that they used when they went to Lake Erie with the boys on day trips in summer.

"It's snug. A good home," Hank said to his wife.

"Yes," she replied. "Homey."

"We'll get a nice table and chairs for the lanai so we can eat outside. Maybe I'll look into getting a gas grill."

"Yes." She hesitated. "A gas grill. That will be nice."

He knew what she was thinking. He stepped behind her, placed his hands on her shoulders and massaged them above the collar bone. "We'll fit. We'll make it work."

* * * *

"You'll end up there permanently one day. You'll see. It's in your blood." Seth expected remarks like these every time he went to visit to his parents. Each year the number of visits increased. Flights from New York to Florida were cheap and plentiful. There were palm trees. Everything he needed for a few weeks—shorts, tee-shirts, toiletries—could fit into the backpack he used to traipse around Manhattan for business or leisure.

"Over my dead body." He suspected his friends might be right. They could afford to know him better than he knew himself. The price they would pay would be far less than the price Seth would have to pay for knowing himself. He would be the one leaving Yoni, not them. They'd only have to put up with him afterward when it was convenient, and hopefully to give support. He, on the other hand, would have to put up with himself always. No getting around that, he knew. And with another failed relationship added to the list. Maybe it would be different in Florida, what with the heat and humidity, the men perpetually clad in shorts and flip-flops.

His friends saw the end of his relationship with Yoni coming, even after twenty-five years. They were good years. Years without serious issues that festered, but years in which the relationship had crusted into a habit; a pleasant one, he thought, but a habit nevertheless. As much as Yoni liked his parents-in-law, Seth was relieved when Yoni told him, "I'll stay back this time, if you don't mind?" and he replied, "That's fine. I understand." He didn't mind at all. He understood that they were straying from each other and wouldn't be able to find their way back.

"*Shpilkes.*" That's what Yoni labeled Seth's departures for Florida. Seth appreciated his humor. Yes, let's keep it light. You understand why I'm leaving. I understand why you're not putting up a fight. They kept it light, but it still hurt.

By the time he made the definitive move, his mother had been dead for two years, his father was rapidly deteriorating, and his domestic partnership with Yoni was spent. "You can keep everything. I'll just take my clothes and my books and my office stuff."

"Nothing of ours?" Yoni asked.

"Not right now," he said. "Maybe later." He got his Florida real estate license to carry on with the business of making money. In the process, he found a modest 3/2 move-in bungalow that was two blocks from the beach and a twenty-minute drive to his father's house. With the exception of the hallway leading to the bedrooms and one bathroom, the interior was open-space, a far cry from years of living with Yoni in a one-bedroom apartment carved out of what had once been the 600 square foot dining room of a 4,500 square foot apartment on Riverside Drive above 115th Street that claimed the entire fourth floor. Here in the house in Atlantique, there was a sweet front and back yard, a large pool recently resurfaced with indigo blue tile surrounded by a large deck that housed a pergola near the pool's left perimeter. The seduction of a tripling of indoor space and the existence of outdoor space, with a pool to boot, was irresistible.

"You'll come visit," was all he had to say to his friends and to Yoni as he stepped into the cab and blew kisses. "I'll come back to visit, too, as soon as I get the situation with my dad in order." His father died one month after the move, before Seth could consult with him about the best place to buy a lawn mower and pool net. He contacted his father's congregation to assemble a critical mass for the simultaneous house-warming and *kaddish* in his open-space living room. David, a friend of his father's whom Seth had never met, obliged to preside. Standing at the head of the newly purchased translucent glass dining room table laden with assorted delicatessen, the elderly stranger recited the kaddish in a monotone that suggested a well-worn recitation:

> *Yitgadal v'yitkadash sh'mei raba.*
> *B'alma di v'ra chirutei,*
> *v'yamlich malchutei,*
> *b'chayeichon uv'yomeichon*
> *uv'chayei d'chol beit Yisrael,*
> *baagala uviz'man kariv. V'im'ru: Amen.*

Seth stood at the other end of the table, reading the translation that he had printed out in advance for those, like him, who didn't read or understand Hebrew:

> *Exalted and hallowed be God's great name*
> *in the world which God created, according to plan.*
> *May God's majesty be revealed in the days of our lifetime*
> *and the life of all Israel—speedily, imminently, to which*
>   *we say Amen.*
> *Blessed be God's great name to all eternity.*

Blessed, praised, honored, exalted, extolled, glorified,
    adored, and lauded
be the name of the Holy Blessed One, beyond all earthly
    words and songs of blessing,
praise, and comfort. To which we say Amen.
May there be abundant peace from heaven, and life, for
    us and all Israel,
to which we say Amen.
May the One who creates harmony on high, bring peace
    to us and to all Israel.
To which we say Amen.

"Amen."

He lowered his copy of the translation and looked around the table at his father's Florida friends. All of the women were dolled up for the affair. Most of the men were wearing shorts and sandals. "If Yoni were here," he thought as he helped himself to some kippered salmon, "oh the character assassinations we could do." But Yoni wasn't present. He'd called Seth the night before. "A work emergency," he explained. "No problem," Seth said.

He surveyed the room again. He knew none of these senior citizens who peopled the daily life of his father and were filling their plates with the free food. One by one, they approached him and paid their respects with a feeble handshake as they held their plate with their free hand. "I've heard so much about you." "I'm so sorry for your loss." "A nice spread." "Your father was a good man. And what a sense of humor." "Lovely home." "Oy, Arthur. Such a mensch." "Are you retired?" He slipped away from the table and made his way to the hallway bathroom, which had a second door on the far wall that opened onto the pool deck. He locked the first door behind him, opened the second door, walked to the middle of the yard. The vegetation was high and thick there, and he sat down on the wrought-iron chair that he'd placed under the poinciana in the event there was a need to feel hidden and small under its feathery leaves and red blossoms. He surveyed his property: the back of the house freshly painted a light terracotta with white trim, the trees, shrubs and flowers he'd selected one by one, the egg-shaped swimming pool, the deck and pergola, the quiet of it all, the stark newness of the life he'd thrust himself into without the approving nod of a father or mother. He could only have one mother and one father, and both were gone, he thought. He was next in line. He considered that he might have another partner in time. Raking his fingers through his hair, he could almost feel the grayness of it and dismissed the consideration of a next love as the whim of a fool. "I'm just another aging man in Florida," he thought. He looked up at the sky above his backyard and prayed it wouldn't pull him into its immensity of darkness. Not yet, anyway.

"How about you move into my house after we're married?" Honey asked Glen. He was renting a subsidized studio apartment on the mainland, and here she was in a sprawling beachside house, the one she grew up in. Her parents had saved enough money for her to go away to university to begin her odyssey into a larger world, but she chose a local community college. She didn't want to leave her world. When her mother died shortly after her father, she asked her sister June, "How about I buy you out of your half of the house?" June was married and living in Iowa. She'd gone off to university in Iowa and met her husband there, a local who, like Honey, didn't want to leave his world. He had extended family and a steady job with benefits there. Why would June want to hold onto half a piece of real estate in Florida? Honey thought it was a sensible proposal. If June bristled at the idea, they'd get through it. They were sisters. They'd gotten through far worse.

With Glen, though, it was different, she thought. She and

her fiancé didn't have a history of getting through things together yet. The risk factor of asking the question was high. He could say no to the proposal, decide she was the controlling type, and give himself the slip. She felt her body flush whenever she thought about him inside her, but this was a test of a different intimacy. It took her a while to ask him.

"Wow. Great!" he replied.

"Really?"

"Are you kidding? Instant set-up. No rent. No mortgage."

Wife, complete with house. House, complete with wife. The deluxe package. Did he love her? She tried to push the thought out of her head. "Think of all the money we'll save. We'll be able to redo the house and make it our own," she said.

"Sure, sweetheart. How about we grab a beer at Ichabod's? Ray and Sharon should be there." She didn't drink beer. Didn't he know that by now?

"Sure, sweetheart." She tried out his phrase, but it didn't ring true. She hoped he didn't notice. He didn't. They set off for Ichabod's, Glen's torso straight and high behind the steering wheel of his Camaro convertible, Honey's stooped over as if contracting herself into smallness.

They didn't get around to redoing the house. Honey didn't know she was already pregnant when she'd asked Glen to move in. She found out after the four days of nausea she suffered during their honeymoon in Key West, especially in the morning. She thought it was all the alcohol and sex. Her doctor told her otherwise. They bought a crib for the bedroom nearest theirs, and she hung sweet curtains in the windows and did a deep cleaning of the house, room by room, until Cal was born. Aurora followed two years later. Another crib, another set of sweet curtains, another deep clean. She was neck-deep in babies and feedings, adult meals and the occasional adult conversation. She no longer saw the tattered furniture, the stains on the carpet, the chipped countertops and cracked grout that her parents had bequeathed to her. She didn't have the time or energy to look around her.

Glen was out all day working. She dreaded his return. "The bewitching hour," she called it. He was hungry and tired, the babies were hungry and tired. It was up to her to take care of all of them, feed them, fill them, quiet them down. "Great dinner, sweetheart," he told her, making a getaway to the living room as soon as he could and taking the children with him only if she asked him to. As she loaded the last dish in the dishwasher, she stood there, waiting to hear the hum of the machine. She would have liked to stand by it during the entire cycle. Its sounds were soothing. She could hear the television on in the living room, the male voice of a news or sports broadcaster, and wondered how the children were occupying themselves while their father was rapt by the headlines. She'd join the family, put the children to bed after an hour, and, if she had her way, watch a classic family sitcom or two. She loved the Petries, the Thomases, the Stevenses, and the more controversial Bunkers. She delighted in watching them live their unremarkable lives. "Such happiness in those homes," she thought as she turned off the television and watched the families and their tame antics dissolve in the black screen. "Why does mine feel so dreary?" Glen was usually asleep on the sofa by then. The more she took care, the less he seemed to care. "Is this it?" she asked herself, feeling a bitterness well up inside that made her understand her mother, who was so irascible. It must be in their blood, she decided.

5

The seven-year itch, give or take a couple of years. Honey liked the phrase. It had the effect of gathering up her conjugal dissatisfactions and dissolving them like antacid tablets released in a glass of water. She also liked the phrase "couples therapy," which appeared more and more frequently in the books and magazine articles she read. She was drawn to the general topic of relationships and more so to the subset of marriage, especially if the concept of "evolving" prevailed. Honey wanted to be that. Evolving and serene with what had been dished out as her portion. Glen was an ample portion. Too ample over time. She wanted him to lose weight and spend fewer hours in his recliner and more with the children. She wanted him to be able to breathe better when he walked, and perhaps breathe some of the old enthusiasm and passion they had for each other. For his fifty-fifth birthday, she considered presenting him with a gift certificate to the local gym but then reconsidered. Too risky. Instead, she brought out a home-made red velvet cake, kissed him on the cheek. "Happy birthday!"

She heard him wheezing when he took a deep breath to blow out the candles. As he pried the dribbles of candle wax off the icing, the left side of his mouth and right eyebrow lifted. She knew that look. It wasn't a reflex as much as a strategy, his way of making a show of taking her needs seriously, even if he considered them to be nothing more than passing moods or whims. He carved out a large wedge of cake and brought it to his plate. She picked at the crumbs that left a trail and waited for one of them to say something.

"Thank you," he said after he finished his dessert and pushed his plate aside. "That was nice." He still had that look.

A year or so before his birthday, she got in the habit of slipping out of the house in the afternoon. "I'm going to church," she told him. "I'm going to the bookstore," she told him. It was the truth, although she soon stopped going to church and didn't tell him. At that hour, the church was deserted. She spent more time at the local Barnes and Noble bookstore than she did at The Church of the Blessed Trinity. Without the presence of others, she was afraid to kneel alone and connect with God. It made her feel too important. She wanted the interference of others. No special treatment for her. Who was she, after all? A woman who was trying to find her way back to the heady feeling of those first few years with the man she loved. Other people had more serious problems to be sure—children who were nothing but trouble, spouses who had no qualms about slapping or punching, credit cards bloated with debt, feel-good pills stashed in unused drawers. She wanted to be in the thick of such scenarios, if only to gain some perspective. But during the week, the church was empty. Where could they be? If they were here, kneeling somewhere near her with their supplications for transformation, she stood a chance of realizing that her own agitations for transformation were nothing compared to theirs, poor things: the son in jail; the eviction notice; the latest bruise from yet another fist-punch. Just like her, she knew, all of them were seeking a route to happiness. Where were they all?

The bookstore was peopled at any hour of any day. She liked a background of people. They distracted her by the histories she could make up about them to convince herself that she was better off than most. At the bookstore, she leafed through books and articles with titles like "How to win back your man," "The benefits of co-joined happiness," "Partners in life, partners in fulfilment." Their tables of contents were like instructions for recipes. She didn't trust herself with recipes, what with all the failed brownies, lasagnas and other culinary fare she'd turned out despite her following a set of precise steps. She left the bookstore empty-handed each time, expecting at some point to be stopped at the exit by a suspicious employee and asked to open her handbag. She was disappointed when it didn't happen. She wouldn't have minded being asked something while she was in the store.

It did happen once, while she was browsing through the Romance section. A salesman was in the same aisle unloading a box of books and lining them up on the "D" shelf. She was at "G." From the corner of her eye, she could see that his movements were slow and careful as he placed the books on the shelf, adjusting each one with the tip of his index finger so the spine was aligned with the other books already on the shelf. She turned toward him. He was about her age. Slim. Handsome. Wire-rimmed glasses. Before she could turn back to the "G" shelf, she noticed him smile at her.

"Is there anything I can help you with?" he asked.

If you only knew, she thought. "No thanks," she replied. "Just browsing."

"Well, if you need anything, let me know. I'm Owen. After I finish this box, I'll be down a few aisles. In the Fiction section."

"Isn't Romance Fiction?"

He looked puzzled and turned back to his box. She left the store, and ramped up the volume on the radio as soon as she'd turned the ignition key.

At home, she kept a paperweight from her childhood on the kitchen counter. She used it to pin down coupons and reminders of things to do that she scribbled on yellow post-its. Its plastic dome was filled with water and housed a country-style steepled church surrounded by pine trees, with flecks of plastic snow at the bottom waiting to be unsettled when shaken. She had to add water from time to time by turning the paperweight upside-down, prying off the stopper under the base, and setting the water pressure of the kitchen spigot to a light dribble so that the steady drops of water could enter the tiny hole. She enjoyed the tumult she could create by giving the object a gentle shake. Such a graceful way to stir things up. She went to the paperweight often after her disheartening visits to the Barnes and Noble. She would hold it in front of her and shake it with a fury to create the blizzard that she knew she could count on. The snow swirled violently around all that quaintness, and she would inhale deeply, holding the air in her lungs until the plastic flecks of snow resettled at the bottom. When a snowflake got stuck on the church steeple or in the branch of a pine tree, she only needed to give a tiny jiggle to make the flake sink back to the bottom and restore the scene to a state of simple happiness.

Glen was a star athlete way back in the day. His exquisite physique evolved organically, and so slowly that he was oblivious to the effect it had on those who saw him. Male or female, they ogled him discreetly in admiration, envy or desire. Honey saw him the first day she arrived at high school. He was shooting hoops in the gymnasium with some other boys. His white jersey had a large, embossed maroon "#1" stitched on the front and back. The hair sprouting from his armpits was long and straight, like spider legs. When he wasn't negotiating his gracefully arced hoop shots, he was sweeping his long blond hair away from his face. Honey was not athletic. Her thighs and upper arms were thick, but she was flexible. She locked herself in her bedroom for hours, bending and stretching, determined to make it through the tryouts and land on the cheerleading squad, if only to be able to watch him dart about on the court and field while she rooted publicly for the team and privately for him. She was in love with him in secret, and she loved her secret. She had to become a cheerleader, to be assured of scheduled times when she could count on being close enough to him that he might take note of her. She was in love with him. He was gorgeous without being a total jock. He was smart without being a nerd. He seemed to be ingenuous enough that he might notice her, even appreciate her. It was too hairbrained a fantasy to share even with her closest girlfriends, she knew. For one thing, she was plain. Her breasts were too small to bob about. Her hair was undifferentiated from the hair of most of the other girls. Boys talked about those things when deciding on a girl. There was nothing remarkable about her to cause one or more of Glen's senses to awaken to her, to desire her among the other girls who, like her, must have been secretly longing to be that for him, too. She contented herself with her pure and private fantasy of one day marrying him and sleeping next to him and feeling his unknown scary part inside of her and making their child happen inside of her, and of her washing their dishes and his dirty clothes, all the while knowing that his secret part had been deep inside of her dark stickiness and made this child happen, who hopefully would look mostly like him but with touches of her (perhaps her nose, which also didn't draw attention one way or the other but didn't have the crook that his did). It was too much to hope for, far too much.

    She went to the three tryouts, limber and primed to do her personal best before the panel of judges. Her name was called after the first round, but not after the second. She didn't make the squad. "What in the world was I thinking?" she asked herself as she trudged to the locker room to change back into her hip-hugger jeans and loose linen blouse.

On their first dates, Glen didn't go at her breasts like a thirsty newborn. Hair didn't seem to register for him either. He did like her nose (his lips landed on it often) and eventually she came to understand how much he appreciated her wide pelvis (his hands gripped it to hold her steady or to synchronize her movements with his). Most of all, he liked her way of not coming on too strong, like the other girls. She guarded her hunger. After the second date, he said to her, "I like you. You're such a relief." Then he kissed her and filled her mouth with his tongue. Several dates later, after he'd felt her small breasts, he said, "I love you. You're such a relief." He fell in love with the relief of her. They married and in due course bred; in due course, whatever sense of connection they had, and the relief that came with it, began to sputter.

"I guess this is what happens," she said to herself. "The natural order." She experimented with keeping herself busy. She signed up for a knitting class, a Zumba class, a Mediterranean cooking class, where she found herself in the company of women, many of whom prattled on about their husbands as they ladled out soup, caught their breath between Latin dance moves, turned the roasting vegetables with tongs. How she could relate to these women, what with all their marital dissatisfactions. She listened to them without contributing. She arrived at each class eager to listen to the next round of prattling, expecting some kind of dramatic arc that would veer toward a neat resolution that could help her understand what she should do when she returned home. There were no arcs, just loops and a lot of sweat. "That's not what I want."

She didn't know what she wanted. She thought about packing a suitcase and hopping on a plane to a Caribbean island or to her old friend Megan in Santa Fe (who was unmarried and childless and proud of it) until she could sort things out, whatever that meant. She thought about entering Glen's bedroom one night, positioning herself on the edge of his bed, and saying "Can we talk?" She asked him this once when they were sitting on the living room sofa about to watch television.

"What's up, Honey?"

She was tongue-tied. "I love you," was all she could say.

He looked at her perplexed. "I love you too." He waited. "What's up?"

"That's enough for now."

He moved closer to her, but not so close that their bodies touched. He reached over and grabbed a DVD. "How about 'Scarface?' It's due back at Blockbusters by tomorrow or the late fee kicks in."

She didn't enter Glen's bedroom to tell him what was up.

She volunteered at the homeless shelter. She was tasked with changing sheets and sweeping. She asked the director whether she could do something where she was in contact with the residents.

"What did you have in mind?" he asked.

"I don't know exactly. But it would be nice to interact with them."

"What would you want to talk to them about?"

"I don't know really. Just show some kindness."

"Do you have any training?"

"In kindness?"

She enrolled in a photography class advertised in the local paper. She enjoyed taking family snapshots with her Polaroid and pasting them into albums. She chose the photos where everyone was smiling; the others she tossed into a large plastic bin that she kept in her closet.

There were men in the class. The instructor was a man. Everyone sat, classroom style, and listened to him as he explained the mechanics of a camera, which was difficult for her to follow.

"But," he repeated continually, "the mechanics are the means to the end. What is the end?" Hands went up.

"Vision."

"Aesthetic."

"Control."

He snickered at each response. "So reductionist. C'mon people. Don't be so lazy."

Honey raised her hand. "When I look through my Polaroid, I feel safe. When I put my eye against the whatever-you-call-it that you look through, there are boundaries. I know that's all I have to work with. I don't need words. It calms me down. Does that count as an end?"

"That's up to you to decide," he replied. "But you really need to upgrade to a real camera."

She treated herself to a Nikon FA. She showed it to Glen.

"What's that for?"

"To take pictures."

"No kidding. What about our Polaroid?"

"That's for snapshots."

"What's this for?"

"For me."

"How much did it cost?"

"A lot. I'll need to buy some lenses eventually."

"Honey, you shouldn't..."

"Yes I should." She went into the kitchen and hung the camera on the hook on the wall, directly above the paperweight. The vibration caused a few flakes of snow to lift and whirl above the steeple of the church. Peacefully.

* * * *

An itch that didn't have a chance to pose itself as an itch.

Marilyn hadn't given the slightest sign of being about to die when the results came in. She and Hank were neck-deep in a long and steady stream of pleasant domestic life, absent of crises of any kind, when the doctor called to invite them in to discuss the matter of a small dark patch on one of her routine X-rays. Probably nothing serious, he assured them, but best to take some additional tests. Just in case. An appointment was made for 6 p.m. Their boys had already moved on and out to other places, but they were visiting when the call came. It was during the Easter holiday. They were off from work. She prepared dinner and told them to not wait for them if they should be home late from the appointment. She reminded them to say their prayers at the dinner table. "You can make them short," she said. "Just don't forget to say them." She knew they wouldn't forget. They were such good boys. Such good men. She and their father would go to the doctor and the boys would have time together to catch up. A lovely thought. They'd eat everything she prepared. They'd clear the table, wash the dishes, and leave the kitchen spic and span. What a blessing, these boys. These men. She hoped Matthew's love-making with his wife (a lovely girl) persisted with ardor. She wanted grandchildren. Matthew, it seemed, was her only hope for that.

After Hank helped Marilyn through her ten-hour labor as she gave birth to Jonathan, his desire for sex with her receded. He compensated with affection and attentiveness. He stood by her side peeling potatoes and folding laundry; he stood by her soul when her face revealed fatigue or disquiet. What a blessing, this life. She thought this often. So did he. They said it to each other at least once a day, year after year, even when Jonathan was at the age when he should have been talking about girls from time to time. Jonathan didn't mention any girlfriends, let alone bring one home for them to meet. So unlike Matthew, who was all bravado and doused himself in colognes and fussed over each strand of hair before going out of the house. Their little one was circumspect in what he divulged outside of his studies and athletics. He was indifferent to cologne and the shape of his hair. He didn't subscribe to the remedies for conventional vanity. There was something special about him. Off. Odd. It troubled them. It harbored a possibility: Jonathan liked boys. They didn't talk about it. Deep down they knew, and they knew that the other knew. Nothing needed to be said about it. Words were pointless.

She never tired of cutting her husband's hair in the kitchen. She carted the boys off to the barber once a month (they didn't protest), but she always cut her husband's hair. It didn't occur to him to refuse. He would have preferred doing other things, but he understood the solidarity of the ritual. As he sat in a kitchen chair with a fresh dish towel wrapped loosely around his neck, he questioned whether he offered similar services to her as a way of keeping them tightly knit without necessarily needing words or God to do so. Certain requests that he made to her came to mind. "Can you pass me that wrench?" "Could you hold the ladder tighter? I have to stand on the top to reach the fire detector." He hoped he did. Haircuts always took place in the late afternoon, when the boys were out playing with friends and the sun was coming in through the window over the double sink and had the color and sweetness of butterscotch. His head in that light was a safe place for her to be so intimate. "Stay still while I trim around your ears." He swept up afterward while she prepared dinner. They were silent, but each knew what the other was thinking. What a blessing, this life. Will Jonathan choose the right path? They hoped that a direct prayer to God wouldn't be necessary.

There were many ways the dark patch that her X-rays revealed could have been nothing. It chose another way. A way to be something. A way that wasn't blessed. A way that tested all of them.

"Dear God, my Father in heaven, I believe that you designed her body to be healthy, so it saddens you to see sickness,

which doesn't come from you but comes from living in a fallen, broken world. My loving Father, please heal her from this illness. Please heal her body and soul to the fullest extent of your will. I know that you will always heal her soul when she prays for help, because her soul will last forever. Sometimes you also choose to heal people's bodies, even though they can't last forever will and eventually die. There's no way I can predict what your healing plans are for her. I do believe that you will respond to my prayers by doing what's best, according to your purposes for my life. For her life. If you choose to allow her to keep enduring this illness, please help us to remember that you would only choose this in order to accomplish some higher purpose, even if I and my loved ones shouldn't understand it in our ignorance. Amen."

The kitchen was spotless when they arrived home from the doctor's office. Their sons were sitting next to each other on the three-seater sofa in the living room. They were watching television. The plate of brownies she'd made lay empty in front them on the coffee table.

They stood up as soon as their parents entered the living room. Matthew stood up. "So?"

The doctor had explained a number of treatment options which they'd only half-heard while they waited for him to arrive at what they wanted to know: "How long?" "How gruesome until the end?" He didn't arrive there, and they didn't ask.

"Nothing definitive," she said, "More tests. I'm sure it will come to nothing." She smiled. "What are you watching?"

"Back to the Future."

"Enjoy, my sons. Wipe the crumbs off the table before you go to bed or we'll be invaded by palmetto bugs." She took her husband by the wrist and led him away from them toward the hallway.

"Shouldn't we have told them more?" he asked her.

"What more do they need to know?" He understood her. They themselves had opted to know less about the thing that might kill her than they could have. They didn't press the doctor for answers. In this, they understood, God humbled them. They realized that knowing more sometimes served less. And besides, they couldn't know everything. Not even close.

"You're right," he said. She loosened her grip on his wrist and slid her hand toward his hand. He interlocked his fingers between hers and gave a squeeze. "What would I do without you?"

Marilyn gave Hank a haircut the day before she died. Her hand was unsteady and the edge of the scissors nipped the top of his ear. It bled. "I'm so sorry," she said. "I was trying to get those white hairs on the edge of your ears. Have they always been there?" She had the presence of mind to get the styptic pencil from their bathroom and apply it to the cut after she blotted the wound with a sheet of paper towel to absorb the pearl drop of deep red blood that was about to spill over and trickle down along the tendoned contour of his ear. She was mortified. She knew what her trembling hand meant. So did he. When the blood subsided, she wrapped her arms around his neck, bent down and pressed her lips to the top of his head. He raised his hands and cupped them over her wrists. They stayed like that for a minute, as if they were practicing the art of waiting with calm. What they were waiting for came sometime during the night while they slept. He woke up as the morning sun was announcing itself through the thin white drapes of their bedroom window. She didn't stir when he rustled the top sheet. He gazed at her, observed her belly, which didn't rise and fall; placed his nostrils under her nostrils, which didn't take in or let out air; pressed his lips against the top of her head which felt icy. Would the boys be awake yet? He started to calculate their respective time zones. Awake or not, this, they had to know. He called them.

The boys flew in for the funeral. All went well. His boys were good boys. They didn't get into scrapes with each other or anyone else. They continued making straight parts on the left side of their head long after their mother had supervised their grooming as they got ready to go to school each morning. Matthew had red hair, which wasn't an easy thing to have. Oh, the nicknames Matthew had to suffer because of his red hair, Hank remembered, and that time at dinner, when he slammed his fist down on the table because he didn't see why he had to gather up the blots of boiled spinach sticking along the edge of his plate and eat them. He apologized as soon as the sound of his fist crashing onto the Formica tabletop echoed above the family. "I'm sorry, Mom. I'm sorry, Dad." Hank marveled at how such instant contrition, such goodness, came to be. Did he really have to apologize? Couldn't he have at least pushed his plate away and glowered at them for a sharp instant before saying he was sorry? Such goodness. Or was it meekness? Whatever it was, he would not take credit for it. Most likely it was God's work. Maybe it was just the luck of the draw. Who knew? He knew. He looked at his wife after the apology and he knew. It was her doing. If it was ever in him to feel his love for his wife waning, her preeminence and her bounty as Mother would have stopped him dead in his tracks. Her patience was as natural as breathing, may she rest in peace.

A year before Marilyn showed signs of dying, they went on a campaign to stop buying items that weren't for immediate use, like milk or ground beef. Their house was chock full of things, as most houses ended up being when they'd been lived in for as long a time as Hank and Marilyn had lived in theirs.

"Time to pare down, don't you think?" he asked her as he tried to close a drawer after stuffing a dish towel into it.

"I'd say it's long overdue," she said. "A nice project for us to work on." She opened the drawer, pulled out the dish towel, refolded it and placed it back inside. The drawer glided shut smoothly. "We really do have more than we need." They didn't talk further about the clutter. Most houses had it, they knew, and theirs was no exception, what with the kids and the hustle and bustle and fads and needs that transpired within their walls over the decades. Like every other family, Hank supposed. That was the point of having a house, even if it meant straining to meet the mortgage payments. Beyond shelter and security, it was a receptacle to deposit tangible evidence of having lived a meaningful life, a structure where any and every item could be set on a shelf for admiration or be shoved into a drawer or cabinet just in case; a combination museum and mausoleum; a way of not vanishing altogether, at least not for a while.

They set themselves to the task quietly and efficiently, confident that the other understood what they were up to and how it would end up: a few pieces of jewelry worth a penny or two, a stack of photos, a hand-made potholder, the kids' drawings. "This was your grandmother's," one of them would say during the purge. "This was your great-grandfather's," one of them would say. They'd arch an eyebrow, shrug a shoulder, and heave most of the items into a dark green Hefty trash bag. Ashes to ashes, dust to dust, bags to Goodwill. Marilyn was in charge of coiling the twist'em around the neck of the bag. When he noticed her hesitating, he recited, "*People, despite their wealth, do not endure; they are like all of Earth's beasts that perish. This is the fate of those who trust in themselves and in each other.*"

Three days after the funeral, Matthew and Jonathan left to catch their planes; there he was, surrounded by everything about her except her. Despite the purging, the house was overflowing with objects on every surface and in every credenza, cabinet, chest of drawers and closet. Everything was positioned at right angles, neat folds and squared stacks. Marilyn insisted on orderliness. It had a way of compressing excess to resemble something more modest, despite all the vases and figurines and other gewgaws on display. "The marrow," she called them. Hank looked around. The living room felt hollow. The objects were empty, as dead as his wife. He thought about getting rid of many of them, but he knew that he'd be incapable of removing any remaining fact of her existence, down to the bobby pin on her night table that he noticed as he was getting into bed that night. He put it in the top drawer, next to her hand lotion, where it wouldn't be so visible. To throw it out verged on the iniquitous.

Without her collaboration, he couldn't bring himself to purge anything else in the house that had been accumulated. In fact, he regretted every single thing she might have thrown out or given to Goodwill without telling him. He always assumed that he'd be first. He'd done the calculations. He was older than she was. He had high blood pressure, like his parents, who died young. Women lived longer than men. His calculations betrayed him: Marilyn went first. Her absence was present everywhere, and his presence was so thin in comparison, he thought. But it required him to carry on. Somehow.

Do not be overawed when others grow rich,
when the splendor of their houses increases;
for they will take nothing with them when they die,
their splendor will not descend with them...

Sometimes he caught himself uttering swear words way inside his head. Not because of anything that happened that was bad or annoying or stupid. Shit, Fuck, Hell. The words came out of nowhere, like the chromosome-shaped filaments that floated in front of his vision before he had his cataract surgery. As soon as the words took shape, they faded away. As soon as they did, his thoughts turned to self-flagellation to get them to stay away. He considered the dish towel draped over the handle to the oven door but decided that even if he wet it to make it smart more (like he and others did in the locker room after phys. ed. class to distract them from the tension of their nudity), it wouldn't do the trick. He almost laughed at himself but three words persisted inside his head. They moved about carelessly and carefree. They careened into each other and melded into a diabolical whole, pushing its way forward toward his throat, where it could pick up volume and voice before exiting through his mouth: "Goddammit." He stifled it, horrified.

He wished he were easier on himself, and on people in general. As time went by, most everyone he came in contact with (Joe at Bible study, for example) seemed to be bent on drawing attention to themselves by talking about what they'd done or what they were currently doing. The drama and anecdotes of the "I." He preferred his attention to be drawn to those who were so in the midst of doing the things they were doing that it didn't occur to them to talk about them. He wasn't particularly interested in their renditions of it. He listened to what they had to say, politely and patiently. He didn't trust their versions. So few of them had something to say and knew how to say it. A few of them had little to say but at least knew how to say it. A few others had something to say but didn't know how to say it. Most of them had nothing to say and didn't know how to say it. They were the ones who went on the longest. It was a challenge for him, this paucity of engagement with others, this lack of anchor, and it should have made him sad. Instead, it made him angry and impatient, with himself and with them, he knew.

Like with Joe, at Bible study. No matter what verse they were discussing, Joe brought his latest game of golf into the discussion. As metaphor ("It's about choosing the right instrument, concentrating and aiming"); as anecdote ("I didn't believe I could bogie after that sand trap, but guess what? I did. We gotta persist in having faith in positive outcomes"); as non-sequitur ("Why just yesterday on the 15th green..."). If Jesus had hit some balls from time to time (and Hank doubted that he had), maybe he could find a path to forgiveness. Joe complimented Hank every time he brought a tray of homemade peanut butter cookies to Bible study and set it on the back table beside the store-bought doughnuts and cupcakes that the other men had brought. The recipe was Marilyn's. Despite Joe's compliment, he still got impatient with him and suspected him of offering up praise in order to hoard the cookies, which he did. The others in his group hoarded attention. Joe hoarded the cookies. Where did humility disappear to?

He carried on, inventing ways to get through each day and reminding himself that eventually he would join her. In time he got used to not being able to get used to the new order, although he lost the ability to smile.

* * * *

The twenty-five-year itch. Chafings before then, but not of the kind to cause scratching until there was blood.

"What's happening to us?"

"Nothing is happening to us."

"Then I don't understand."

Seth looked hard into Yoni's eyes and grabbed his wrists above the watchband and copper bracelet. "I just said it. 'Nothing is happening.'"

Theirs was a smooth and steady coupling for a long time. Years in the making. When their friends and colleagues weren't cowering under a black cloud of envy, they felt the reassuring shafts of light of their steadiness. It was possible after all, what these two men had. Smooth and steady. Legitimate. Just what

Yoni dreamed of and couldn't believe was happening to him. With a man, no less. Seth wasn't as trustworthy. He needed to chip away at things and turn them this way and that. It had something to do with his notion of free will and the modest portion of it that everyone had at their disposal if only they were brave enough to seize a moment, an event, a condition, yell inside "It's my life! My one and only life!" and challenge it, take control of it, to the death. He visualized line graphs, where he could discern and study trends and draw conclusions about how he and Yoni were faring, and why. He wasn't on the prowl for the easy drama of treacherous peaks and steep drops, but neither did he want flat terrain, which would make him yawn even when he wasn't tired. (He only had to think back to those endless road trips to the seashore he took as a child, and the torment of the highways that didn't curve or dip or climb and had nothing to show on their shoulders and exit ramps except clots of scrub and the same rest-stop chain restaurants. Thank God they would arrive at the ocean. Oh, the ocean.) Or worse than yawn, God forbid, succumb to complacency.

When Seth went to Japan for a short business trip, he added four post-business days in order to peel off from the hotels and conference rooms and see what there was to see in a place so far away that had once been called The Orient.

"I'm going to have to bow out this time," Yoni told him. "Bunch of stuff to do." He didn't elaborate.

Seth didn't inquire. "It's okay. There'll be other occasions."

Theirs wasn't a cloying relationship. They looked forward to sporadic separations and their promise of a stretch of time when they could allow themselves to let certain private and neglected zones fill up with something other than each other, musty spaces that they could air out or redecorate or invite some stranger into for an hour or two. Seth had a fantasy of island-hopping by bicycle during cherry blossom season, even though he didn't know what bicycling through Japan entailed (were there clusters of American tourists doing the same in bike lanes? Were there bike lanes?) or when cherry blossom season in Japan was (was it the same season as in D.C.?). He rented a bicycle through the service desk at his hotel. He biked each day, but the rigor of his pedaling didn't pull him beyond the gravitational pull of downtown Kyoto and its teeming humanity. Breaking through the city limits and into the countryside carried the risk of his venturing into unpeopled spaces. People fueled the tumult of possibility, what with their individual histories and stories that he could create for each and every one of them he passed and knew nothing about. A panorama of cherry blossoms provided a different nourishment. It was gorgeous and aromatic to the point of intoxication. But that was what it was supposed to be for one such as him, who might stop for a moment or two in order to settle into a meditative state of appreciation. After twenty-five years with Yoni, Seth was settled enough.

"You can pull over here," he told the taxi driver on his way back to his hotel after dining with colleagues and the insufferable shop talk.

"This isn't your hotel," the driver said. "Three more blocks."

"I know. It's fine here. I can use a walk." He got out of the taxi and looked at the building in front of him. The street number painted above the door corresponded to the address of the gay bar he'd located on Google while he was in the taxi. The door was thick and heavy, as if it had been constructed to give access only to those who had sufficient resolve to leave the anonymity of the sidewalk and enter into the possibility of something more intimate, more disruptive.

He opened the door and entered. Inside its pinched and claustrophobic interior were two local boys too young to be legal in such a place and one heavy-set tourist seated at one of the three banquettes. He left and walked back to his hotel. The lobby was empty, but he lingered there hoping someone would push through the revolving door or exit the elevator to be deposited in the lobby, where they would find each other and their way out of an evening of solitude in The Orient.

The revolving doors didn't spin around; the elevator doors didn't slide open. People weren't happening in this place, at this hour. Oh well, he thought as he surveyed the lobby for anything he might have overlooked that would steer him away from his own company before the evening ended.

Among the brochures splayed fanlike on the coffee table next to him was one that held his gaze because of the font, Bahnscrift Condensed, which gave form to the one word on the brochure cover. It was a font he was familiar with but rarely came across, much like certain names of people—Agatha, Brent, Millicent, Lionel. He admired the parents of children with such names. They must have chosen them with painstaking sensitivity to the shape, sound, feel and life-force of a single word that frame their progeny for life. Bahnscrift Condensed was like that, too, he thought, as he read the only word on the cover of the brochure: "*Kaizen.*" He didn't know the word. The "Complimentary copy" label affixed to the brochure cover didn't offer an explanation. He took one of the brochures to his room, grabbed a single-portion bottle of vodka from the minibar and hopped into bed. A marketing brochure accompanied by alcohol. The perfect recipe for nodding off into a deep untroubled sleep.

The brochure kept him propped up on his pillows and attentive. The inside panels elaborated on Kaizen, as he'd expected. He'd also expected to quickly shrug his shoulders and say, "Oh, please." Instead, in this random bed at this dark hour, he continued to read the brochure's roadmap to happiness and fulfilment without his usual tendency toward haughtiness about such matters. "If I'm such an expert on happiness and fulfilment," he thought as he punched the pillows to check for dust, "why haven't I gotten close to feeling either of these things? I'll put this in my suitcase and take it home with me." Something to carry back to his life at home, with Yoni, to save them from a more permanent separation. One never knew. Unions ended for the silliest of reasons. They patched themselves together for the silliest of reasons. They held together for the silliest of reasons. He continued reading.

Kaizen. A pale blue sidebar on the second page offered a summary, with key words in bold: continuous improvement… incremental steps to better things…lasting and powerful change…one small step followed by another…avoid a major disruptive effort that sets off alarms in the brain and shuts down power. He imagined arriving home and getting one solid night's sleep before downloading the brochure's proprietary spreadsheet where he could enter the shared and compatible goals and components of his life with Yoni—complete with quotients of happiness—to arrive at scores computed and neatly tallied at the bottom of each narrative column. The complexity of living pounded into crisp numbers was a kind of magic that he was willing to believe in, especially if it pointed in a direction that he wanted to go in.

He dozed off in the hotel bed as he was reading the flip side of the brochure. When he woke up, sunlight was pouring in through the bleached-white bamboo shades. He closed the brochure on his lap, back cover side up. Blurbs proclaimed that the methodology had been tested by Boeing, Toyota and the U.S. Navy. Underneath were photographs of the backs of men looking towards planes and cars and boats. Their faces couldn't be seen, but their shoulders were broad and upright, their heads held high.

"Yuck. What was I thinking?" He got out of bed. On his way to the bathroom, he stopped at the coffee contraption beneath the flat screen television hanging on the wall to figure out what buttons to push, what packets to open, where and how to place them, in order to get the coffee going while he took a piss and a dump. Under the coffee machine was a waste bin. He tossed the brochure inside.

Sitting on the toilet, he imagined a line graph of "My Life with Yoni," which was as flat as a Kansas prairie. Had Yoni been privy to it, he would have exalted in the security of its levelness. "That's what a relationship is supposed to provide," he would have said. He'd said it during their therapy sessions as a counterpoint to Seth's restlessness and gloom. The therapist listened to Seth unravel, egged on by her studied silence and intense gaze. She listened to Yoni, too. He didn't say much except that for him all this accrual of steadiness meant solidarity. The two men couldn't make their polar interpretations find a way into a harmonious intention, despite years with Dr. Hollis, who was expert at nudging them just a tad further than where they expected to be able to arrive by the end of each session. They could have gone on forever with her, talking to her in a civilized way about their chafings and knowing that they would leave the session with some new scrap of meat to toss into the stew and stir gently. They could afford her fee, too. Or one of them could choose not to go on forever. Seth chose not to.

"Can we stop keeping ourselves stuck in this?" he asked her while staring at Yoni. "We're going in circles. It's making me dizzy and bored." He took a sip of water. "It feels like progress, but it's more like a confessional. Said the Jew to the Jew."

"Go on," she said to him. "Did you have something else in mind?"

"No. Just ending it. That's all."

She turned her head to focus on Yoni while she maintained her crossed legs, her upright back, her hands folded in her lap. How tight she is, Seth thought. How loathsome her profession.

"How does that make you feel?"

Yoni looked at her, then at Seth, then back at her. "Like a piece of shit. I want to hear more from him." He glared at Seth. "End it?"

"Would you like some more water?" she asked them.

"Why not," Seth said. "As a matter of fact, do you happen to have a lake in your bag of tricks? I wouldn't mind doing some laps right now."

She rose from her chair and went to the credenza to fetch the pitcher. Thin discs of lemon were floating on its water-filled surface. How chic, he thought, as he stood up and held out his glass. What an eye for detail. What a farce. What a rip-off. I will not give in to this coddling. Can't she simply help me end it already?

The two men held out their empty glasses. She went for Seth's glass first. At this, Yoni let his glass slip through his fingers. It fell to the area rug. He nudged it twice with his foot before it rolled onto the parquet floor, where he stomped on it until it shattered. "Fuck you," he said to the fragments. He lifted his head to her. "You too." And then to Seth. "You too." He walked out, closing the door gently.

"I gather this is what you've been wanting for quite some time. We should talk about that, but our time is up for today. Should we schedule another appointment?"

Seth rose from the sofa. "Yes, this is what I wanted. Maybe. Maybe not in this way. But this is what I wanted."

"I understand. Next week then?"

"I'll let you know. I'll call you. Let me help you clean up."

"Thank you. I can take care of it." She opened a small drawer by the side of her chair and extracted a dustpan and brush. "Tools of the trade."

"I'm not the first."

She smiled.

"You should use plastic glasses. More practical tools of the trade."

"I'll wait for your call."

He didn't call her during that first week when Yoni's disappearance tormented him with competing moments of panic, guilt, second thoughts, and relief. He didn't call her at the beginning of the second week, after Yoni called him to arrange to pick up his possessions and they hardly squabbled over the phone as they negotiated certain items that both tried to convince each other of having a legitimate claim to. He didn't call her toward the end of that second week, when Yoni arrived in a U-Haul truck and with an infuriating tenderness and grace in his movements and expressions proceeded to remove each and every trace of his material existence from the apartment. Their apartment. He brought lots of empty boxes with him. "We'll talk eventually," he said to Seth, with a trace of a smile as he worked his thumb and index finger through the cloth loop of the truck's back panel and pulled it down after he'd loaded the last box. Seth noticed that his ring finger was no longer ringed. "Be well."

As he watched the U-Haul speed off and he lingered on the sidewalk hoping for Yoni to stick his arm out the window to wave and perhaps slow down, stop, turn the vehicle around and come back to him, he considered calling Dr. Hollis to make an appointment for as soon as possible. The U-Haul vanished around a curve in the road without Yoni having demonstrated any weakening of his resolve. He trundled back into the apartment and began to take in the new empty spaces on walls and shelves, and later in the day the emptiness in the enclosed spaces of drawers and cabinets. Much to be filled up with. He was sad, but he was hopeful. He looked forward to the day (and it would come, he was sure) when they came around to being able to be together in a way that didn't make them roll their eyes so much. He didn't want Yoni back in the old way. As much as he would miss him, the old way wouldn't work and would serve only to undo all the resources (energy, time, money) that they spent, and spent in earnest, to change the course of things, even if the push toward change was a continual punch in the gut. But he didn't want him gone entirely, as it seemed could be the case when Yoni didn't wave or slow down or put the car and U-Haul in reverse to turn back. Seth started rearranging the furniture, asking himself whether, when all was said and done, Dr. Hollis had been a waste of time and money. Perhaps none of this would have happened if he and his partner hadn't been seated together on a sofa in front of her for so many fifty-minute sessions watching her nod her head most of the time. Perhaps it would have happened anyway. It didn't matter. The old way was no longer. The new way had yet to unpleat itself. Until it did, the apartment would be quiet, which would be a relief if only it weren't so disquieting. He didn't call Dr. Hollis again. Her job was done. He was single.

It would take time to get used to, this amputation of half of him. At times, he could almost feel the raw and exposed nerves and capillaries sprouting new growth, lush and fulgent. Other times, he felt nothing of the sort and repeated to himself, "Think withdrawal. A partner becomes an addiction. I'm going through withdrawal." The trick, he knew, was to not get sucked back into the habit of him but to find a practicable alternative, some part-time way back to him; a path strewn with the kindness and laughter and buoyancy of those first years, but minus the appetite for physical coupling that held them together like glue. No. No sex. Not that. How utterly puritanical, he thought as he moved his tee-shirts, which were sharing the drawer where he kept his undershorts, into the empty drawer above (where Yoni had kept his underclothes). So much space now. He breathed in deeply, trying to make all the space inside him and in these empty drawers feel like a balm, a blessing. The breathing felt too forced.

After he rearranged the furniture, redistributed his clothes in the chest of drawers, and got used to eating dinner alone, he brought a cat home from the local shelter. He named it Max. Two days later, he realized he was a she. He kept the name, and he kept the cat, even though she didn't do for him what he hoped she would do: bridge the gap between being alone and being lonely. Max was a sweet presence, but not an overly demanding one. She liked to be petted and fed, but without insisting on it. Sometimes she slept with him, but most of the time she didn't. She was just what he thought he wanted, just what he thought would be enough. She wasn't, though. She never involved herself enough with him to irritate him and make him feel the taut muscle of responsibility. He gave Max a pep talk about getting a dog and graduated to Winston. He fell in love with him. Max was independent and aloof. She didn't seem to mind. She picked the hitchhikers stuck on Winston's paws from his walks while he licked the inside of her ears. They kept themselves occupied while Seth went about his business. The threesome figured out how to make it work. Feline, canine and human navigated need, affection, devotion and reliability with ease. Seth watched the beasts as he went about his business in the house. Everyone seemed to know their place, their function, their portion of happiness. What was the deal with two people trying to pull off the same arrangement?

6

The fish weren't biting, except for the usual whiting, which Hank unhooked from his line and threw back into the ocean with the expertise of the pitcher he used to be throughout elementary, junior and high school. Whiting were too scaly. They didn't have enough meat on them to make it worth his while. He didn't like the bluefish either. They were too dark and oily. He preferred pompano, with their thin skin, easy-to-remove comb-like scale and white fleshy meat. It was rare that he caught one. The pompano seemed to know how to stay one step ahead of the different shaped weights and colors and flavored lures he attached to the end of his lines. No wonder pompano cost so much on the menus of the two restaurants that he and Marilyn went to on special occasions. It wasn't that he was against splurging on special occasions. But if he was going to splurge, he wanted it to be on something that his wife didn't prepare at home. And he brought enough pompano home for her to prepare. Most of the time on their nights out, he gave in to the surf 'n turf, choosing a double order of coleslaw over the French fries as his sides. He hadn't been out to eat since Marilyn died.

He pulled off his baseball cap and wiped the sweat off his

forehead with a red and white paisley handkerchief that he kept handy in the left back pocket of his fishing shorts. He had several pairs of shorts that he designated as fishing shorts because of their many pockets. They differed only in color. Some were beige, some olive, others navy blue. He kept them freshly laundered and without stains; he gave especially close scrutiny to the beige ones, spraying Shout on any suspicious blots before placing them in the washing machine. The fishing shorts were barely distinguishable from his other shorts, except for their age and the extra pockets. As soon as any pair of shorts, fishing or otherwise, began to fray at the hem or reveal a stain that couldn't be removed, he would cut them up into multi-purpose rags—for dusting, removing grease from the stove vent, wiping down the patio furniture or toilet bases—and deposit them into the recycle bin after a single use. Better that than going through rolls of paper towels, which weren't cheap. He didn't need to micro-manage money, but it felt like it was the right thing to do. He read the opening paragraphs of articles about the Green Revolution.

    He also liked to cook, although he would have preferred that Marilyn be still alive to tend to the preparation of their three daily meals. The routine of sounds and smells that she produced from the kitchen as he busied himself at his desk—paying bills, reviewing bank statements, sorting through the junk mail—or tinkered in the garage was a source of comfort to him. It reassured him that what was under his control was being attended with efficiency. Each time that Marilyn called out "Dinner's ready" in her sweet voice whose volume adjusted itself to wherever in the house he happened to be (she always knew where he was), he felt the rightness, the appropriateness, of everything that unwound from the spool of their union. In those moments, and they were many, he didn't forget to close his eyes and thank God.

    Now that she was dead, his cooking steadily approached

being as good as hers, although with one difference: he often had to consult recipes. Some had been written by her on three-by-five cards and placed in alphabetical order in a pink and gray plastic recipe box that he kept handy on the kitchen counter; others required thumbing through her recipe books to find the spots where she made an asterisk in ink. Marilyn didn't need any instructions. Despite her recipe books and three-by-five cards, she rarely referred to them after several years of marriage and up until her death. On occasion, he tried his hand at something that she never prepared. Like the pizza. It felt daring, verging on mean-spirited, as if he were taking revenge on her for dying by showing her, and himself, that he could manage just fine, if not better. He knew this wasn't true. He was simply making time pass, or trying to pass through time, without the pang of nostalgia or the agony of loss.

Another bite! The line was tugging furiously, causing the fishing rod to arc in a serious way. He dug his feet into the sand and began the pull-and-release play of the rod and reel that was necessary to prevent whatever was on the other end from either snapping the line or dragging him into the ocean more than thigh-deep, where gravity would be working against him and in favor of the fish. He didn't expect such moments. They were rare. He also didn't expect fishing to be an act of exertion as much as one of decompression. A gentle sport. When such moments came, he felt exalted. Nothing mattered anymore except this simultaneously instinctual and strategic give-and-take battle that was taking place between mammal and fish. There were no other moments in this moment. Never had been. Never would be. Any and all meaning was to be found here, nowhere else. Total presence. Survival of the fittest playing out in a matter of seconds.

Hank had the upper hand. He reeled the living thing in, watching it wriggle desperately as he turned the handle of his rod and until it was above the water and immersed in the life-depriving air. A young barracuda, about a foot long, inedible and of no use to him. He unhooked it and as he pitched it back into the ocean, so much returned to him, including the ache of Marilyn and the guilt over feeling that God had given and had taken away. "Guide me," he beseeched out loud. Under his breath, he murmured "God damn you," raking his foot back and forth along the sand to smooth away the signs of his combat, his victory, his renunciation.

He walked home downtrodden and fishless. He removed a frozen dinner from the freezer and placed it in the microwave, setting the auto-defrost to high, which would give him enough time to go to his desk, an imposing piece of mahogany furniture that belonged to Marilyn's father. The Bible on the upper-right corner was his father's. He pulled the red string taut and toward the left to open it to the place where he last left off reading.

"*...Rise up, my love, my fair one, and come away. For, lo, the winter is past, the rain is over and gone; the flowers appear on the earth; the time of the singing bird is come, and the voice of the turtle is heard in our land; the fig tree puts forth her green figs, and the vines in blossom give their scent. Arise, my love, my fair one, and come away. O my dove, who art in the clefts of the rock, in the secret places of the cliff, let me see thy countenance, let me hear thy voice...*"

The microwave beeped three times. The temperature was reached, which meant the packet needed to be stirred once and set on high for another two minutes. He didn't remember what was inside the aluminum tray. There were pieces of chicken, noodles, a creamy sauce. Chicken tetrazzini? He stirred briskly and asked forgiveness for his breach into profanity, hoping somehow—surely it would take a miracle—that he would soon come to understand why his wife had to die when she did five years ago. He also prayed that the woman with the camera hadn't taken photos of him in such a state.

He'd noticed from time to time that she didn't stop clicking when he happened to pass within her field of vision, and he dreaded the possibility that, in her daily efforts to capture what he assumed was the dawn of a new day she might have ensnared him and stained the glory of her photos with the intrusions of a simple mortal bemoaning his personal and trivial fate. Shameful. He wouldn't be able to bear it. He looked in the oven again. Is the dinner hot enough? He was hungry and he felt empty.

* * * *

Calm ocean. Not a soul in sight. Just Seth and Winston. Graceful lines of pelicans, six or seven per line, aggressively breaking their formation as one bird after another torpedoed down through the ocean's surface to nab some prey. Where were the local fishers on such a morning? Didn't torpedoing pelicans indicate the promise of a good catch? Seth was sure that, contrary to their fly-by-night appearance, the local fishers had a secret knowledge of the complex conditions that had to converge to make the time they spent ankle-deep in the water at this God-forsaken hour worth their while. The same was true for surfers who on some mornings, Seth noticed, would suddenly appear at the water's edge in clusters, like lemmings obeying some higher order. As they paddled out to sea in formation, he asked himself what they knew about this endless mass of undulating liquid that drew them here. Were there mermaids they could see? Sirens they could hear? Or were they simply drawn to being around their own kind—lithe, broad-shouldered youth, clad in boldly colored bathing trunks, leg rope dangling from the back end of each board waiting to be fasted at the ankle—at such a magic hour and with no reason in the world to utter a word?

He walked along the deserted stretch of sand and also

asked himself what called him here. There was Winston, of course, who needed to exercise and sniff and do his business. At this hour? They could go out later. And in this place? They could walk around the neighborhood. Seth didn't believe in callings. They were too mystical-like. He believed in intention, in a modicum or more of control and of deciding and sometimes willing the course of things to take their course. He had little patience for people who uttered, "It is what it is" in the face of difficulty; of others who opted for "It was meant to be." Resignation and passivity didn't sit well with him. Walking on the beach at sunrise with Winston—a man and his dog—gave him the satisfaction that came with intention and deliberation; in this case, to ease up on rigor and structure and drink up the empty, quiet time along a stretch of beach that has been here forever at a time of day when the sun appears as it has since forever.

    He recognized Cap'n Tommy in the distance, the white shock of hair, the turquoise shorts, the four fishing poles that he plunged into the sand as he always did and then twisted with a downward spiral motion until they were deep enough to hold a sturdy upright position, and the large white plastic bucket that he used for his catch. "An old bucket of house paint," Cap'n Tommy told him when he inquired. Involuntarily he quickened his pace, as if he were instinctively drawn to the possibility of human contact, even if he relished the possibility of no human contact. Winston was uncharacteristically indifferent to Cap'n Tommy. With the exception of the captain, the sighting of any living animal—person, dog, cat, squirrel, bird and the rare rabbit—caused his tail to elevate in anticipation of affection and of play, or his body to become taut and attentive to the possibility of conquering or at least subduing his sighting. But Winston passed by Cap'n Tommy as if this well-meaning and jovial man was a presence devoid of consequence or appeal to his canine instincts. Seth and

Cap'n Tommy joked about it, to lighten the sense of slight and to find something to be able to talk about as they passed through their momentary intersection.

"Morning. Any luck?"

"Nah. Too much seaweed."

"Ah."

"Waste of time."

"Nah."

"Sure it is. Look at the bucket. Empty."

"Hang in there. You'll catch something." He smiled and waved his arm above him in a broad sweeping motion in order to make it clear that he was already saying good-bye. The last thing he wanted to do was to stop beside the Cap'n and commit himself to a conversation. The pleasantries were accomplished. He didn't care whether Cap'n Tommy caught something. Winston was already several yards ahead, muzzle in the sand, sniffing furiously for something that didn't present itself but was surely there, somewhere underneath. Passing safely beyond the zone where it would have been possible to veer toward Cap'n Tommy to stop and chat more, Seth felt the usual vexation over his competing needs for solitude and the breaking of solitude. He both resented and missed Cap'n Tommy as soon as he saluted him, exchanged quirks, and went on his way without looking back. The sun broke through the horizon, overlaying the weaker pinks and purples surrounding its entry point with more forceful shades of yellow. In the distance, Seth could make out the woman with the camera. She was using one of her long zoom lenses. She was as constant a presence at sunrise as the sun itself. He was comforted by the reliability of her presence at this hour. It gave him the option and luxury of arriving at her and communing, should he become bored with himself during the walk. Winston spotted her too, he noticed, but didn't seem to be particularly interested in her either.

When they arrived home, after back-tracking on the same path they'd taken to arrive at the spot where Seth decided to turn around, Winston was panting heavily but contentedly, and the sweat on Seth's chest blotted his white sleeveless t-shirt like a Rorschach panel. He stripped down, draping his sweat-soaked clothes over the top of a deck chair and dove into the pool. Winston lay down in his usual morning place on the deck where he could keep an eye on his master but not bake further under the intensifying sun: the small rectangular spot next to the glass table shaded by the hibiscus overhanging the roof of the pergola. Seth did a few laps, got out, toweled off and looked at the clock on the wall next to the patio door. 8:30 a.m. How would he pass the remaining 14 or so hours before he lay down in his bed and let the dream state take over? He went inside to the kitchen. He wasn't particularly hungry, but he knew that eating something after a long walk and a swim was a good thing to do. He read somewhere that when the body feels threatened by food deprivation, it has a tendency to hoard any remnants of food-energy stockpile them in the stomach area, which explained the spare-tire effect of most of the men within ten years of his age. He was acutely aware of the asset of his leanness and adhered to the principle of not eating only when pangs of hunger demanded it, and of not of eating until fullness demanded a stop to it, but simply of eating just enough to nourish his body in a relatively clean and predictable way—of starting before he was hungry and stopping before he was full. He pulled out a mango yogurt from the fridge, along with the stick of butter that he sliced into membrane-thin panels to spread across a sheet of matzoh sprinkled with freshly ground sea salt. "Thank you, Bubby," he said to himself. His grandmother lived with the family until she died and ate a sheet of matzoh every morning. She'd bite into it before she could sit down. "*Illitumen vie di veldt,*" she'd say. It was true. A simple sheet of baked flour and water was as delicious as the world.

7

"I've got it." Seth stooped down to pick up the peach that cascaded off the pyramid of so-called "tree-ripened" peaches in the produce department of the supermarket and landed on the polished cement floor. Most of the peaches were hard enough that had they fallen they would have bounced and rolled toward the rack of romaine lettuce that was programmed to eject tiny jets of mist overhead to keep the leaves perky. However, this peach was soft enough to make floor contact with a thud.

"That's okay. I'll get it." Hank reached for the peach at the same time as Seth, his back bending over to minimize his need to stoop and risk setting off a pain in his right knee that had started up recently out of nowhere. He retrieved the peach and added it to the plastic bag where he'd already deposited three peaches that didn't have the bruises which marked too much handling and rejection by others.

"You're keeping it? Look at it, poor thing."

"It's my fault. I pulled this one out from the middle row. I'm surprised the whole display didn't come crashing down. The least I can do is pay for it. It's good enough. I'll eat it tonight after dinner. I can't just put it back." He smiled. His eyes were naturally radiant.

Seth smiled back and headed toward the cheeses without consulting the list he'd prepared and shoved into the left pocket of his shorts. He liked to do all the aisles and then extract the list to see if he forgot anything as a test of his memory and the possibility of early-onset dementia.

Six of the fourteen cashiers had their "open" lights illuminated. He quickly scanned the possibilities; although he could spot Hank unloading his cart at Cashier 2, there was a customer behind him with a full cart. Cashier 12 was empty. He turned into lane 12 and placed his items on the conveyor belt, making sure to put his canvas bags first so that it was clear he didn't need plastic.

"Did you find everything you need?" the cashier asked him. Her name was Tiffany. It was embossed in white on the gray pin affixed to her smock. Her smile seemed sincere.

"Yes I did. And more." It was his standard reply, and one he was sure Tiffany had heard thousands of times before in the largest supermarket in Atlantique. He looked her directly in the eye when he replied. He'd read somewhere that sincerity lived only in the eyes.

The bagger appeared. His name tag read "Dylan. No tips allowed." "That's okay," Seth told him as he unfolded his three canvas grocery bags. "I'll take care of it. You can help someone else. I like to bag my groceries." He hoped that Dylan would move on to another cashier. He didn't want to be persistent and have to pronounce, "I don't need the chicken, beef and fish to be quarantined in individual plastic bags. They're already wrapped in plastic. I don't need the precision of a long-haul moving company. I live ten minutes from here."

"Are you sure?" Dylan asked.

"I'm sure."

By the time Seth was wheeling his cart out of the automatic sliding exit doors, Hank was placing the last of his many plastic bags in the trunk of his car. Hank didn't mind all the plastic bags. He had five hooks evenly spaced on the pegboard that covered one of the walls of his garage. From each hook he hung one plastic bag, and each bag was filled with other plastic bags—some beige, some white, some yellow—depending on the store where he made his purchase. "Five is enough," he calculated. "I don't want to hoard, especially in the garage. I need room to maneuver in there." His table-saw and horses were laid out on the far side, along with all of his tools arranged on the pegboard hooks. Hooks for tools; hooks for plastic bags. "A place for everything, and everything in its place," Marilyn had a habit of saying to him. He didn't need reminders. They saw eye to eye on that, especially when their modest home seemed to shrink and carry the risk of being transformed into a chaos of ever-accumulating objects as Jonathan and Matthew grew in size and in need. They were lucky, he reminded himself. The boys didn't plead for many toys and gadgets and they put their things away most of the time. It wasn't until pre-adolescence that they made a foray into rebelliousness. He put the last of his bags in the trunk and remembered the fuss they made about the part in their hair that he and Marilyn insisted upon from the time the boys went to the barbershop for their first professional haircut and needed to sit on a stack of three phone books. They must have planned it, he thought. They no longer needed phone books to lift them out of their meekness. They ranted about the part. Hank and Marilyn didn't make a fuss. The boys were such good boys, and the part no longer served a purpose, as long as their shirts were still tucked in when they arrived home from school. He closed the trunk. "They are good men. Decent men."

Seth didn't notice Hank in the parking lot. By the time he reached his 2005 Dodge whose silver paint was chipping on the roof and hood but still ran like a dream, he had forgotten to think about looking for him. He was scrutinizing a scrappy thirty-something man—tall, gaunt, baggy bathing trunks, bare-chested, rubber flip-flops—who was bending over in his pick-up to adjust something on the seat before closing the door and heading to the supermarket entrance. Watching the man's sun-bleached strands of not-so-clean blond hair and the darker hair on his thin sinewy legs, Seth tried to imagine how he might smell. As he finished unloading his canvas bags into the trunk of his car, he lingered until the man stood upright and he could see his face and decide whether the fantasy was worth continuing while he drove home. He knew that if it was, he was eminently capable of going back into the supermarket under the pretext of having forgotten something (he was running low on matzoh, he remembered) to shadow him. "I've done worse in my day," he said to himself. When the man finally made his face visible, it wasn't an attractive face. It was ruddy, the cheeks too sallow, the beard too straggly. It suggested someone—and there were many of them in this area, Seth reminded himself—who was a "recovering" something. "Steer clear. They want something in exchange. Money, a fifth, a joint." He knew the type. They made him understand before they had sex that he wasn't an object of their sexual desire. It prevented him from getting hard.

    He closed the trunk of his car, got in, and started the ignition. Hank was already out of the parking lot and on the coastal highway headed home to attend to one of the next items on his list: the wobbly table on the patio, the cracked caulking around the bathtub in the second bathroom, the dead sea-grape leaves scattered about the front lawn like crisp frisbees or oversized potato chips, the cobwebs in various intersections of walls and ceilings, and on and on. By the time each man was on the highway, Hank listening to a non-strident religious radio station and Seth to NPR, their chance encounter above the bruised peach had lost whatever resonance it might have had. The episode of the peach didn't even resurface when each of them was slicing peaches that evening after their solitary dinner.

8

"The coming of the Kingdom." Hank placed his notes and King James Bible on the small table in front of him. He tucked his yellow pencil behind his ear. "This is probably the most difficult passage in Luke that we'll be looking at," he said to the group of twelve men sitting in fold-out chairs that were laid out in a circle in the Activity Room of the local church. His hands were shaking slightly. Despite the hours he'd devoted to preparing for the session, he felt he was on unstable ground. The weekly one-hour men's discussion group he'd been attending since Marilyn became ill was informal. The men arrived wearing shorts and a tee-shirt, and sneakers or sandals; everyone stacked on their paper plates the doughnuts and Danish that a different man was assigned to bring each week. He knew all of the men, some better than others, depending on whether they came to every meeting or only sporadically. Nevertheless, he treated his shifts as facilitator with the gravitas of someone preparing to deliver a Nobel Prize acceptance speech. These men were important. So was God.

He picked up his Bible, opened to the earmarked page and read. "'The Pharisees asked Jesus when the Kingdom of God would come. They were impatient to hear some tidings of its approach.' Did you know that the term 'Kingdom of God' appears 35 times in Luke's gospel? If it appears that many times, it's important that we understand what the term means." He took a sip of coffee from his paper cup and would have liked to take a bite from his doughnut but thought it better to wait until someone else took the floor before he reached for the simple glazed ring he'd selected from the tray. The silence that accompanied his taking a bite of the doughnut could be uncomfortable, unless someone intervened while he chewed and swallowed. He wasn't willing to take the risk.

"Jesus answered them. He told them when the Kingdom of God would come. It's there, in the Bible you have in your lap. Some of you use the King James Version, some the New King James Version, some the New International Version, some the English Standard Version. So many options. Does anyone want to read Jesus' answer from your text?"

Hands were raised. Hank reached for his doughnut as he called out three names: Joe, then Earnest, then Richie.

Joe read: "The Kingdom of God is within you."

Earnest read: "The Kingdom of God is among you."

Richie read: "The Kingdom of God is in your midst."

Hank swallowed his second mouthful of doughnut and washed it down with some coffee. As he returned his paper cup to the table, he saw that his hands were no longer trembling. The discussion had begun in the way he'd hoped. "Within. Among. Amidst. They sound different to me. The Greek is *entos*. I don't know what that means, but for centuries scholars have come up with the three translations that you gentlemen offered. My questions to you are: Are they the same? Are they different? And if they are different, how so? And if they are different, which one is right?" His eyes swept the room like a lighthouse beacon. "What do you all think?"

Carl, the jokester of the group, replied, "I say we call it a day and play some golf."

Hank smiled. "I knew I could count on you, Carl. Let's deserve to play golf first. Let's try to work through this. Any thoughts? Are they more or less the same? Does one exclude the others? Do they overlap?"

He abandoned the protocol of calling on those who raised their hands. Instead, he let the men speak when and as they wished. In reality, he wasn't looking for an answer to the question. It was a centuries-old question that couldn't be answered by thirteen retirees in Florida who probably came here each week as a way to chip away at their interminable days and be grateful for the minutes and hours spent out of the house and away from their solitude or their wives, who were also probably struggling to chip away at an overall sensation of tedium only to arrive at the thing they too feared the most: the end of their time and the wide-eyed realization, "That's it?" He knew that most of the men present at these plenary segments used them to segue into some pressing and personal anecdote—the sick cousin, the overdue mortgage payment, the latest MRI results. Hank didn't intervene when they digressed. He allowed the segues and non-sequiturs to find their place. It must be what these men need, he reminded himself. God knows, I need it too. These meetings were as much an opportunity for release and commiseration as they were for religious and spiritual enrichment. He believed his task in all of this was simply to be one of promoting a sense of communion and fellowship, even if individual moaning and groaning ended up being the order of the day. Who was he to judge?

He let the men spill while he walked to the fold-out table in the back to get some more coffee and a piece of Danish and to listen to their variations on a larger and more painful theme of something that he couldn't give a name to, but which he too felt most of each day since Marilyn's death: Why did this happen to me? Listening to these men unleash their woes helped him to understand that he wasn't alone.

Seth listened to the menu of melodies and said "Stop" to the salesperson of his new cell phone when he heard the sequence of do-mi-sol-do. He'd asked the salesperson to program the phone so that the sound of incoming text messages was different from the sound of incoming emails. "Every time I hear a noise coming from my phone, I have to look," he explained. "If I knew it was an incoming email, I could hold off."

The salesperson looked at him quizzically. "So you want this sound for your texts?"

"Yes."

"Anything else?"

"No." He felt ridiculous.

The first high-pitched and trilled arpeggio of an incoming text message arrived that evening. "Hey. It's Ed. Free tonight? Can stop by. Got the itch. How about you?" The message gave him pause. Ed was the only hook-up he saw on a regular basis since he'd moved here. The sexual and emotional boundaries between them had been set after two encounters. They were wild but contained, provided the mood and the moment were right. Seth quickly came to understand that hook-ups were about heat. Sometimes the heat was on high, sometimes it had to be coaxed to produce that blue inner flame, and sometimes it simply couldn't be generated. Ed was the second type. Some kindling would be required.

"What did you have in mind?" he replied, hoping that an erotic response from Ed would do the trick. He wanted to want to have sex.

"You know what I like."

"I sure do. Anything else you'd like to explore?"

"What did you have in mind?"

The flame wavered. He felt the need for something more or suggestive or daring.

"I'll get back to you in five minutes."

"Okay."

He took a stroll through his house, stopping to look at the 50-inch television screen on his living room wall (he could watch a movie), the computer at his desk in the study (he could write some emails or surf the internet), the books and magazines strewn about (he could catch up on some reading), the queen-size bed in his bedroom (he could carry on with Ed). He paused at the threshold to his bedroom, imagining that he'd just led Ed down the dark hallway to this spot, where they would kiss before entering. Perhaps here, while they kissed, one of them would begin unzipping the other's shorts. He looked at his bed again. Four pillows, in stacks of two, were propped up neatly against the headboard. The metallic blue top sheet was folded into a thick band over the blue and beige striped quilt, which would give way softly when one of the two men pushed the other down onto it and the play began in earnest. It wasn't working, and he wasn't in the mood to conjure another scenario. Walking back down the hallway, he pulled out his cellphone. "Can't tonight. Having dinner with my brother. Could be late. Another night. Soon, I hope."

He sat down on the sofa and picked up a magazine. "Do-mi-sol-do." It was Ed. "No problem, man."

Case almost closed. Seth read the message again. There was something about the moronic word "man" on the heels of the astuteness of the comma that set off another spark. He was tempted to fuel it again, to relent and type in a time for them to get together that evening. He resisted. Had Ed been an unknown man, a new man, he thought, he would have jumped at the chance, even canceled dinner with the brother he didn't have. But Ed was familiar territory. They had a history of encounters, unavailabilities, last-minute cancelations. He would get through this one as well. He placed his cell phone on the side table and looked out the window toward the strip of sky that was visible above the tree line. The evening lay before him like another empty promise. Long evenings and empty promises weren't new to him. The final years with Yoni were proof enough.

He picked up the remote for the television and walked to the thermostat on the other side of the room to switch to air-conditioning. The room was stuffy. "Heat," he thought. "It's overrated."

9

Honey missed a morning. She wasn't able to schedule Glen's colonoscopy appointment late enough for her to make a quick hop to the beach with her camera. If she trusted that her husband would continue fasting without her hovering and would take his last dose of Mylicon before the procedure, she could have slipped out. But he wouldn't attend to these matters, she knew. After more than forty years, she knew a thing or two about him. He liked to eat too much, for example. Anything and everything was fine by him, as long as he felt full. He liked to feel full. It was a need that at first she felt obliged to try to coax him out of with patience and persistence. She failed. Then she tried guilting him into stopping by being shrew-like about his eating habits. She failed. The options were narrowed to accepting his appetite or leaving him. She chose acceptance and purchased belts for him that were progressively one size larger but nevertheless had to make a severe arc under his belly before he could fasten the buckle. Rising from her bed, she heard his labored breathing in the adjacent bedroom and wondered whether the breathing would give up. She wondered whether she would too. And if so, when.

It was still dark. Her heartbeat raced. "Beach sunrise. Glen colonoscopy." Both of her essential relationships couldn't be accommodated that morning. She went into a panic, as if she were about to go AWOL in a huge way and would pay a heavy price. Damn him and his ways, she thought.

She entered her husband's bedroom. "Time to get up. I'll get your Mylicon ready."

That morning, Hank and Seth noticed the absence of Honey at the same time but from different vantage points: Hank was walking along the beach from the south and Seth from the north. Although neither had ever approached her or greeted her despite her radiant smile, they took note of her and, like the willets darting at the ocean's edge, assumed that she'd always be there. This morning, however, she wasn't there. Her absence verged on the dramatic, as if a centuries-old lighthouse that they'd always seen but never visited (after all, it's always there and they could visit it any time) had been mysteriously removed overnight, eliminating the beacon of light they'd counted on since as far back as they could remember, even if they weren't sure why.

Converging at the spot where she usually positioned herself and her paraphernalia—beside a large and many-branched driftwood trunk that had been there as far back as they could remember—they held each other's glance for that extra split second that made it necessary for someone to say something. Both men said simultaneously, "She's not here."

"Do you know what her name is?" Hank asked. "I don't. I've never spoken to her."

"I haven't either. I did wave once or twice. Strange."

"What do you mean?" Hank asked.

"I mean that I can see the same woman in the same place on the beach almost every single day and not even say hello."

"I suppose so," Hank replied.

Seth looked out toward the sun, which had finished breaking the horizon and was a brilliant yellow-orange. "By the way, how was your peach?"

"Sorry?"

"How was your peach? The one that dropped on the floor at the supermarket. How was it?"

Hank looked directly into Seth's eyes. "I thought you looked familiar. I cut away one small bruise. The rest was fine."

"You have better luck with peaches than I do. If I buy them before they're ripe, they never get ripe. And if I buy them when they're ripe, they have the texture of a potato. So much for tree-ripened fruit."

"My wife taught me everything you need to know about picking fruit."

"I never had such luck."

"Well, it's not like women instinctively know how to pick fruit."

"I didn't mean that. I meant that I've never been married."

"Ah."

Seth waited for Hank to bite the bait and tug. He didn't. "Anyway, I should keep going. I'm on a cardio fitness routine. Can't stop for too long. Seth, by the way."

"Hank, here. Nice to meet you."

"Likewise."

They shook hands. Seth tried to look intently into Hank's eyes, but they were cast downward toward the sand.

"I'm sure we'll run into each other again. We only have one sun and one supermarket."

"I come here almost every morning."

"Me too."

"Then, I'm sure we will."

"Enjoy your walk, Hank."

"You, too, Seth."

As they turned to go their separate ways, Seth paused. "Hey Hank." Hank turned around. "I'm going to say hello to the woman with the camera the next time I see her. Even if I have to go out of my way a little bit. How about you promise to do the same? A gentleman's agreement."

Hank looked puzzled. "I'll do my best."

Seth smiled. "If you don't, the next time I run into you at the supermarket I'll make the whole display of peaches fall around your ankles and say it was your fault. You've been warned."

Hank smiled back uneasily and continued northbound.

* * * *

When she sat next to her husband during intake and discovered that the procedure and recovery period would take at least two hours, she said to him, "How about I leave and come back later?"

"Sure, honey. Go have a nice breakfast for me."

"We'll do that together afterwards. I'll just drive over to the beach and take a walk. Get some exercise for you instead."

"You don't let up, do you?"

"You don't either."

"You'll come back to get me, won't you?"

"You'll find out soon enough."

"If you do, there's a Denny's down the street. We'll celebrate."

She gave him a peck on his full rosy cheek and headed toward the glass exit door to the parking lot of the facility. She hadn't hung the handicap parking placard on her rear-view mirror when they arrived, thinking it would be good for him to walk the extra few feet. Now she was regretting it. The heat was already intense, the sun's waking spectacle was long over, and she was having second thoughts about going to the beach after all as she trudged across the broiling asphalt to the far side of the parking lot. She got in the car, turned on the air-conditioning, switched on the radio, which was already set to her favorite station of hits from the Seventies and Eighties, and sobbed.

* * * *

Beth Ha Tephila. The House of Prayer. Seth passed the synagogue almost every day on his way home after some errand along the main drag. It was a modern building, round and with lots of glass bricks stacked in abstract shapes to let in the light. But it was only one story high and set back from the road. It didn't want to announce itself. He found this to be the case with most synagogues he saw wherever he went: structures that were zealously studied (and here the Talmud came to mind) in their effort to be understated but united in a voice that gently insisted on embracing the past but not at the expense of the present or future. He admired the *schuls* in America and the people who conceived them. He admired American Jews for the most part, architects and otherwise. He felt proud to be one of them and didn't question his sense of belonging except when it came to how he went about doing sex, especially before and after his practically setting up a full-fledged domestic partnership with Yoni. Surely he wouldn't be excommunicated for indulging, anonymously and habitually, in men, let alone uncircumcised ones, after his one long-term Jewish love. Surely he wouldn't burn in Hell for eternity, since there wasn't a Hell to burn in, if he'd understood correctly. But acceptance? A sense of belonging? He had his doubts and steered clear despite the inviting architecture.

 He stopped at the hardware store on his way back from the beach. From the large picture windows of the synagogue looking out onto the street, he saw clusters of people inside lingering around large round tables encircled by metal fold-out chairs. It was the first time he'd seen the temple peopled.

Up until now, it had been devoid of human activity, a kind of static monument or monolith to something that he felt excluded from, whatever it might have been a monument for. Now it was abuzz with movement. People of all ages—and many of his age, he noticed—milling about with what looked like those plastic glasses of wine that had a snap-on stem and base. They were dressed casually: no white shirts buttoned tight at the collar; no dark, ill-fitting slacks with dark leather tie-shoes; no loose-fitting dresses falling below-the knee. Here, through the picture window of a place of obser-vance, he observed people in jeans—shorts even—and Izod shirts and t-shirts and blouses that revealed cleavage and an occasional *pipik*, and sandals and sneakers. With so many people, it must be some kind of holiday that he'd forgotten about, he thought. Some Jew he was. There they were, so many of his age, of his kind, shielded from him behind the thick panes of glass, as if to say to those like him on the other side, "You think you belong, you may want to belong, and maybe you could belong. But you've chosen not to. You may observe us through the glass bricks. Hurricane glass. Bullet-proof glass."

* * * *

Curious man, Hank thought, walking back to his house. Nice enough, but.... And here he searched for a word that was kinder than the one that had immediately presented itself: cocksure. He pulled on a thread hanging from his shorts, and his thoughts were about to turn to the matter of checking the hamper as soon as he got home to see if it was full enough for him to do a load of laundry. But the image of the full hamper dissipated when he saw his neighbor Jane stooped down and digging with her trowel along the flower-edged border of her recently repaved driveway.

"Good morning, Hank. Nice sunrise?"

"Morning, Jane. Yes it was. Best way to start the day."

She jabbed her trowel into the mulch and earth underneath it and stood up from her digging, brushing the few strands of gray hair that escaped the black elastic band triple-looped at the nape of her neck. "Oh, the weeds. No end to them."

"No end to sunrises either," Hank said.

"They appear overnight. It's unbelievable."

"Keeps you busy. Out of trouble."

She smiled. "And what kind of trouble could I possibly get into? A woman my age. Hank, my trouble-making days are long gone."

"I never had them," he replied.

"It's never too late," she said.

Hank lowered his eyes to make the conversation go away. It was his fault, that last remark of his about keeping out of trouble. He shouldn't have. His fingers groped for the hanging thread again and pulled it off. He flicked it toward the gutter but it was picked up by the breeze and off it went in a swirl. He resumed his walking. "Have a nice day, Jane."

"You, too."

His house was three identical houses down from hers, and the proximity worried him. He looked forward to running into her. At the same time, he didn't want it to happen often enough that a line would be crossed, as he feared it just had. As he separated the key to his door from among the other keys on his key chain, it occurred to him that he didn't know where Seth lived. Probably in this general area. A curious man, he thought again. A lonely man. Like Jane. Like the woman with the camera at the beach. Like me, he supposed.

* * * *

Honey and Glen were seated side by side at the oncologist's office. The chair seats were thick and resilient, like shock absorbers.

"We didn't find any polyps," the oncologist said.

"Is that good news?" Honey asked. She reached for Glen's hand but it was clenched in his lap and wouldn't open to meet hers.

"It's not cancer," he replied.

"Then what does my husband have?"

"We'll need to conduct more tests."

"What might he have?"

"Best not to speculate. But we can eliminate cancer."

"That's a relief," Glen told her as they walked out of the doctor's office.

"It is. But you do have something." She watched as he rested his arms and hands over his mound of belly as if he was with child. "Whatever it is, you should lose some weight."

"I didn't hear the doctor say that."

"It certainly couldn't hurt," she said.

"Lay off, will you?"

A third person could have fit into the space they maintained between them as they walked down the main corridor toward the hospital exit. Honey expected the visit with the oncologist to produce a condition with an actual name, even cancer, and a treatment that included a leaner and cleaner diet.

The main corridor was painted a toothpaste green, and the fluorescent overhead lighting cast a glow of overall unhealth, despite the polished floors. "Let's get out of here into the fresh air," she said to her husband. "I need to breathe."

Glen started to have trouble breathing after he married her and stopped surfing on his free mornings and rarely went out with his men friends on free evenings. When the children were born, Honey hoped he would rise to the occasion of fatherhood. Instead, he became sulky, sedentary and overweight. The bottom shelf of the refrigerator was allocated for his beer, which he drank in the evenings in front of the television. The children were bundles of energy, joyous. She gravitated toward them, exhausting as they were. "Glen, come look at Cal. He's trying to pedal your exercise bike." "Be there in a minute," she heard him call from the living room, knowing that he wouldn't arrive, that he might never be there for her or for them. She felt inadequate. Wasn't it her responsibility as wife and mother to fix all things breaking or broken? "Something is wrong with me," she thought.

They walked toward the car in silence. She considered bringing up her stock of remedies for change: counting calories, reducing his intake of red meat and processed snacks, getting on the Home Gym that she bought him for Christmas, taking a power walk in the neighborhood before he went to work. But she knew better. That topic of conversation was already depleted. Even if he had followed any of her gems of advice, were these the changes that would matter in the long run? Yes, he might return to a semblance of his surfer-dude physique, although without the crowning touch of his unruly blond hair, which had thinned considerably and turned gray-white long ago. But was it really about that? It certainly couldn't hurt, she thought as turned on the ignition. But still.

"Let's do Denny's," he said. "I'd say we have something to celebrate."

"Denny's it is. Why not," she replied. She knew how it would play out at Denny's after he pretended to study the laminated menu. He'd choose what he always chose—the All-American Slam: three scrambled eggs mixed with shredded cheddar cheese, bacon bits and slices of sausage with a side of hash browns plus two slices of white or whole wheat toast. She watched him as he fit himself with effort into his side of the booth like a large round peg in a small square hole. She surveyed the other booths. Most of them held elderly couples who weren't talking to each other. She wasn't the only one.

"I'll have the All-American," he told the server. "An extra

side of whole wheat toast."

The server walked off and she watched her husband move the dish of butter pats individually wrapped in gold aluminum to his side of the Formica table. "He'll take eight this time," she ventured. "Give or take two." She enjoyed these time-worn habits of his. They gave her a respite in the form of predictability. "Let's see if I'm right again," she thought. Most of the time she was on the mark, which gave her a moment of satisfaction. The moment passed and her bitterness and frustration returned. "Christ," she said under her breath. "Does he have to? Again?" But she held her tongue.

They didn't find much to say to each other at breakfast. They finished their meal quickly and returned home.

"I'm gonna lie down for a while," he said.

"Good idea. Get some rest." She went to the refrigerator to put away the Styrofoam box that held the wedge of omelet and hash browns that she'd lost her appetite for shortly after they ran out of things to say. The shelves were full. She found a tight spot above one of the Rubbermaid containers. She couldn't make out what was inside. The turkey meatloaf? Or was it the mac 'n cheese with bacon? Two of Glen's favorites. She wasn't particularly fond of either.

"Call me if you need me," she yelled out as he trundled down the hallway to the bedroom. His bedroom. As she closed the refrigerator door, she noticed her camera sitting on the granite island countertop. She slung it over her shoulder. In a soft voice that she knew he wouldn't hear, she said, "But I won't be here."

10

The onset of evening was a difficult time for those who were in the habit of waking up in the morning darkness and, feeling too rested to go back to sleep, took themselves to the beach to bear witness to the sun announcing the beginning of another day, another chance to undo some wrong, get something right, or touch down with greater understanding on some vaster and more nebulous terrain—like love or happiness or fulfillment. For them, sunset was like a slowly closing door. The sun itself sunk way over to the west, sequestered behind trees and buildings long before slipping through the actual horizon line like a coin into a pocket. The air at that time of day was heaped with heat, humidity and torpor, not something meant for humans to inhale without the discomfort of yet another weight to endure. Whatever suggestions it could make about another chance, about hope, were muted, less dramatic and insistent. At sunrise, on the other hand, the heat and humidity had dissipated into the night darkness. The air of the burgeoning day felt cleansed and breathable, like a balm or a promise. Better to stay indoors at sunset, in the cool A/C while prepping dinner and thinking about what film or television show to watch afterward, what websites to surf, what mixed drinks to concoct, how to pass through this chunk of darker and heavier time until it was time to go to bed. Love, happiness, fulfillment indeed. They could be thought about again tomorrow.

After dinner, Hank watched the third episode of a detective series that was showing potential; Honey opted for another romcom, grateful that there seemed to be no end to the genre and that her husband would repair to the den at the far end of the house to watch a sports channel. Seth was still undecided between yielding to the television, resorting to a hook-up site on his computer, or reading a book.

Had one or more of their windows been opened, which few people in Florida did on a summer night, they would have heard the sounds coming from those who preferred to venture outdoors as the sun was setting. Sounds of lawn mowers, of hoses being uncoiled from their spools to spray jets of water on thirsty shrubs and filmy cars, of children releasing their last shouts and flailings before being called indoors for the balance of the evening, of frogs and cicadas readying their throats for the full performance to take place when the moon was at its apex. They would have smelled evening smells. Smells of damp, steaming grass and driveways, of meat-laden smoke billowing from charcoal grills, and the more generalized odors of natural life about to ease up and repose.

Their windows were not open and they were subjected to the sounds of news bytes clamoring for attention on computer or television screens, of sizzling and boiling coming from pans and pots on the stove, of the whirring of the microwave as it rotated the almost-ready meal to an acceptable temperature, of the hum of the central air-conditioning passing cooled and dried air along its subcutaneous foil ducts and releasing it from small grillwork frames embedded in the ceiling. The sounds of the great indoors.

Hank had leftovers aplenty: thick-slice ham, parsley potatoes and green beans. He arranged them on one plate, covered it in plastic wrap and placed the plate in the microwave, which he set for one minute. He would eat at the small table in the breakfast area, as opposed to the dining room, which he rarely used. The lattice-work placemat was down. The cutlery was placed on top of the paper napkin, which he sometimes folded into a triangle and at other times into a rectangle, depending on his frame of mind. The Bible was stationed above the placemat, pre-opened to kick off the meal-time prayer. All he needed was to hear the beep of the microwave and dinner would be ready. He marveled at modern technology. He was also skeptical. What nefarious machinations lay in those microwaves and the food they penetrated as they heated it up? But they were convenient, especially for someone whose meals no longer had anything to do with the rites and rituals of family, of gatherings of friends, of a hoped-for compliment.

Honey moved her camera off the kitchen table and carried the casserole to the lazy Susan in the table's center. "Dinner's ready," she called out to her husband, allowing for the possibility that he in turn would call out that he wasn't hungry and preferred to stay in bed, which he did. She brought her camera back to the table and began taking photos of the uncovered oval Corningware casserole that housed a mixture of ground meat, macaroni, oregano and pre-shredded packaged cheddar cheese that lay hidden under a coverlet of melted mozzarella. As she waited for the rising steam to dissipate so that her camera lens wouldn't fog up, she poured herself a glass of white wine from the half-gallon screw-top bottle and treated herself to a long gulp. She had this idea of taking a close-up of the peaks and valleys of the cheese so that they could be interpreted as one of any number of possibilities, depending on the viewer of the photo that she imagined standing in a gallery where the series of photos was being exhibited, each framed and matted in white, signed in the bottom right-hand corner: the Alps in winter; shades and multi-levels of white;

or, simply, a close-up of a 1950s-style casserole. She continued snapping and sipping, knowing that in all likelihood the photos would remain deep in the internal mechanisms of her camera and that the wine would end up being her dinner before she settled down to watch a romcom, but not before putting together a plate of food and placing it on a tray to deposit in the den by Glen's side, where she would find the plate empty the following morning when she went to retrieve the tray while he lay asleep.

Seth baked a salmon steak dribbled in white wine and butter and flanked by quartered redskin potatoes that he coated with olive oil and fresh rosemary, all of which were laid out in a Pyrex dish that he slid onto the oven rack when the temperature reached three hundred fifty degrees. He didn't spend too much time in the kitchen, but he steered clear of prepared or processed foods, preferring to nourish his body with items that he considered clean. As he prepped his dinners, he promised himself he'd devote more time to them, if only to have greater variety. After all, what was waiting for him after dinner besides some vague hope that there *was* something waiting for him after dinner? Or some*one?* Standing over pots, bowls and utensils in the confines of his small, windowless kitchen hardly seemed a path to the unexpected. What was the time saved in the kitchen really going to lead him to or bring to him?

He ate his meal with a book splayed open under the lip of his plate, held firmly in place by the steak knife crossing the top margin of the open pages. He was hoping that the pages he read would persuade him to continue reading after he finished his meal, rather than closing the book and drifting toward the lure of his computer or phone. The book, one that had been reviewed positively in the Times Literary Supplement, held his attention. He reached the end of a beginning chapter as he was raking up the bits of bits of salmon that had found their way to the edges of his plate. He asked himself whether he should start another chapter, perhaps moving to the living room and spending the evening reading something worthwhile instead of again dwelling on how the idea of cohabitation was so distasteful but how the reality of solitude, especially at his age, was so frightening. The book seemed promising. It might do the trick.

* * * *

The half-hour before getting into bed, and however long it took to fall asleep after getting into bed, were difficult for them. At that hour of night-black sky, rituals were simple and automatic enough to not require full concentration on the rituals themselves: locking front and back doors, turning off lights, slipping into pajamas, brushing teeth and applying rehydration facial creams in the bathroom. But bathrooms did have a mirror, and one fleeting glance at the face reflected in it was all it took for them to see and to feel the weariness and the toll exacted on the many of those like them, those who had passed through enough time and enough disappointment for as long a time as they had. The bathroom mirror at night was to be avoided at all costs. The front-lit bulbs above and the absence of any natural light behind cast a harsh verdict. The mirror couldn't be avoided. At some point, any slighted dabs of cream on the face had to be spotted and massaged into the thirsty pores and crevices; the toothpaste had to be spit into the sink and form a foamy globule that seemed like an infection: and as the head lifted itself from the sink, the eyes wouldn't be able to resist meeting their doppelgangers in the mirror and scrutinizing, if only for an instant, the irrefutable evidence inscribed on the entirety of the face that things weren't supposed to have ended up this way: a diminished body and soul, hoping for hope (but against all hope), eyes filmy and crow-footed with disillusion, cheeks hollowed by an onslaught of failures at fullness, hair whose lost luster had also decamped from many other places, real and imagined. In short, overwhelming weariness and melancholy. Mirror mirror on the wall.

On the other hand, rising from bed in the dark was easy for them, almost joyful. They didn't set their alarms to go off with a shrill tone that catapulted them out of their beds against their will. They trusted their bodies to stir when it was time, at which point they looked at the digital numbers (blue ones for Hank and Seth, red ones for Honey). If the three or four numbers on their clock indicated that the sun would be rising in an hour or less, as if to say, "Have another go at it," their bodies didn't think twice about ceding to the feeble seduction of sleeping for just another bit. For them, the darkness before dawn—the end of darkness—was altogether different from the darkness at sunset—the beginning of darkness. The beginning of darkness carried the possibility that the sun might call it quits and the darkness would have no end. One never knew.

In that morning darkness, however, artificial light had to be switched on to move about, pajamas had to be removed, teeth brushed anew. In those minutes before the sun's awakening, the mirror put a wholly different slant upon the prospect of the upcoming day that lay ahead of them, one that carried a possibility or two of things that might finally be different from the many days that had transpired up until then, especially when they splashed cold water on their face to wake up completely and they saw hope their reflection. Another day, another glorious beach sunrise. Its spectacular colors and wild shapes above the inexplicably perfect line separating ocean and sky suggested a gorgeous story, perhaps preposterous but nevertheless compelling each and every time. A story of the possibility that today, against all odds, things could take a turn toward something resembling a transformation or, if one were truly lucky, an epiphany. Knowing that this awaited them, they slept well on most nights.

11

First Friday in Atlantique was a decades-old tradition. Cotillion Boulevard, the main street in the so-called "historic" district, was closed to vehicular traffic, and rows of white canvas pavilions were erected along the newly liberated two-lane band of asphalt that stretched ten blocks. Local art was the main offering: oil and water-color paintings (mostly seascapes but some portraits); driftwood and/or shell sculptures, mobiles and windchimes; artisanal jewelry that veered toward the clunky and hastily thought out; and odds and ends of offerings that eluded categorization, unless the reaction "You've got to be kidding" could be construed as a category.

The art pavilions were given breathing space by food stalls and trucks serving hot dogs, hamburgers, beer and the like, and by the occasional not-for-profit organization manned by one male and one female representative handing out brochures and soliciting donations for their cause. In the intersections where side streets criss-crossed with the main drag to create spaces akin to piazzas, local bands and individual musicians installed themselves with their instruments, amplifiers and gangly cables to test their efforts in the public sphere, beyond the safe confines of their garage or bedroom. Strangely, the shops along the main street didn't extend their hours until ten o'clock to accommodate the storm of visitors. Perhaps it wasn't so strange. Most of the visitors to First Friday in Atlantique wanted to get out of the house and into the great outdoors to guzzle a few beers, feel the buzz of a crowd, and converge at the intersections to hear the blare of the music.

For some time, Hank had been trying to overlook a piece of wall in his living room that could clearly do with something framed to fill its too-naked space. Occasionally he walked past the wall untroubled. More often than not, its expanse of whiteness bothered him. Deliberating whether he should go to the art festival, he considered the possibility of finding the right picture there. Moreover, he reminded himself, he hadn't used his car for a few days and didn't want the battery to die. Crowds and noise threw him into a tailspin of anxiety. At the same time, he was reaching his threshold for the silence produced by his routine, a condition that he recognized as soon as it illustrated itself in his mind as a type of reverse electrocardiogram: when the steady line began to blip and make small peaks of life, for him it was a sign of an agitation provoked by isolation that needed to be leveled out.

He put on a pair of his "dress" shorts (large white and blue checks with a permanent-press crease down the middle of each leg), a short-sleeve white linen button-down shirt, and a pair of white sneakers whose heels weren't yet worn down at their outer edges by the pressure of his slightly bowed legs when he walked. Before leaving the house, he made a pit-stop in the bathroom to comb his mostly brown hair, and opted to not wear the cap he usually wore to guard against the sun, since the sun had already begun its descent. He also took a quick pee, which he tried to remember to do whenever he was about to leave the house. A prostate thing combined with an age thing. He wasn't exactly looking forward to going out, but the alternative was to do what he always did. If nothing else, he could gain a measure of satisfaction from the simple fact that he had actually gone out in the evening. The car started up right away.

* * * *

The municipal parking lot was full; Seth had to weave through the side streets of the downtown area for a good twenty minutes before he found a parking place. He was unperturbed. He'd lived in Manhattan for more than two decades. Finding a parking place after circling for only twenty minutes was a stroke of luck, verging on a miracle. He delighted in the shift in perspective and still couldn't believe that he didn't need to return to his coveted parking place in forty-five minutes to secure the spot again by feeding four or more quarters into the meter. No parking meters here. In their place were volunteers, all of them senior citizens, who cheerfully cruised the streets in golf carts to search out transgressors of the "one-hour parking" signs posted along the sidewalks. For those uniformly white-haired golf-cart drivers ("Q-tips" they were called by the permanent residents of the area), their steadfast patrol conferred power and purpose, even if little was required on the part of those who violated the parking signs to sway the Q-tips to soften up and exempt them from the pink ticket. All it took was just enough chit-chat to hold a compliment and a thin excuse for the infraction. The Q-tips weren't looking to punish. They were looking for contact.

    Despite the wind, Seth unbuttoned one more button of his shirt. He considered his chest an asset, even if he understood that in a setting like an art fair in a place like Atlantique, and what with this wind, his chest would have little if any impact on anyone. The side street where he parked was quiet. He looked forward to the chaos that was teeming only a few blocks away.

The pavilions' simple aluminum frames began to sway back and forth as the wind picked up, and their white canvas tops to billow upward and then suddenly collapse downward as the wind current shifted. The sole purpose of these structures, and the tedium of their assembly, was to provide shelter to the works of art within. They were as fragile as a house of cards. Had there been menacing clouds to accompany the wind, one could have foreseen the likelihood of a flash thunderstorm and have chosen to stay home behind closed doors and lowered windows. The sky was clear. There was just a light breeze moving aimlessly like a bored and restless thug itching for a situation. Anything could happen. Welcome to the tropics.

In front of one pavilion, displayed prominently on an easel, was an enlarged photograph of a stretch of generic beach that Hank and Seth wouldn't have recognized if it wasn't for the piece of driftwood, a large tree trunk in the shape of a Y, that had found its way and settled onto *their* stretch of beach, the one that both of them travelled each morning and where each of them noticed the woman with the camera standing on every morning. Hank recalled waving toward her one time as she positioned herself between the tree trunk and the ocean after she deposited her camera bag in the joint of the Y.

Hank and Seth arrived at the easel at the same time. They were drawn to it at the same time. And at the same time, they systematically (although in different directions, Hank gazing clockwise through the pavilion and Seth counter-clockwise) cast their eyes about for the photographer—is it her?—who was standing and smiling behind her fold-out table laden with business cards and reproductions of the originals in small- and large-copy formats that she'd stacked vertically in wooden boxes like index cards in a library of days gone by. Her smile was unflinching as she reconnoitered the passersby for potential admirers and, even better, buyers. Her art had its entrepreneurial side.

As the eyes of the two gentlemen surveyed her piece of turf, a gust of wind lifted the display photo off the easel. It flew to the sidewalk and landed face-down.

She moved from her spot behind the table as they moved from their spots near the display, to retrieve the photo and restore it to its designated place.

"My goodness. Some wind!" she said into the space around the easel that encompassed them and a few other passersby.

"It's always something," Seth replied. "Wind, rain, heat. I love how people here just keep on trucking, as if catastrophes are always around the corner. Kind of diminishes the catastrophic nature of a catastrophe."

"It's just wind," she replied. "It's happened before. I really need to remember to bring some clips."

Seth smiled at her as he stooped down to retrieve the photo.

"I've got it, Seth." Hank grabbed the frame on its sides.

"You're too kind," she said.

"Hank, I didn't recognize you without your hat. Let me help you." He stooped down to grab the frame along its top and bottom. Together they placed the photo back on the easel.

"Thank you, gentlemen," she said.

Seth looked at the photo. "I know that place."

"So do I," said Hank. "I see it, and you, almost every morning."

"I'm flattered," she replied. "And a little creeped out."

Seth softened his eyes. "No stalking. Promise. I walk the beach every morning at sunrise. I see you there," he said, pointing to the driftwood Y in the photo. "Right there, with your camera bag sitting in the crook while you take pictures."

"I do too," said Hank.

"So you both see me?"

Seth laughed. "Yes. But not together. The closest I got to him was in the supermarket, when I saw him make a peach fall to the floor." He looked toward Hank and smiled.

Hank lit up. "Ah, the peach!" He extended his hand. "Now I remember. Hank here."

Seth extended back. "Seth." They shook hands. Seth's eyes tried to meet Hank's, but they were gazing downward.

"Honey."

"Which one of us are you referring to?" Seth asked.

She laughed. "That's my name, if you can believe it. No comments please. At this stage in my life, I've heard them all."

Seth didn't break his attempted eye contact with Hank. "Honey. Okay. I can believe it. My mother almost named me Silas."

Hank withdrew his hand from Seth's and extended it toward Honey. "It's a pleasure to meet you."

The three of them felt the strain of appearing at ease in this unexpected emotional breeze that was tampering with their normal ways of going about the things they were in the habit of going about until the inevitable minor variations reminded them that routines were supremely vulnerable. Their smiles were protracted and accompanied by a silence that was just long enough to make each of them aware of their discomfort. It was Honey who broke it.

"Don't make yourselves so invisible at the beach next time."

"See you at the Y tomorrow then," Seth said.

"Your photos are very nice," Hank said.

"I'll explore some more art. What about you?" Seth asked.

"I'll be heading to my car. It's the other way."

"Good to see you."

"You too."

Seth went further into the crush of people and noise. He wasn't relishing the idea, but wasn't the crush of people the point of the outing? If he wanted quiet, he could have stayed at home. As he paused to let a large and rowdy group of young men (students from the local community college, he assumed) work their way around him in small clumps, he turned his head back toward Honey's pavilion. Several feet in front of it he saw Hank walking away from the crush and noise and toting what appeared to be the fallen photograph, which was now secured between his right armpit and the curled fingers at the other end of his arm. He, on the other hand, was going home empty-handed.

12

The dark sky, still brimming with stars, was slowly losing its battle against the oncoming light gathering force below the horizon line. Holograms of puffy clouds were emerging in the dying nightscape like buoys of reassurance that the day would be fine. Just enough birds could be heard chirping and trilling to indicate no rain, at least not in the next hour or two. These were the small promising signs that those like Honey, Hank and Seth sought out as they stirred in their beds at four o'clock in the morning. Oh, blessed mornings such as these.

"Verse 24: *To be in God's future kingdom requires faithful readiness in the present. You know how the whole sky lights up from a single flash of lightning? That is how it will be on the Day of the Son.*" Hank spoke these words softly as he knelt by his bed in the waning darkness, eyes closed, hands clasped in prayer. "*His return won't be of a secret nature, becoming known only to a select few. It will be as observable as lightning that illuminates the sky.*" He looked out the window and thought about whether he should hang the photograph before or after his walk on the beach. He lowered his eyes again.

"Verse 31: *When the Day arrives and you're out working in*

the yard, don't run into the house to get anything. And if you're out in the field, don't go back and get your coat." He struggled with the verse, feeling that the language wasn't a suggestion that such activities should necessarily be accomplished but that it was a kind of dramatic caution against constant preparation. He then thought of Lot's wife, as he felt the discomfort of his kneecaps against the hardwood floor. And he thought of Marilyn. She would have liked the picture he bought, even if it cost a little more than he'd expected. It was quiet, simple, suggestive, and the tree trunk wasn't too intrusive. Where would she have suggested they hang it? Would she approve of the living room wall? Or would she have chosen another place, even if it meant his having to take down other pictures already mounted on the walls and propping up the new one in their place as she stepped back, shifted to the right and to the left, in order to let her keen eye determine yes or no. Part of him wouldn't have minded at all, the part that admired the authority and assurance she issued when sizing up such things, whether it was a picture to be hung, a dress to be hemmed, a simple meal to be arranged on the table—the way she slowly took a few steps back and squinted her eyes as if she had to strain them into the shape of quartered almonds in order to discern the proper placements of the parts that were intended to create the whole. But there was another part of him that would have been irritated by her always taking command and by his inability to stand his ground in the face of her decisiveness. Sometimes he resented her strength more than he resented his weakness. He said prayers to make the resentments go away. They didn't. He wondered about the meaning of marriage, the meaning of prayer. But there were the boys, their boys, now men. Such good men. She would have been proud. The two of them would have stood together watching their sons going about their business, and they would have been proud together. How he wanted to be with her. But he didn't want to be with her where she was, he thought. He wasn't ready. Funny how sometimes he was and sometimes he wasn't. Right now, he could think of nothing better than for her to appear before him, place her hands gently on his shoulders as he knelt by the bed, and ask him, "Anything special you'd like for breakfast?" But he also knew that he wouldn't be able to decide. He would leave the decision to her.

He rose from the floor. If he got dressed quickly, he could still make it to the beach before the light was too light. The picture to be hung would be a daylight chore, to be undertaken after his beach walk when he was starting to feel fidgety. Before leaving the house, he pulled two oranges from the refrigerator to squeeze when he returned from the beach. They were the last two oranges. "There," he thought. "Hang picture. Buy more oranges. The morning is full."

"There," Seth said to Winston. "Clean break, good place to stop for now." He clicked the "Save" icon and got up from his chair, satisfied. An hour of work put in and the world was still asleep. He brought his mug of coffee to the bathroom with him to comb his hair and shave, Winston trailing behind him, tail at half-mast in anticipation of the outing. There wasn't much hair to comb, but it was morning hair, tousled and unruly, for his eyes alone, he thought. Venturing into the public view, he preferred looking put together, even at five-thirty in the morning. One never knew who one might meet. The least one could do was to have combed hair and a clean tee-shirt without stains or too many wrinkles. God knows, he thought as he looked at himself in the mirror, he had enough wrinkles on his forehead and on the sides of his eyes. He refused to belong to the company of men, especially elderly men, who shuffled about in clothes they didn't bother to change for days. "It starts with the clothes and then the showers," he thought. "I will not go down that road with them." It was enough that this company of 60+-year-old men couldn't escape sharing certain gruesome physical conditions—the enlarged prostate, the dreaded erectile dysfunction, the high cholesterol and pre-diabetes. Seth wasn't ready to be a full-fledged member of the club. He kept himself apart by wearing simple clothes that were clean, crisp, unwrinkled and without the trace of a stain. By sheer luck, he had been spared the inevitable physical conditions of his age demographic, with the exception of a bald head and an increasing difficulty in ejaculating when his own hand wasn't doing the work.

He dressed quickly. The sun would be rising soon. Winston was already positioned at the front door, waiting for his master to put the harness around his neck to start the adventure. As they made their way down the street toward the beach, Seth looked up at the sky. Once again, he'd timed it right. After decades of city living meted out by clocks and watches, he couldn't believe how swiftly he'd transitioned to the position of the sun and the moon as the markers of the day. He felt like an honorary farmer, one without acreage or crop yields or years of labor in fields. And of course, he reminded himself, there was Winston and his animal instincts at the front door to give him a jump-start.

As they paused at the intersection of their street and the highway that they needed to cross before reaching the semi-hidden path to the beach, it occurred to him that he hadn't thought about, or searched out, sex that night. They made an unnecessarily mad dash across the highway, and Seth felt a breathtaking sense of liberation. Winston was panting happily.

* * * *

When Honey got out of bed that morning to begin her day, the darkness didn't offer up the tranquility she took for granted. It was as if she couldn't quite fine-tune the channel for clear reception. Glen was in his bedroom, sleeping soundly, as he always did at this hour. Not a peep. Interference was coming from those two men who'd approached her at the festival and spoke with her. She feared she'd have to greet them if she saw them on the beach, perhaps engage in conversation them. Why hadn't those two men come to understand that certain distances shouldn't be breached? Didn't they know how that disrupts the order of things? At their age they should know better.

Before opening the front door, she unhooked her camera bag to sling it over her shoulder, as she always did when she was going out at this hour, although she wasn't convinced that she would use it this time. Hank and Seth, she thought. If they were at the beach, they'd come to her, they'd talk to her. Sweet men, kind men. But still, their words, no matter how kind, would break the spell of the solitary morning that she was so used to.

She replaced her camera bag on the hook and headed back down the hall, trying to think about God before she arrived at Glen's room to peek inside. She liked the idea of God, especially since it held the dual promise of simplifying and consoling. She'd tried to use the expression "It was meant to be" but it rang false.

She heard Glen's snoring before arriving at his door. She didn't open it. "He's alive. That's all I need to know," she thought as she climbed back into her bed, the one place where she was sure not to run into her husband, or Hank and Seth. As soon as she lay down, she knew she wouldn't be able to go back to sleep. She got up again, went down the hall and unhooked her camera bag. She slung it over her shoulder and went out the door. "There," she said to herself. "Time for some focus."

Hank and Seth spotted her on the beach at the same time. Although from different vantage points—Hank heading south,

Seth heading north—they recognized her. They recognized each other, too. As imprecise as their figures displayed themselves in the distance and the dark, the others knew who they were. There they were, the three of them, where they found themselves almost every morning, taking their walk and letting their thoughts travel freely to comfortable places or uncomfortable places, depending on their mood and the degree of complicity of the sky and waves. They ambled along the shoreline and took pleasure in identifying objects along the way: wild daisies pushing through the dunes, sand dollars clustered in the sand, willets darting the incoming waves on feet as thin as thread. Such objects were like small anchors, assuring them that they wouldn't stray too far the demands of day as they bobbed about in the magic of their individual solitudes. This morning was different, however. The three of them felt it. There were new anchors, anchors with more weight, anchors that now had names—Honey, Hank, Seth—and that would require them to stop and chat.

13

Honey was first. "Hello!" she called out southward toward Seth as she waved her arms over her head like someone who was stranded. She made an about-face north toward Hank and continued the gesture, "Welcome!" she called out.

Hank and Seth smiled at her, then looked at each other and extended their hands. Winston sniffed the strangers' legs, and his muzzle found its way between Hank's legs. Hank bent over and scratched the dog's ears.

"Hands will *not* do," Honey said. "This place demands hugs." She opened her arms and glanced first at Seth, who obliged easily, and then at Hank, who proceeded more slowly and barely let the contours of his body skim the surface of hers as accommodated her. "Thank you, gentlemen. For the hug, and for saving my picture from the wind the other day. But more for the hug." She was barefoot. Her hands were slightly red and chapped. Her shoulder-length gray hair was pulled back in a loose ponytail held in place with a thick pink cloth band that was quadruple-looped and took up two inches of the tail. She was wearing a pair of denim shorts and a blouse that looked like the smocks that matronly art teachers used to wear in elementary school back in the day. She was as far away from slovenliness as she was from meticulous. Most of all, she looked supremely comfortable, in her element.

"No no no no," said Hank as she aimed her camera toward him.

"Superstitious? Don't worry, I won't capture your soul."

"I just don't like my picture taken."

"Not a problem."

Seth pretended to be fixing the necktie that wasn't around his neck and raking his fingers through a mane of hair that wasn't on his head. "You can take one of me. I don't mind. It's the ham in me, finely cured over many decades."

"Sorry. You're too easy," she said. He looked offended. "Just kidding." She began to click. "Better?"

"You're not the first to say that to me." Seth strolled toward the ocean, which was pierced by a sliver of sun. Winston trailed behind him. "Christ, did you see that?" he shouted just as a fin disappeared under the water after arcing briefly above the surface. "A shark!"

"It's a dolphin," Honey and Hank said in unison.

"How do you know?"

"Was the dorsal straight or curved?" she asked.

"Curved."

"Did you see the tail?" Hank asked.

"No."

"It was a dolphin," Honey and Hank said in unison.

He walked back toward them. "Are you sure?"

They smiled. Honey said, "It's rare to see a shark around here. You can let it go."

"Christ, that's a relief."

"And no need to bring Christ into the picture."

Seth looked at her. She held her smile, but her eyes looked serious. "I'm so sorry," he said. "I didn't mean to offend you. It's just that..."

"It's fine. There it is again. I think it has a companion." She pointed a finger. "Focus your eyes over there. If you hold it long enough, eventually they'll pop out again. So beautiful. Especially in pairs."

Both men heeded her instructions and sure enough they witnessed several times the double arc of two mates cajoling each other in a playful dance of provocation and seduction as they made their made their parallel trajectories thirty feet out.

"Stunning," she said as she moved away from them to position herself to click away in case the dolphins should break through the waves just when the entire orb of the sun was breaking through.

Seth turned to Hank. "So you bought the picture."

"Yes. I'll hang it today."

"Need any help?"

"I can manage. Thanks though."

"It's a nice picture."

"It is."

"I like the way she framed the Y of the trunk. Not too prominent. Not too insistent. Not too in-your-face, if you know what I mean."

"It's a nice picture."

"Yes. A nice picture."

Winston pried his muzzle between Hank's legs again. Hank bent over and rough-housed the dog's unkempt pompadour and ears.

"Sorry. He loves anyone and everyone. He assumes that the world is a benevolent place. Not such a bad thing, I guess."

"He's very sweet."

"Yes, he is. I don't remember what life was like before this guy. So easy. So devoted. What more could you ask for?"

Hank looked at him puzzled. "I'm a widower."

"I'm sorry."

"Almost three years. My wife and I talked about getting a dog. But we didn't get around to it. Not sure why."

"I never had one until I got Winston. I wanted one for years. It never seemed right. And then it seemed right, and I got him."

"You did a good job. He's so sweet."

"He is. I'm not so sure how much credit I can take for it. For that matter, how much credit we can take for how our charges end up being. I just feel grateful. I mean Winston is, well, almost perfect."

Honey returned to them. "Done."

"Satisfied?" Seth asked her.

"I think so. Don't want to be too satisfied. Otherwise there'd be one less reason to come back tomorrow. On second thought, there's really no reason to have a reason to come back. At least not here." She extended her arms toward the sun. "How can you resist?" She gathered her belongings deposited on the Y. "Time to head home."

"Me too," said Hank.

"Me too," said Seth, glancing down at Winston lying on his side directly under his feet. "This creature needs to be fed. He's collapsed and wilting away. I could do with some breakfast too."

They turned toward the dunes and the abandoned house rising above the band of sea grapes and sand daisies. "Such a shame," Seth said. "Look at that place." It was a modest two-story house, whose many large pieces of plywood fastened to its façade must have once been picture windows. The sloped roof was sunken in places, and the large deck was rotted. Sea oats pushed up through the planks and were chin high. A curious construction. For one thing, it was detached. Although the beachfront strip was not yet invaded by high-rise hotels, it did have its share of low-rise condominiums that filled up in the winter months, emptied out after Easter, and came to life again around Thanksgiving—the so-called snowbird migrations. Detached homes were a rarity. The driftwood trunk in the shape of Y had settled directly in front of it.

It was the house that made each of them slow down at that particular stretch of sand, rather than continuing on to the local public-access beaches where they could pick up a doughnut or cup of coffee. Before the house came into view each morning, they strolled along fantasizing about things large and small. Sometimes they dwelled upon a particular thought, sometimes they let it go on its way in their effort to land on something that would make them different from who they were and make their sense of the world appear less imperfect and troublesome than they saw it to be. But when the house came into view, they would ease up on their walking. For each of them, it suggested a suitable structure for encasing their life once they had come to terms with the shortcomings of their life and their souls were more at ease. The house had nothing special about it, except for its timelessness. There it was. It was always there, or so it seemed to them, as if it were an accretion of debris deposited by the ocean over the centuries, or particles of dust gathered high and solid by eons of time. It struck each of them as a safe place to slow down. To stop. To look out, back, and ahead.

"Do you know what the story with that house is?" Seth asked.

Honey and Hank shook their heads.

"One of us should find out. I've wanted to, but I never seem to get around to it," she said.

"It would be interesting to know," Hank said.

"I'll get on it, then. Have a wonderful day." She made her way to the dunes. Seth veered north, Hank toward the south. The triangle they formed expanded as each went their separate way toward their home and the life that awaited them within its sturdy and familiar walls.

14

Hank looked at the wall above the plaid sectional sofa. "That's the place," he said out loud to himself. "The picture will look very nice there." If only Marilyn had seen the Y before she died. Was it even there, he asked himself, when they took their almost-daily walks along the beach? If it was, and if they'd taken note of it together in the early days, he would have lifted her up by her slender waist and installed her carefully in the crook. Maybe he would have taken a photograph. Had it been in the latter days, they would have admired it, approached it, perhaps rubbed their hands along it and privately realized how the rough and weathered texture wasn't unlike certain parts of their own limbs—the back of the heel, the elbow, the knuckles. But the piece of driftwood didn't wash ashore to figure into the rituals between Hank and his wife. It appeared, just like that, after Marilyn had died, during one of Hank's unsettling solitary morning walks of mourning. He didn't notice it then. It took him a year of solitary morning walks to notice it.

The picture was large. Getting it positioned at the right height on the wall, and perfectly parallel to the ceiling and floor, was going to be more complicated than he anticipated.

He already arranged everything he thought he would need on the low rectangular coffee table in front of the sofa—hammer, brass picture hook and nail, level, sharpened pencil. As he laid them out, he noticed a fine white dust on the table and thought to give it a good dusting after the picture was hung. What he didn't consider was the height of the hole that he would have to make in the wall. It was too high to make by simply dragging the sofa out a foot or two and standing on the floor behind it, stretching himself upward with his hammer and pounding the dot he would have first inscribed with the pencil. Two solutions seemed possible: standing on top of the back of the sofa to make the pencil mark and pound the hole, hoping the sofa wouldn't fall backward from his weight as he hammered against the wall; or bringing out the ladder so that he could do the job on a more secure footing. The problem was that over the past three years the ladder had become entrenched behind stacks of unlabeled boxes that he'd gradually piled up, one on top of the other, during the bouts of emotional strength that he mustered in order to pack up those objects that provoked too much pain or grief after his wife died. The sturdy ladder that was hard to extricate, or the precarious sofa? If Marilyn were there, the picture-hanging would have been straightforward. He would mount the sofa back as she knelt on the sofa cushions, clutching his calves and saying "Please be careful" as he pounded the hook and nail into the spot that they'd agreed on. She would trust him with his hammering as much as he would trust her with the steadying of his calves. She made things so smooth and easy. Why did she have to die? he asked himself as he came to understand that without her he wouldn't be able to hang the picture just yet. It would take time. Too much time to hang a stupid picture. A word was forming in his head, a word that was entirely inappropriate for the man he aspired to be ever since he could remember. A word that in this moment carried rage instead of love. A word that could be used in so many ways, and one that he heard just that morning in a way that horrified him: Christ. He put away the hammer, the brass picture hook and nail, the level, the sharpened pencil. He went to the kitchen, opened the door under the sink, and took out the microfiber dust cloth. At the very least, he thought, he could restore a bit of a shine to the living room. As he passed the cloth across tables and chairs and picture frames and various electronic components housed in the entertainment unit, he asked himself why dust, of all possible things, was the only substance that could be counted on to ultimately be anywhere and everywhere. Where did it come from, anyway? Why was it one of the only things that didn't stop accumulating? What about compassion? Empathy? Forgiveness?

He stopped dusting when he arrived at the sofa. Its frame had soft curves, its legs were adorned with elaborate curlycues. He was tired. He knelt in front of the sofa, rested his elbows on the center cushion, joined his hands together and closed his eyes. "Forgive me, for I have taken the name of your son in vain. I did not speak it, but I thought it. I don't understand why you took her from me when you did. There is much that I don't understand but try to accept. But this, I do not understand. Forgive me. Show me. I beseech you."

He made an effort to rise slowly. Slow rising was new to him. It took mindfulness and discipline. His knees and his back had been giving him problems lately, especially if his movements were too abrupt. He wasn't used to abruptness.

* * * *

Shortly after he moved to Florida, Seth stood in what he called the "conservatory," a large space in his house that stood empty for more than a year while he waited for it to announce it how might be used in a way that would make it a space that he used. He considered giving up on the space after six months, or of playing up its lack of necessity by creating a Zen garden there. Not some desktop version of the *karesansui*. That wouldn't do. Something more along the lines of a vast frame constructed in the center of the terrazzo flooring that he would fill with pea gravel and where he'd place a *BangBangDa* somewhere in the mass of smooth stone for him and others to rake. He'd lay pillows around the frame and, under the windows lining one side, sleek black wooden troughs filled with slender bamboo trees to fracture the light coming in. He and his friends and other guests could spend time sitting in that space and... And there the vision stopped, overpowered by the taste of his grandmother's Sunday blintzes and a sense of betrayal. How un-Jewish could he allow himself to be? The idea of *karesansui* was tempting. It was fashionable. It hinted at some kind of privileged point of entry to a deeper appreciation of things that would be completely lost on those who were less privileged. He was reluctant to carry it out. He wasn't really one of them. He barely got around to raking the leaves in the front yard, let alone pebbles inside the house.

After six months, the empty space in the house suggested something more practical: Fill me up with a baby-grand piano on a cream-colored area rug. Seth knew how to play the piano, so the space would be used from time to time, although as a private space, never a performance space. If anyone should be impressed by the imposing aesthetic when they came to the house and say something like "Oh, do you play the piano?", he would respond, "I play *at* the piano" and hope to end the conversation there. Ivory keys won over pea pebbles. It seemed right. He scanned the space again. "Yes," he said to himself. "It should look very nice there."

The next and last piece of the house to tackle was the third bedroom, another piece of unused space, although one that he'd furnished sparingly but comfortably for those rare but inevitable occasions when enough visitors arrived at the same time that a third bedroom was necessary. Surely it would happen, he thought. Especially in winter or during Easter break. The ocean was around the corner, Disney World a forty-five-minute drive. But how often, he asked himself. He considered knocking down the wall between the conservatory and third bedroom and opening up the space. If there was too much company, he could always relinquish his own room and sleep on the sofa bed in the living room for a night or two. On the other hand, if he wanted to sell the house one day—and at this he pictured himself old and infirm, perhaps incapable of taking care of the house—how many single-family homes had only two bedrooms?

Then again, the idea of hiring someone to take a sledge hammer to the wall was tempting, if only so he could observe the aggression that was sanctioned among those men whose professional success lay in their capacity for smashing cinderblock and dry wall until they tumbled, and to flail their burly arms about in their attempt to dissipate the dust and rubble of their aggression. He didn't mind being rattled in this way from time to time, or watching such men. He stood there and, once again, he hesitated. "Jesus," he shouted, staring at the wall. "It's just a wall, for Christ's sake." He went back and forth—resale value of a conventional three-bedroom house versus being privy to the erotic spectacle of a demolition crew hard at work? He let the wall come down. How many compartments does a solitary life need to inhabit?

* * * *

On the mornings after Honey and Glen didn't sleep together because she could no longer bear his bouts of snoring and slipped into the spare bedroom in the middle of the night, she tapped lightly three times on the wall between the spare bedroom and what was gradually becoming Glen's bedroom. The tapping had become one form of their private shorthand over the past few years, one more way of not resorting to words to communicate. In this case, it was their code for two straightforward questions: "Are you awake?" and "Should I start breakfast?".

She waited for a knock in reply, or silence in reply. Either way, she would know how to proceed, which was the point of her tapping. She waited a few seconds, tapped lightly again, and waited again. Silence. Another restless night, she thought, convinced it was the blue light coming from the 50-inch flat screen television on the wall above the dresser that he'd bought recently and that made her understood that she was no longer needed in their bedroom. "He's found a new diversion," she thought, "One that doesn't ask for anything in return." His snoring was one thing. It couldn't be helped, and she was the one to decide to remove herself from their bedroom, if only to get a good night's sleep. But the television was another matter. That was his decision. She felt banished. It took him a week to notice her absence for seven nights in a row. When he did, he objected.

"I don't fit here," she said.

"Of course you do."

"How?" she asked. "Where?" she added. "When?"

He patted the empty half of the mattress. "You're just overreacting."

"And you're just horny."

"You got something against that?"

"You're all alike," she said as she walked out of the room.

"What nice men they are," she said to herself on the morning after her encounter with Hank and Seth at the festival. She went to the kitchen and squeezed herself a grapefruit to drink and took a single-serve plain yogurt out of the fridge, along with a fistful of raspberries that she pulled from a bowl and inspected one by one for mold. "Very different from each other but both so nice. Genuinely thoughtful, not just polite. Hank and Saul." She paused. "Saul?" No, that wasn't quite right. Hank was right, but Saul? It was something short, she recalled, and it started with an S. She could feel it. As she dipped her spoon into the container of yogurt to blend the liquid that had formed in the center, she ran through single-syllable names that began with S: Sal. Sam. Sid, Sol. So Jewish, she thought. Scraping the spoon along the inside edges of the bowl, she hit upon Seth. Yes, that was it. Seth. Hank and Seth. And good-looking for their age. Fit, too. Nice men.

She sat at the island thinking about them after she finished her yogurt-berry mixture. She heard a faint tapping coming from the bedroom wall down the hall. She ignored it.

15

The sun was where both Hank and Seth calculated it to be as they walked down their respective paths through the dunes the next morning. The strip of sand was there, wider than usual because of the half-moon, which was barely visible to the west, and the low tide. The ocean was there, its waves still in a semi-sleep state as they lapped lightly against the shoreline. In the distance, the "Y" of the driftwood was just beginning to emerge in the early morning mist that floated above the beach like a swath of gauze. All of it was there, as it was each morning, although with variations. This morning, for example: the sound of small waves making bubbling noises as they were absorbed by the sand; the rough texture of the sand granules with their peaks and valleys underfoot; the barely discernible odor of fish and seaweed, which would intensify as the sun heated up the vast murky broth below it like some upside-down flame. Yes, all of the usual ingredients were there. Except for Honey. She was not there. The "Y" was stripped of her photography equipment and was on its own.

Seth was the first to reach the trunk. He'd been fully prepared to wave to her from the distance and yell "Hello" to her as he neared her. He'd even readied himself to stop and chat once he arrived. "Of all times for her not to be here," he thought. He saw Hank approaching and paused at the trunk. Maybe Hank would stop, too.

He waved to him from the distance. He hollered "Hello" when it seemed like Hank was within earshot. He waited to see if Hank would stop when he reached the trunk. Hank slowed down, but it wasn't clear whether he would turn away from the ocean and pause to join him.

"She's not here," Seth called out to him.

"I noticed," Hank called back as he turned right and headed toward Seth.

"It feels strange, like not finding the ocean here one morning."

"Yes, it does feel strange."

"How much we take for granted. But the ocean is still here. I think we can count on that."

"I hope we can." Hank approached the trunk. "I hope everything is all right with her."

"I'm sure it is. Maybe she's still recovering from the festival."

Seth extended his hand as Hank approached. "I sure was exhausted from it, and I only spent a half-hour there." Seth didn't feel the assertiveness that he was hoping for in the joining of their hands.

"Did you hang the picture?"

"I tried, but the place on the wall where I think it should go is difficult to get to by myself."

"I can help you."

"That's okay. Thank you, though."

Seth looked at Hank hard and smiled. "I don't mind at all. Let me help you. Didn't you just say that you can't do it on your own? Unless you already have someone lined up."

"It's nothing."

"It's nothing for me to give you a hand either. Just tell me where and when. I'm assuming we live near each other. I'm in the neighborhood behind the junior-high soccer field. The neighborhood with the 50s-style bungalows. The one with the streets that start with 'Avenida de' something."

"I know it. I'm in the complex of townhouses across from the elementary school."

"Right. The 'Chalets de' something. All these languages here. You'd think we were some international hot-spot."

Hank looked at him blankly.

"Anyway, the chalets are five or six minutes from my house in the Avenidas."

"Is that how you pronounce it? I thought it was 'a-VEN-i-da' Not sure I'll remember that."

"We can head back together and I can stop at your place, if that works for you. I don't have any plans this morning. I rarely do. And your place is on the way."

"Well, sure," Hank said. He added, "Fine," and then, "Okay," each time feeling his throat tighten at the prospect of his morning ritual taking a deviation, and of his house taking in a visitor. Ever since Marilyn died, he kept his house like a monument to her life. A kind of mausoleum. He never had a living thing pass through its front door since the gathering he held after her wake. Everything inside, he felt, had to be preserved, untrammeled and uncontaminated by things outside. She was his inside, as was their home. To allow a new form of human activity within its walls meant that he was moving on, and away, from her, what little he had left of her to hold onto. That could not be.

He swallowed hard. "Do you have Honey's phone number? Maybe we should give her a call." He regretted having said "we." The word was presumptuous. It made it sound like a friendship that had traveled great distances, one that could be taken for granted and pushed further.

"I don't. I'm sure she's fine." Seth swiveled his left foot in the sand, making a small arc, and thought of the Zen garden that ended up as a showcase for a piano that he played less than he thought he would. "That's one of the down sides of routine," he said out loud to himself.

Hank continued gazing out toward the rising sun. "What do you mean?"

"I was just thinking about when I moved out of my parents' house. Almost half a century ago. I was seventeen. I remember loading up my car with the last of my belongings and was backing down the driveway for the last time, and my mother saying, 'We'll talk every Sunday.' I said, 'No we won't.' I was a pretty obnoxious teen. And precocious, now that I think about it. Then I said something like 'We'll call each other whenever we have something we want to say to each other. If we arrange to call every Sunday and it doesn't happen one Sunday because one of us has other plans, the other will think that something horrible has happened. Let's just keep it loose, Ma.' It made sense, but it was still obnoxious." He smiled at Hank, who turned to him midway through his discourse.

"Seventeen? Goodness. That's young. I didn't leave my parents' house until the day after my wedding."

"Don't get me wrong. I got along fine with my folks. At least I think I did. I just felt ready. I was working part-time after school and saved money and was making good money at that time and at that age. I figured, 'Why not?' There was a giant world out there, and I wanted to dive into it."

"And they let you?"

Seth laughed. "Like I said, I was precocious and obnoxious. When I told them, it wasn't like I was asking their permission. It was more like I was informing them that I was doing it, as an arrogant courtesy. At least that's how I remember it." He was about to add "Jesus" but refrained.

"And they let you?"

"They probably knew me well enough to know they

couldn't stop me. And deep down I believe that they trusted me. They may not have liked the idea, but they didn't think that I was going to tumble into some deep dark hole either. And I didn't. I don't think I did, anyway." He stopped digging his feet into the sand.

Hank realized that he was staring at Seth. He lowered his eyes. "I should get going. I haven't had breakfast yet."

"And your picture?"

Hank slowly started to pull away. "Maybe tomorrow. It's nothing urgent."

"I guess not. Hank, it was nice talking with you."

"You, too. Maybe Honey will be here tomorrow," he said as he turned away toward home.

Seth remained by the trunk with Winston, who was pawing furiously for crabs. Before they left, he covered up the arcs and dips made by his and Winston's feet, even though he knew that the advancing tide would level out all traces of their diggings.

* * * *

Honey wasn't there the next morning. Neither was Hank. "It looks like it's just you and me, buddy," Seth said to his dog, who was going about his business, indifferent to the absence of a human or two.

Seth was annoyed at himself. How easily the labor of finding equilibrium in solitude could be blown to hell by the brief and inconsequential company of another, and the expectation of it happening again, he thought to himself as he and Winston turned back toward the dunes and the exit. On their way out, he waved to Cap'n Tommy, whom he saw fishing in the distance and who never caught anything except tangled clumps of seaweed and an occasional mullet. He wondered why the Cap'n persisted with his four rods and large plastic bucket that was always empty. He imagined a shrill wife at home. He could be so catty sometimes.

He walked past the complex of townhouses where Hank lived. It wasn't out of the way; in fact, it was one of the alternative routes that he and Winston took back home when he was tired of seeing the same houses along the same streets at the same hour of another morning. On those occasions, Winston was perplexed. He'd pause, look at his master with head cocked and tugging at the leash. Unlike his master, he didn't tire of revisiting the same sequence of objects: the Bismarck palm at 201 Riverside Lane, the jatropha at 203, the hydrant on the corner at 205, the gutter grill on the other side of the intersection of Riverside and Tropical Way. He delighted in their familiar smells and whatever new ones might have infiltrated over the course of one day and one night. And so, predictably, he looked up at Seth with his head cocked, and tugged at the leash. "C'mon buddy!" Seth said. That was all it took. Winston resumed his loping gait, tail up and wagging, muzzle close to the ground and sniffing out all that the sandy earth might have to offer up.

As they approached the block of townhouses, Seth imagined spotting Hank going down his driveway (which one would it be?) to check the mail, or doing some lawn work, or sitting in a chair on the front patio leafing through the newspaper. Images that would shift the encounter between the two men from public places to more private ones. He would wave, Hank would wave back; he would pause at the bottom of driveway, Hank would head toward him; they would start talking by the mailbox and Hank would keep the conversation going until he saw a sign that Hank either wanted to invite him in for coffee or have him go on his way as soon as possible; Hank would invite him in for coffee and he would accept; they would have their coffee and as they drank and talked, Seth would take in the objects of the house and try to construct a greater whole out of the parts and amass an accelerated history between them that wasn't there. He circled the block and saw only one person, an elderly woman on her knees spreading mulch around the verbena she'd recently planted along the edges of her frequently power-washed driveway.

"Good morning," he said, breaking into a smile when he noticed a suspicious look on her face.

"Morning," she said, easing her harsh expression. "Beautiful dog."

"Thank you." He continued on his way. "Have a nice day."

"You do the same." The woman waved, trowel in hand. A chunk of dirt dislodged itself from the tip of the trowel and fell onto the pristine driveway. Seth didn't say anything. Surely she noticed it.

He considered going around the block again, but he saw that Winston was beginning to drag. "I'm dragging too," he thought. "And hungry." Suddenly the impulse behind his idea of a repeat circling around the block struck him as adolescent silliness. There were bagels in the freezer, lox and cream cheese in the fridge and, if the mood struck, he could text Ed to propose a mid-morning quickie. He wanted to want him.

*　*　*　*

"What is the principle of Verse 33?" Hank recited aloud, notes in hand at the dining room table. "Jesus states the principle. 'Whoever seeks to keep his life shall lose it, and whoever loses his life shall preserve it.' What does this mean?" He took a bite of his toast with strawberry jam. "It means that if you try to save your life, in this case striving to live it out the way you think best and to preserve it according to your own wisdom, then Jesus states that you will lose it. According to Solomon in Ecclesiastes, the end result of materialism, hedonism and the desire for confirmation is vanity, a pointless chasing after the wind. And worse than that, your soul is lost and you will be damned by God for eternity." He struck out the last sentence. The verdict seemed too merciless.

Hank didn't enjoy facilitating his Saturday morning men's group. It meant a week of doing research, taking notes and practicing what he was going to say. "What do I know?" he asked himself continually as he practiced. He didn't feel up to the task intellectually or spiritually, but he felt it was his duty to his brethren and to his god. It also gave him something to do.

He took another bite of toast, this time rewarding himself with the one whole strawberry at the center of the slice. "Our purpose in life is to glorify Lord God our Creator by doing His will. It says it in Matthew 6:33. 'Your life is in His hands and He has already promised to meet your needs for life as you seek first His kingdom and righteousness.'" That worked. He continued. "If you do this, you not only gain a life that has meaning and purpose, but your soul is saved and you will spend eternity in the joy of Heaven."

Had Seth stopped and looked in the right window of the right house along the block of townhouses, he would have seen Hank licking his fingers as he said "joy of Heaven" and would have at least known in which townhouse, among the twenty-odd townhouses of the complex, Hank lived. At the place where Hank's driveway met the sidewalk, Winston was fixated on a squirrel across the street, and Seth had to keep an eye on him and have his fingers at the ready on the retractable leash to make sure that the beast wouldn't be driven by instinct to make a mad dash in order to force his desired prey up a tree and out of reach.

"So what does it mean? Think about it. To be so attached to the things of this earth that we want to hold onto them more than we want Heaven is to jeopardize our eternal soul. To let go of all the things that the world values and to live in the light of Jesus' coming will result in ultimate and final salvation." Hank penciled out "ultimate and." "There," he said. "That should do it." He knew he would go over his notes a few more times so that he wouldn't have to look down at them too much when he stood before the group. At the same time, he didn't want to sound rehearsed. Inspiration was key, he reminded himself. But still, it was worth skipping the beach to review the notes, he thought as he ate the final piece of toast. He brought his plate to the sink. "What will I do later in the day?"

One possibility presented itself unexpectedly as he looked out the window while depositing his plate in the sink: Seth and Winston. They were at the bottom of his driveway. Seth's face was glancing up at the sky and Winston's nose was scrutinizing the bottom of the mailbox. He backed away from the window, out of view, and stood in the middle of the kitchen, seized by panic. He could rush to open his front door, greet Seth, invite him in for coffee, and the two of them could hang the picture; or he could remain where he was for a few more seconds, stepping back from the window above the sink to see if the coast was clear and, if it was, wash his plate and knife and move through another day in the way he was accustomed to. Marilyn would insist that he invite Seth in for coffee. If he hesitated, she'd say, "For goodness sake" and open the door herself to invite Seth and the dog inside. He wasn't Marilyn, though. And Marilyn wasn't there to intervene. He could feel a slight trembling coursing through his body and at first didn't know how to interpret it. Was it the prospect of slogging through the tedium of another day? Or was it the prospect of disrupting the tedium of another day? He stood there well beyond the time it took for Seth and the dog to continue on their way and remove the need for him to have to decide whether or not to open the front door. He grabbed the dish towel draped over the oven handle. As he wiped his hands, which were wet from a combination of sink water and sweat, the trembling subsided and he understood its cause to be the usual one. He said it out loud: I'm incapable of making a decision. I can't take a stand.

Standing in the middle of the kitchen, he recited, "If you try to save your life, in this case striving to live it out the way you think best and to preserve it according to your own wisdom, then Jesus states that you will lose it." He recited it perfectly without his notes, although he no longer found the aphorism compelling. He looked at his watch and calculated that another 14 hours had to pass before he could fold down the patchwork bedcover, climb into his queen-size bed, adjust the pillow, and call it another day gotten through.

16

Over the next week, both men thought about Honey from time to time. They didn't speculate to each other about her, since they hadn't run into each other. Her gradual acquaintance and sudden disappearance were momentary considerations in the course of their days. But they did think about her existence in the face of her absence. Hank tended toward the gloom and doom: she was in the hospital; one of her children (did she have any?) needed her in another part of the state/country; or, Heaven forbid, she was offended by something he said the one time they spoke (at this, he tried to recreate the brief exchange they had under her vendor's booth but nothing that could be remotely construed as offensive came to mind, unless she took issue with the "Bless you" he said to her as he was leaving with the picture tucked awkwardly under his arm). Seth tended toward the more banal: she was away; she decided it was her week to sleep in; she simply wasn't in the mood to go to the beach (at this, he thought of the few occasions when he himself wasn't in the mood to go to the beach and how on one, two at most, of those occasions he acquiesced to his mood and regretted it as soon as the incantatory interval between night and day had passed and he had nothing to show for it).

During that week, Seth shifted his morning route to include a walk around the perimeter of Hank's complex. During that week, Hank looked out his kitchen more times than usual as he brushed the breadcrumbs from his breakfast plate into the garbage disposal, washed the plate, fork and knife, and placed them in the dish rack to the side of the sink (he stopped using the dishwasher after Marilyn died). For three days their timing was off; neither saw the other. On the fourth day, at the beach, each spotted the other from a distance. Hank was installed by the "Y" and was the first to notice the other. Rather than turn around and head back toward home, as he usually did, he waited for Seth to arrive.

Winston began to tug at the leash as soon as he saw Hank. Seth unhooked the leash from the harness. "Go get him!" he shouted. As Winston took off, Hank stooped down with open arms to welcome him. Then he stood back up and let Winston push his way through his legs as if the dog were going through a car wash.

"Sorry about that," Seth said when he arrived at the "Y," short of breath. "Winston has no shame."

"He is such a sweet dog. You've trained him well."

Seth extended his hand. "I can't take credit for it. He's always been this way. I don't think I had much to do with it. Maybe nothing even."

Hank grasped Seth's hand and gave it a quick firm shake before retracting his hand from the coupling. "I doubt that," he said. Both men looked out toward the seam between ocean and sky. The sun hadn't yet perforated the perfect line dividing the two elements.

Seth broke the silence. "It's good to see you."

"Likewise."

The spectacle of the sun inching above the horizon—always a sight to behold with reverence—gave them an excuse to resume their silence. On this morning, there were no clouds to dab the sky with color. The sun ascended as a clean, fierce circle of yellow. The air was still, a signal to the squadrons of pelicans that they could soar in unswerving chevron flight, a seascape photographer's dream.

Seth turned toward Hank. "It's strange," he said. "I can't tell you how many times I saw you and Honey on the beach before we actually stopped and introduced ourselves. You were fixtures. Blurry ones, but there. Like the abandoned house over there. Then we introduced ourselves, and since then, I haven't seen either of you here. As if by speaking we broke some kind of spell."

Hank stooped down to pat Winston, who was belly-down at his feet and splayed on the sand like a salamander. "I've been here. Just later than usual. I haven't seen Honey either."

The bottom of the sun pushed through. The show was over. The usual heat and humidity would soon be upon them until sunset, and the probable thundershower in the late afternoon would do little to make the outdoors more bearable until the thick of night.

"Did you hang your picture?"

"Not yet."

Seth could feel the light and air intensifying minute by minute. The harsher edges to the day had kicked in. Another day. "In that case, I'm inviting myself," he blurted. "Let's go."

Hank was caught off guard, although it didn't feel threatening to him, even in the smallest way. "Okay," he said. "But you'll have to forgive me. The house is a mess."

"I don't forgive in advance," Seth said. "But I think I can cope. Winston, let's go!"

Winston cocked his head up and got to his feet, tail wagging. "Looks like we've got no choice now."

The two men, and the dog, headed south. Together.

"Would you like something to drink? Water? Coffee?

Juice? I have some doughnuts," Hank said as the two of them and Winston entered his house on the fourth morning that Honey didn't appear at the beach.

"Coffee would be great, if you have some ready. Don't make a special pot," he replied. "I already had a mug at home before my beach walk."

"There's some still in the pot. It should be warm."

Winston made a beeline for the living room and Seth followed him while Hank was getting the coffee ready. Walking around the small, comfortable space, he noticed the picture, still wrapped in brown paper, leaning against the wall next to the olive-green three-seater sofa. He eyed the many other pictures on the tables and walls; most of them were framed photos of what he assumed to be Hank and his family—a man, a woman, two boys—during different moments of a two- or three-decade period. On the wall behind the dining room table and above the credenza was a small cross. It was only then he realized how little he knew about this man other than several characteristics of him he thought he'd discerned: that he was soft-spoken, reserved, kind and attractive. As he lingered in front of one photograph of the two boys when they were teenagers (so handsome, he thought, but at his age he believed almost all adolescent boys to be handsome), he felt almost silly. Here he was, standing in a stranger's house, egged on by presumed qualities of character but without having the faintest idea as to how those qualities played out in the facts of the stranger's daily life, whatever they might be. In fact, were these his sons? Was that woman even his wife?

Hank appeared with a tray holding two cups of coffee, a sugar bowl with a lid, a matching creamer (the leaf pattern was the same on both), two teaspoons and two white paper napkins folded into triangles. He placed the tray and its contents on the dining room table. "Here we are. Please, help yourself."

"Thanks so much," he said as he approached the table. "You have a very lovely family, by the way. I was looking at your pictures."

"Thank you."

He removed the lid of the sugar bowl. "Sugar cubes. I don't remember the last time I saw sugar cubes." He placed three cubes in his cup and stirred vigorously. He glanced around the room. "Where's the mess?"

The men raised their cups at the same time to take a sip of coffee, each looking anywhere but at each other.

"So you live alone, like me."

"Yes." Hank took another sip of coffee.

"I've never been married."

"I see."

Seth sensed a dead-end to this conversational path. "What do you say we get this picture hanging where it belongs?"

Hank put his cup back on the tray and pointed to the large empty space on the wall. "I was thinking it should go there," he said. "Let me go into the garage and get what we'll need."

"You want a hand?"

"That's okay. I can manage just fine. I'll be right back," He swiftly retreated into the kitchen. Seth heard the sound of a door opening and figured it was the inside door to the garage. He remained standing by the dining room table, although he would have preferred to sit on the sofa. He'd been on his feet since he and Winston left the house more than an hour ago. He was tired.

As he stood there, holding his cup and saucer breast-high, he surveyed the room: nondescript furniture, mostly dark wood whose curled legs and rounded edges made him think of the Colonial motif; lace doilies and porcelain figurines stationed here and there; flower-patterned toss pillows on the sofa and chairs; thick drapes with pulley cords; low-pile wall-to-wall carpeting. Not my taste, he thought. Did Hank like these furnishings and accents, or did he defer to his wife in such matters? Would Hank redo the décor now that his wife was gone or would he keep everything intact as a tribute to her, down to the doilies? There was this large new picture about to be hung. His cup rattled against the saucer. His hand was trembling lightly. Who is this man? Why am I here?

He heard the access door click. Hank reappeared in the living room with a small carpenter box. "Why don't we move the sofa out first. What do you think?" He laid the tools—drill, hammer, level, picture hooks, level, molly bolts, three sharpened pencils with pristine eraser nibs—on the coffee table.

"That makes sense."

Hank moved the coffee table toward the center of the room and went to the left arm of the sofa. "No need to lift it. We can drag it across the carpeting." Seth took one of the pencils and stuffed it into the pocket of his shorts, in case it should be needed at a delicate moment during the operation.

They dragged the sofa several feet, positioned the framed photo, repositioned it, penciled dot marks on the wall where the hooks should go, drilled holes and inserted molly bolts, and hung the picture. After moving the sofa back against the wall and the coffee table in front of it, both men stood back and looked at the fruits of their joint labor.

"It looks really nice," said Seth. "What do you think?"

"It's fine."

"We can try another place if you want."

"No. It's fine here."

"Are you sure?"

Hank cast his eyes down. "I'm sorry. It really is fine here. I'm glad I bought it. Marilyn would approve."

"You miss her."

"I do. Three years and I can't get past it. Probably never will. Probably don't want to." He took a sip of coffee. "So you were never married?"

Seth slowly brought his empty cup and saucer to rest on the coffee table. He needed time to which response to give. Here we go again, he thought. He'd been through it many times. The harmless question and the myriad answers to it: "I'm gay"; "I'm separated"; "My life partner and I are separated". In the end, he reiterated what he'd said before: "Nope, never married." His instincts told him that Hank was polite, reserved, taciturn, and he wouldn't be interrogated further.

"Would you like some more coffee?" Hank asked.

"No thanks. I've had my quota for the morning. I should probably be heading home." He wasn't particularly pressed to go home, but it seemed like the right thing to say and do. If Hank wanted to know more, he could see him to the front door or suggest that he stay by making a simple offering—something to eat or another modest project in his home that required more than one set of hands.

"Thanks so much, Seth. I couldn't have done it on my own." He accompanied Seth and Winston to the front door and held the screen door open for them. When Seth reached the bottom of the driveway, he looked back toward the house. Hank was at the screen door, his left arm poking out and waving. Seth waved back.

At the soccer field down a ways, equidistant from their respective houses, Seth calculated, Winston started to "circle the wagon". Seth reached into the pocket of his shorts to extract the roll of turquoise plastic poop bags he made sure was there at the beginning of each day. He didn't feel it. Strange, he thought. He checked the other pocket and pricked the tip of his thumb on the sharpened end of Hank's pencil as he was feeling around for the roll. He recognized it immediately as being Hank's. He let his hand glide up and down the pencil. It was hard and thin and made him think of the erection of a scrawny young boy he might have come upon who knows where. It also made him regret that he hadn't chosen the easy reply to Hank's question about his marital status. "Hank might be taciturn," he thought, "but I'm the coward."

He continued stroking the pencil, trying to evoke an image less pathetic than a randy young penis standing at attention because of his appeal. Something softer rubbing against the flesh. Like flannel pajamas. Yes, flannel pajamas.

* * * *

The blue ones. The ones his mother had brought home for him in August when he was ten. Even at that unknowing age, the purchase seemed strange to him. She never arrived home with clothing as a surprise. Clothing was something to be bought only when a shirt was frayed or stained beyond remedy, or a pair of socks had a hole in the heel the size of a half-dollar, or a pair of pants were up to the ankles and the cuffs had already been lowered as far as they could go. The pajamas must have been marked way down, father and son thought. "A steal," as she would say.

She put the pajamas in the bottom drawer of her son's chest of drawers, keeping them safeguarded in their thick plastic wrapper as her way of letting him know, "Not for immediate use." No price tag hung from it, only a small rectangular frame of grime etched onto the upper left corner of the packaging where once an orange label had been stuck on and removed when the product didn't sell. She probably removed it. He didn't really care about the price. Parents paid for stuff. The pajamas were beautiful. He couldn't wait to wear them, even if they were flannel and it was August.

From the front side of the wrapper, he could see that the shirt part had some kind of pattern. Something boyish—cowboys alternating with geometric shapes, or maybe they were rounded shapes, like soccer balls or baseballs or basketballs. He didn't remember the specifics of the pattern. It was so long ago. But it insisted on maleness and made him feel uncomfortable, despite the brilliant royal blue of the flannel pajama bottoms. Those bottoms were mesmerizing, the stuff of catwalks. Their dazzling color. Their loose fit that could be windswept and sexy, like the photographs of men he pined over in his mother's fashion magazines. Yes, he would be a model one day! If the word "glamorous" had been within his reach when he saw the pajama bottoms, it would have flashed as bright as a Broadway theater marquee.

He didn't think twice about waiting for the cooler autumn air to arrive in order to ask her, "Hey Mom, can I put on those new pajamas now?" Unable to resist slipping the soft, thick bottoms on to sleep in that very night, a warm night, he didn't bother to ask her at all.

"Wait," she would have said. "Why don't let's wait until September, when it's cooler."

He could have given her any number of reasons. The window air-conditioner would keep him cool enough. If not, he could kick his horse- and geometric-patterned quilt down to the bottom of the bed. He never showed interest in horses, and her choice of such a pattern for him, her son, was a mystery. Yes, he would wear the pajamas on a hot August night and in the morning he'd fold the bottoms along their pre-formed creases and ease them back into the wrapper. No one would notice a thing. Then he remembered: his father was waking him up at five o'clock; they were going on their annual one-day father-son fishing trip. No. No no no no no! How would he get up in time, on his own, to put the pajama bottoms back? Worse still, how would he get through an entire day with just his father? What could they possibly find to talk about in the car during the three hours it took them to get to the river they went to each summer for a day of father-son fishing? And then the fishing itself, with even less space and distraction than the car, where he would have no choice but to respond to whatever his father put forth to him in the way of conversation. However much he tried to stare out at the water in a posture of meditation that might ward off having to talk in order to prove himself with this gruff and unshaven man, the litany of questions his father came armed with made it clear that the annual fishing trip was about just that—proving himself to his father—in the same way that his mother's purchase of items of clothing for him carried with it a laser-sharp lens into who this son of hers was. She needed to know how to best prepare herself for what he was, to what degree to accept and encourage it, to what degree to reject and push it in a different direction.

So did his father. And his father was a more immediate concern. If he didn't wake up early enough, his father would bang on the door and say, "Son. It's time to get a move on." He'd have to quickly stuff the pajamas back into the wrapper and hide it until he could more carefully arrange its contents to make it seem like he'd never opened it, indifferent as he needed to demonstrate that he was. He had to wake up on his own that morning. He had to bear being trapped with his father in a rickety rowboat rental in order to partake in the world of the masculine. To make matters worse, he would have to pee in an empty soda can when he couldn't hold it in any longer. His father made sure to keep the first empty can under the left oar.

For his father, time was short. The stock-taking had to begin in earnest as soon as he shut off the motor and the first fishing line was cast into the water. For the son, there was no escape from the questioning. The only redeeming feature was his father's breath. It was strong and bad, and whiffs of it could be detected until about lunchtime. He could smell it in the closed car and in the open air of the boat, especially when his father aspirated his Hs. It smelled like something animal-like in an advanced state of decay. It was a smell that came uniquely and exclusively from way inside his father, like some private secret that couldn't be held back. He turned his head away when his father spoke to him from too close, but he always turned it back in time to breathe some of it in. How could he not be drawn to something so unintended and, as a result, intimate? The lure of that odor enabled him to suffer the questions.

"How were baseball tryouts?"

"I noticed that you're hanging out with Christopher at the bus stop. He's an ace athlete. Solid student, too. Why don't you invite him over some time?"

"Can you flex your arm? Let me see those biceps."

"I like your haircut. Nice and trim. Did you want to get it cut that way? Or did your mom put you up to it?"

"What do you say we stop with the piano lessons? You don't seem all that enthused. Then you'd have time to go out for track. What do you think?"

"What do you say you spend more time on science? Your English grades are good enough. Gotta bring up that C in the hard-core stuff."

"Ellen is cute. She's smart, too. I can tell she likes you. Is she going steady?"

His father's effort to coax masculinity out of him was as relentless as a persecution. So many questions. So much subterfuge for his young mind to cope with and strategize about if only to gain the approval of his father on his father's terms. Strictly manly terms. His father needed his own confirmation: that his son, the boy's strange ways, would end up manly. And the sooner the better.

Fishing day. It made Seth want to contract into a fetus, unformed and buffered with tepid fluids. That wasn't possible, he knew, despite the endless expanse of the river waters lapping at every side of the small, rickety boat his father rented each summer. He couldn't answer his father boldly and directly, though. The risk of him having to put up with his father sermonizing to no avail was too great. And if by some miracle his father were to yield his all-male stance and take the leap to listen to what his son had to say in order to understand him instead of to build his all-knowing adult male case against him, the unprepared boy wouldn't have a clue as to what to say anyway, besides something that wouldn't make any sense to him either. Something like "Dad, I don't like any of those things." He hated his father for not understanding things about him that he himself was too young to understand. He didn't yet understand this.

He suspected his mother put his father up to these hellish annual fishing excursions. His father didn't like to fish as much as he didn't like to fish. He would have preferred to stay home and hover over his mother while she baked a cherry pie, especially when she laid the strips of lattice-work on the top. Female engineering. Maybe it was a conspiracy between his parents to have the father-son fishing trip. He doubted it. His mother listened to him. She wanted to understand him, and not necessarily to preach to him. He wished she would preach more because he trusted the things she said. But she wasn't one to preach. Whatever she thought about what he said she kept tucked away while her eyes shined bright and attentive. Her quiet, absorptive capacity was breathtaking.

That night, as she did on every night in summer, she set his bedroom window air-conditioner to Medium. He thought to set it on Low for this particular night but then realized that setting it back to Medium would be one more thing he'd need to remember to do before his father knocked at the door on the door and said, "Time to get up. We're going fishing!" He opened the bottom drawer of his chest of drawers, extracted the wrapper with the pajamas, slipped the royal blue pajama bottoms out from the wrapper and put them on. He let the elastic band snap around his slender waist as he rubbed his hands up and down the fabric to make the flannel pants slide up and down his thighs and assure him of their gentleness. The pajama bottoms felt like the kind of home he wanted to live in. A soft home, one filled with women. He jumped into his bed.

Time was short. All too soon, his father would wake him up with a knock at the door, to begin a day devoted to things that were supposed to matter to real boys. Thanks, Dad. Here were these fabulous pajamas with their texture and their color. Thanks Mom. She must be on to something about him. Flannel in August? Divinity blue?

He didn't sleep well that night, feeling the pressure of having to get the pajama bottoms back into the wrapper before his father knocked on the door and cracked it open to announce, "Let's go. Time to get ready. Getta move on, son." Most of the time, he wished his father was someone else. He didn't know who, but someone more like his mother. Mothers and fathers, he thought, as he entered his first brief round of fitful sleep. Do they have to be so different? Can't the father-person simply disappear after his sperm fertilized the egg? Then again, he remembered, there were bills to be paid, pajamas to be bought. A sticky state of affairs. Complicated.

When he woke up from his fifth and final fitful bout of sleep, the illuminated numbers on the dresser clock emitted 4:45 and his second pillow was stuffed between his thighs. He sat up with a start. There's enough time to put everything in order, he thought. He rose from his bed to slip off the pajama bottoms. As his thumbs extended the elastic band and his other eight fingers clasped the fabric to pull the pajamas down, his two index fingers landed on a damp, viscous spot slightly above the pee-slit of the fabric. He switched on the light at the corner of his night table and saw an identical spot on the pillow that was between his legs. The two spots were white and had the texture of a flour-water residue stuck to the sides of a Pyrex measuring cup. Pee? No way. Then what was it? He didn't understand. And then he remembered his dream. The same dream with a strange man, a handsome man, standing in the semi-darkness. A hairy wrist with fingers extended on Seth's head pushing him downward toward the zipper of the trousers, which the man was opening slowly with the fingers of the hand that wasn't pushing the head of the young boy into a kneeling position in order to situate those young eager lips directly in front of his unzipped pants. The same dream, but this time it left a sticky residue on his pajamas and bed linen. He knew what it meant. In the school cafeteria, he overheard enough stories to even know what it was called. "Nocturnal emission," or something like that. At the cafeteria tables where the athletes congregated, he strained his ears to be privy to the words they tossed about, as if they were passwords to an exclusive club. Jism, cum, wad, load. There they were, spilled onto his pajamas and pillowcase. He felt ashamed.

    He crumpled the pajama bottoms into a ball, making sure that the cloudy blotch was buried deep inside the mass of flannel, and slid them under the bed. He hoped the blotch would fade, or at least dry, and he hoped he would remember to put the despoiled gift back in the wrapper when he returned home from fishing. He also prayed that such dreams as he'd had that night would find another person to play themselves out in. Otherwise, the trying day would be even more difficult than it was already poised to be. Nocturnal emission. Cum. Jism. It was supposed to happen. It was a consummate milestone, he knew. But why these spurts of masculinity when he was defenseless in the night?

    "Good morning. Time to get ready, son."

    He tossed the incriminating pillow against the head of the bed, stain-side down, and his other pillow on top. He looked at his wrists and wondered if the fine baby hair could ever possibly thicken and darken. For other boys, sure. For him? "Almost ready!" he called out to his father. He knew he could never be ready, at least in the way his father expected him to be ready. He dressed himself in the clothes he'd laid out the night before, clothes befitting a randy boy going fishing with his dad, and suspected that he would always feel alone in this thing that he didn't understand.

* * * *

Hank closed the door behind him as Seth and Winston headed home. He went to the living room to admire the newly hung picture. He noticed a small roll of blue plastic on the living room carpet. Now where did that come from? The shade of the blue made him feel the marrow in his bones so hard that it felt like a cruelty he'd participated in only once before, when the baby hair on his legs started to darken and thicken. Twelve? Thirteen? Somewhere thereabouts.

Yes, it was an act of cruelty. Or was it the work of Evil incarnate? Or of simple and harmless rebellion? Which? At thirteen or somewhere thereabouts when the incident took place, he couldn't decide. Who could at that age, when body and mind were in upheaval and one had to experiment, act out, in an effort to find a new order, even among the students at the reputable parochial school he attended and where he was known for his prowess in algebra. Hank was a born abstractionist with a preference for numbers. The fact that something as complex as $\frac{(x)^3 + 8x + 12}{\sqrt{2x}}$ could be reduced to a simple 18 when $x = 12$ calmed the coursing in his veins. Formulas slowed the internal high tide. They had a way of reassuring him that, among the infinity of random incidents that would come his way as he lived his life, a few of them (and maybe more than a few, if he was lucky) would point to irrefutabilities. They steered him in a way that almost everything else didn't.

Maybe cruelty didn't reside at the same level as Evil itself. Maybe it was to be found on a lower rung; a subset of Evil. Sets and subsets. Placing scenarios in a schematic and running them through a formula to arrive at a clean and simple solution. Here, in the woods, he understood the relevance of certain distinctions, even those he couldn't understand. Here, in the woods, after he'd contributed to what had taken place, he wanted to run away, but it was too late. He told himself that he'd done nothing but stand back and watch (except for the gathering of twigs), but the mere fact of his presence made him an accomplice. Up until then, that spot in the woods across the street from their neighborhood had been a benevolent place with a touch of magic, a place where he and his neighborhood buddies escaped to go about their harmless busy-ness outside of the purview of their parents: to search for treasures; dare each other to climb trees whose ancient branches seemed fragile enough to snap (and the risk of breaking was the point) under the burgeoning energy of their bodies; rummage for the umpteenth time through the skeletal rooms of the abandoned house, pausing at the mattress and condoms with their foil wrappers strewn about like an aura when they glistened in the sunlight, and realizing that this place wasn't so secret a place after all.

This time it was different. A girl was with them. Phoebe. She lived in the neighborhood and was younger than they were, but only by an inconsequential year or two. Her most noticeable quality aside from her red hair was her innocence. They wanted to give her innocence a harsh lesson. They brought her here to punish her with the force and arrogance of a gavel crashing down to pronounce an unjust verdict. Torture, they called it, the price to play for losing a game that they'd convinced her to play so that she would lose. A simple game: a race from the top of the Armstrongs' sloped and serpentine driveway to the end of the cul-de-sac that it gave onto. Phoebe was on the chubby side. Her flesh was too young and unformed to be considered voluptuous. She probably spent too much time alone sitting on the linoleum floor of her family rec room playing with dolls. They, on the other hand, were wiry and wild, their flesh raw and hungry. Their parents gladly released them, boys and girls alike, into the great outdoors of the neighborhood to roam here and there on their bikes, skateboards and rank sneakers. Anything to free themselves up from the constrictions of perpetual care and concern. The adults needed a break.

Hank didn't have a skateboard. His sneakers were washed regularly, and they were replaced as soon as the outside heels showed signs of erosion ("Good posture begins at the feet and the shoulders," his mother insisted). He did have a bike. When he heard the cajoling of the other boys as they braked their fancy racers at the four-way stop sign at his corner, he tore out of the house and leapt onto his three-gear vehicle leaning against the garbage bins in front of the garage door. He thirsted for the goings-on of boys who weren't members of his Boy Scout troop or church choir or science club. "Hooligans. Up to no good," his mother called the boys who'd slipped through. What kind of no good, he asked himself.

They hadn't planned the game or its booby prize. It simply unfolded in the course of a late morning in the neighborhood among kids passing time outdoors until lunch was ready. The boys were riding furiously, intent on shifting gears and feeling their knees rise above the boy-bar as often as possible. It was a sign of prowess, of victory. In the distance, Phoebe was wobbling on her girl bike as if the training wheels had been removed only recently. The basket attached to the handlebars was filled with flower petals and pebbles that she'd been collecting.

"Hey, Pheebes!" Harold called out. She rode up to him.

They talked. She joined them in the ride, in their game comprised of speed and budding male hormones, and in the consequence of her losing.

"Now you have to do what we say," Harold told her after she lost. He was tall for his age. His legs and armpits were already hairy, and any adult who got near enough to him couldn't help but breathe in certain adult smells that he hadn't yet learned to wash off. Hank noticed them, too, every time they played together. And his name. Harold. So nerdy. Maybe his name was what egged him on to be so aggressive and creepy so much of the time.

Following Harold's instructions, the band led her deep into the woods until they arrived near the abandoned house. No, not to the mattress, Hank thought. Harold stopped at an oak tree. "Okay you guys, go and gather some small twigs. I'll keep an eye on Phoebe."

"What are you going to do?" she asked.

"Don't worry, Pheebes. It's part of the game."

The three boys set off in different directions. Hank chose the direction that led to his house in case he decided to abandon the game and go home, but he knew he couldn't. He picked up two twigs and brought them back to Harold. The other two boys arrived shortly afterward.

"Okay, guys. Hold them out, like a bouquet of flowers," he said. Turning to Phoebe standing against the trunk of the tree, he said, "Pick one from each."

She pointed to three twigs.

"Good. Now pull down your pants and underpants."

Hank watched as Phoebe did what she was told. He was sure she didn't want to do it, but there she was, one girl against four guys. What choice did she have? He wanted to say, "Let's not do this," but there he was, one boy against three boys. She grabbed the waist of her pants and the elastic of her underpants and pushed them down at the same time, stopping when the two garments arrived at her knees. Her pants were beige. Her underpants were a royal blue. Hank had never seen such a color before. It fixated him. Heaven must be a color like that, he thought.

The boys looked at the secret spot where her thick thighs met and then at Harold, waiting for further instructions. He was the one in charge, thank God. No instructions came. He took the three twigs that she'd indicated, plucked them out of his friends' fists, and inserted them into her secret spot just enough so that they dangled there without falling out. Then he ran away. The other boys followed. Hank remained behind and turned his head away from her as he removed the twigs. He let them drop to the ground. One twig fell to the left of her left foot. The other two landed to the right of her right foot, one on top of the other and almost perfectly perpendicular, like a cross.

"I had no idea that we…"

She pulled up her underpants and pants, one by one.

"I'll walk you back."

"That's okay. Go ahead."

He approached her.

"Don't come near me. You're not like them. I know that. But keep away."

He turned away and ran down the well-worn path to the street, arriving home as his mother was pulling a Pyrex dish of bubbling macaroni and cheese out of the oven. "Go wash your hands," she said to him. "You're late."

He lingered at the bathroom sink, his hands fixed under the flow of water that he set to hot in order to make each and every possible impurity wash away. But those twigs, inside her and then on the ground afterward. No amount of water could wash them away. He turned off the tap and dropped to his knees.

"*Lord Jesus, I need You. Thank You for dying on the cross*

for my sins. Thank You for forgiving my sins and giving me eternal life. Take control of the throne of my life. Make me the kind of person You want me to be."

His mother's voice was shrill. "Lunch is ready. It'll get cold!"

He joined the family and offered to say the prayer. He repeated what he said in the bathroom. Afterward, his mother and father and looked at him proudly. His mother pointed to the casserole. "Help yourself," she said to him. "You can go first today. You deserve it."

He plunged the stainless-steel serving spoon into the corner of the casserole, scraping the spoon against the glass walls to dislodge the crunchy parts of the macaroni.

"That's enough," his mother said. "You'll end up with bits of glass in your macaroni."

Wouldn't I deserve it, he feared. His prayers didn't work. They were supposed to make him feel better. They didn't. How cruel he'd been to Phoebe. How evil. How could he atone if God wasn't listening?

"Don't forget to take some salad," his mother said.

He didn't especially like salad.

"C'mon, child. It's good for you."

He wanted to please her. He needed her, especially now, even if he knew that he could never tell her what he'd done that morning. He piled a mountain of healthy greens onto his salad plate and reached for the bottle of Ranch dressing, which was his mother's favorite. He liked the cello shape of the bottle. He liked the cello. The few times he'd heard the cello, it seemed to orchestrate the refrain of his own frequent melancholy but without the sharper edges. It made it bearable, poignant, something that could be borne if it were to be a permanent condition. He didn't discount the possibility.

"Thank you, son."

* * * *

Honey knew from the get-go that she wasn't her mother's favorite. June was the one who was fussed over most, since June was the one who got into trouble and didn't have the savvy to avoid being caught. She, on the other hand, was so good at being good that her parents could afford to ignore her. She tried to not mind their disinterest. Posing as the model child freed her up to peck about the terrain of her childhood world, and the boys who inhabited it, without being monitored by her mother, who strived to be a gentle soul, but still. As long as she got good grades, everything else did or didn't do slipped off her parents' radar. After her fourth-grade report card arrived with straight As, she understood the power of accumulated As to cast a wide net for her to go about other business in freedom. The simple formula was a curse and a blessing. There was mileage to be gotten out of it.

Honey understood this when she was an adolescent and had arrived home with another glowing report card on a Friday afternoon. At eleven o'clock that evening, she snuck out of her bedroom window to meet the neighbor's boy. He was three years older. Behind the hedge of pyracantha where they'd arranged to meet, she let him feel her up under her training bra. She didn't know why he would want to do such a thing, but she'd come to understand that this was what boys wanted to do, so she let him. He was nervous. She could feel his hands quivering as he tried to figure out how to unbutton her blouse so that his fingers could probe deeper in the Vee until they could pry open the bottom of her bra in order to arrive at the soft small mound that he needed to arrive at so if only to tell his buddies at school the following Monday, "I got to second base." His quivering hand traveled over the small dome of her breast. She didn't feel anything special but liked the way his breathing got heavier and the way the smell of his acrid breath on her face suggested something extremely important was taking place between them.

"Honey, would you mind setting the table?" her mother asked her five years later.

"Sure, Mom." She quickly came to understand that saying "Sure, Mom" in tandem with achieving straight As was the surest path to casting the net of her mother's trust even wider, so wide that she would be able to invite her latest boyfriend T.J. to dinner one day (he was already a senior in high school) and her mother would think him a fine boy, incapable of doing wrong by her daughter—which he was doing at least three times a week (under the bleachers, in wooded areas, behind the stack of logs in his back yard; and she let him as each time she tried to understand what the big deal was). "Butter knives or steak knives?"

"Let me see. The meat might be a little tough. I cooked it for two hours, but it wasn't a prime cut. It was on sale. Why don't you put out the serrated knives, just in case?" She smiled at Honey. "Sweetheart, you think of everything."

"Where's June?"

"Cheerleading practice. She'll be home on time. She promised. Did you see how her hair came out today? She was on to something with that crazy beer and egg concoction. It really works. Stinks like the dickens but boy does it bring out the highlights. She looked like a Tahitian who's blonde. Positively exotic."

Honey's hair was the color of nothing in particular and fell formless on her head. Her upper thighs had burgeoning clumps of excess flesh that weren't dissimilar to those found in small-curd cottage cheese. Her eyebrows were naturally arched, but she was knock-kneed. Her breasts were ample enough but didn't stand proud. She was in the lowest range of average height. The sum of her physical parts pointed her toward a future whose accomplishments, whatever they might be, would not be furthered by the fruit of any physical excellence. In that regard, she was unremarkable. Her sister, on the other hand...

"I folded the napkins into triangles instead of rectangles," she said to her mother. "Something different. Is that okay?"

"Nice touch. You really do think of everything."

She did think of everything. She told T.J. to meet her at the corner at seven o'clock. She figured that June would storm in at six o'clock on the dot, as promised. She knew her sister. As different as they were, they both understood the mileage to be gained by giving in to parental obedience at strategic moments. Dinner would be brought to the table by six-fifteen, and the two siblings would scarf it down and clear the table in the space of a half-hour. That would leave her a precious fifteen minutes to primp in the bedroom before slipping out to meet T.J. with the usual excuse that was always accepted by her mother and received by her sister with an arched eyebrow: "I'm going to Maxine's to study math."

T.J. entered her that night. Her desire for it won over her terror of it and the pain that she expected it to bring, which it did, especially when she felt him first begin to be inside her and all she wanted him to do was to stop. She knew that if he stopped, it would be over before it was supposed to begin, and she needed for it to happen until it was over and she could say to herself, and perhaps a few others at the cafeteria table during lunch, "Guess what. I did it!" His initials were so cool, so sexy. Maybe he would be sexy, too.

It was fast, disappointing. "That's it?" she thought after his heaving subsided and he pulled out and lay on his back beside her without touching her, returning them to the awkwardness they felt when they knew they were about to start. It was over. Like that. She hadn't even seen it, touched it with her fingers, put it to her lips. She'd finally been fucked and still didn't know what a penis looked like.

Over the next two weeks, she let him do it do her three more times before things started to fit together more smoothly and the pain stopped. But the pleasure? Where was that to be found? In the absence of the pain? That's it? She couldn't locate the pleasure beyond that absence. Still, it had to be there. That's all her friends talked about. She'd discover it in time and then she too could call it Love as they did. After the fourth time he entered her, she no longer felt pain. She was impatient for love.

"I love you," she told him. She wanted to wrap herself around him and cling to him like a vine, but he was already safely on this side of the bed, hands cupped behind the back of his head, elbows extended to the edge of his pillow, eyes staring blankly at the ceiling.

"Cool," he said.

"I'm sorry. I'm being my stupid self." She regretted backtracking. "But I do," she added. "I love you."

He produced a wisp of a smile as he patted her head. She could feel it, them, being over.

It ended the day after. "Honey, I really like you." The note she found in her locker the next day started like that. She didn't read further. There was no need to.

She went on getting her As and setting the table and looking for every occasion to say, "Sure Mom." Easy stuff. No sweat. She set herself to the task of allowing a smorgasbord of boys she was indifferent to enter her until Glen brought her to her first climax and stayed on top of her, kissing her all over her face instead of rolling on his back and wanting to decamp. He kept his eyes open all the while. Clearly he'd been around, she thought. With him, she could keep the lights on, she could match his open eyes with her open eyes, she could let out animal noises or she could articulate instructions to him for her pleasure, or his. She married him after she convinced him to propose to her. They were lying on the bank of the creek in the local park. Her thighs were still warm and sticky. His head was against her breast and she could feel his temple pulsating against her heart. "Would you ask me to marry you?" she whispered into the night sky.

His head was turned upward just enough to try to locate the Big Dipper. He lowered his eyelids until all was darkness and he could concentrate on his deep inhale. "I mean, if you want me to," he said. As he released the night air, he said, "Okay. Let's do this. How about marrying me?"

She turned toward him and waited to see if his eyes would open and his head turn toward her. If she stayed like that long enough and remained silent, he would eventually have to shift position and perhaps look at her, extend a finger to her face and let it travel gently through its geographies. He sat up, bunched his knees into his chest, and returned his gaze to the stars. She couldn't believe how perfect his physique was. She lay there, looking at him and waiting for him to look at her. She thought about how her beautiful sister June would be beside herself over this conquest of such a beautiful man, even as his gaze continued to be focused away from her.

"I will," she said. He lowered his head. They looked into each other's eyes. He smiled at her. He ran his fingers down her cheek. She couldn't locate the pleasure that she expected to be had from this sequence of gestures. He had entered her. His unclipped fingernails had grated against the flesh of her cheek in a what was supposed to be a moment of tenderness and connection. He'd asked her to marry him. Throughout his maneuvers, she didn't feel that she was about to embark on belonging to something larger than her dull and dumpy self. She still felt alone.

17

Honey didn't forget about Seth and Hank entirely when she began the speech she'd prepared for the occasion. "O Lord, you who are the Father of mercies and the God of all comfort; look with compassion, we pray, upon all gathered here now, that our minds and hearts shall be at your command. Grant that this service of comfort, which we now hold in your name, may bring to all a sense of heavenly nearness and great trust in you. And may the peace of Christ, even the peace that passes all understanding, abide with us and rest upon all these dear ones. We pray through Jesus Christ our Lord. Amen." Something about the words "comfort" and "nearness" caused the two men to be present, if only in her mind, as she continued with her speech.

The bottom half of Glen's wooden casket glistened under the mini spotlights embedded high up in the church ceiling like a starry night lured to the indoors. Long white gladioli and a broad spray of baby's breath lay across the top of the polished mahogany box. Its upper half was open, revealing a face at peace, chemically distended to erase the wrinkles that inscribe into the flesh the passing of time and the weariness of the passage through it. Glen's face was slathered with some kind of mauve-colored pancake to cover the habitual red blotches and tiny broken blood vessels that had erupted over the last few years. His upper torso was outfitted in a navy blazer and tie, and a white button-down shirt. He didn't look younger, but for the first time in many years he looked like a healthy and dapper version of someone his age and heft, even though he was dead. Or maybe he looked like that because he was dead, Honey thought. As she returned to her seat, the priest began his eulogy.

"The family would have me to thank all of you for the beautiful flowers, the warm handshakes and embraces, and the sympathetic statements of the last few days. From Romans 17, verse 7, 'For none of us liveth to himself, and no man dieth to himself. You are a different person as a result of this loved one's life. His life will continue to speak meaningful things to those he touched as long as they live.' This loved one has become a part of each of you; he will always live on in your memories. I know that there are many things that you haven't even thought of in the last few days that will eventually come to mind and will become a living memorial to him as long as you live."

She was flanked by her grown children, Cal and Aurora. They, like her, were wearing black. She tried to remember whether black was the combination of all colors or the absence of all colors. She extended her hands from her side; each child took one. Sweet children, she thought. Kind.

"Blessed be God, even the Father of our Lord Jesus Christ, the Father of mercies, and the God of all comfort, Who comforts us in all our tribulation, that we may be able to comfort those who are in any trouble, by the comfort wherewith we ourselves are comforted of God."

"Mom, if you don't mind, I'm going to step outside," Cal whispered in her ear.

"Not at all," she said, wishing that she could slip out alongside him, invisibly, like a speck of lint on the sleeve of his charcoal black linen jacket. Only last week she'd been to this very same church to celebrate a birth and baptism of a neighbor's grandchild. Now here she was again, so soon, in the same church but this time in the front pew and flanked by her children who'd flown in from out of state (Aurora from Vermont, Cal from Wisconsin) to hear the same priest give a sermon, but this time over a death. Her husband's death. She listened to his words and was unmoved. His inability to make his words heartfelt reminded her of how she felt during the baptism a week ago: here was a man who was simply doing his job. Efficiently meeting the expectations of his congregation. No more, no less. Was she doing the same?

Aurora let her hand glide from her mother's hand to her upper arm. She squeezed it tightly. Honey couldn't tell whether the pressure from her five fingers was an effort to bolster her or to siphon support out of her. From the corner of her eye she could see that her daughter was attentive, absorbed by what the priest was saying, even if the man of the cloth had to frequently glance down to refer to his notes spread across the lectern like sheet music to a composition that wasn't particularly captivating. How she would have liked to slowly go down the aisle with her daughter, push open the front door to the church, and take a deep breath as the chaos of natural lights and sounds outside insisted on a larger precariousness to the order of things. But she stayed in place. All eyes were upon the lady in black in the front pew, observing her performance as a widow. She held tight, even during those moments when the priest needed to shuffle his notes to find his place. "My God," she asked herself, "how am I to give everyone the degree of sadness they expect?"

"Regardless of how deep our personal faith in God and His providence, the death of a loved one makes each one of us feel keenly the personal loss. There is a sense of an aching void as we think of one that we loved who is gone. We miss the companionship of our loved ones and our grief is deeply personal. In times of loneliness and sorrow, the presence of friends and loved ones can be so meaningful. Certain strength comes by the close, personal presence of those who are dear to us. Because we all belong to the great fellowship of Jesus Christ, we are able to encourage and strengthen one another. God has mercifully provided that the deep wound we initially feel when our loved ones leave us can be somewhat healed through the passing of the days, the months, and the years. This is not to say that our grief is not genuine and deep. Whatever friends and loved ones may do or time may bring, God is our supreme source of comfort. He calls upon us to find refuge in Him."

Her son didn't return from outdoors, and the asymmetry she felt by his absence from her right side was distracting her from trying to fill her heart and lungs with the generic sermon. She also felt a rush of adrenalin—the type triggered by anger, she realized—coursing through her veins and causing her forehead to perspire. She knew it was toward this son of hers, the renegade, who too often chose inopportune moments to be anti-conformist. She envied him in a way. *Maybe he isn't as kind as I think. Maybe not as mediocre.*

The church was across the street from the beach, several miles south of her morning beach. She pictured Cal crossing the highway as he loosened his tie and pulled out his pack of Marlboro Lights, ready to light up and maybe even take off his shoes as soon as his feet touched the sand. *He is a good man,* she thought. *A kind man. But unexceptional and misguided. He'll have a tough time with life.*

"Okay. You can let go now," she told Aurora when she heard the priest say, "In conclusion." Aurora released her hand. The priest continued. "Dear God, we ask you to heal the broken in heart and bind up their wounds; mercifully look upon those who are at this time bereaved. Be near them in their sorrow, and let their sorrow draw them nearer unto you. Now that earthly joys and comfort fail, may the things unseen and eternal grow more real, more present, more full of meaning and power. Let your strength sustain their weakness. Amen."

"Amen," she repeated, feeling nothing except the desire for a cigarette, even though she'd given up smoking some ten years ago. She walked slowly down the aisle, accompanied by her daughter. Her head was tilted downward and her eyes faced the floor, although she occasionally lifted them ever so slightly in order to glance out toward the left and the right of the aisle to take stock of who was there and who wasn't. Family, friends, acquaintances, neighbors, strangers (members of this church who had nothing better to do, she assumed), a respectable critical mass of solemn figures clad in dark shades (except for one woman, whom she didn't know, who was wearing a fire-engine red dress and matching hat. Where did she come from, she wondered). Then there were two figures who didn't belong to any of these categories. To the left of the main aisle she was traveling, seated in the back row, was Hank; to the right, seated in the next-to-last row, was Seth. She nodded to both of them, and the trace of a smile lightly etched itself onto her face. Such kind men, she thought. They nodded back, each in his turn. It was clear that each man didn't know that the other one was there, she realized, and that each had decided on his own (but how did they know, she asked herself) to pay his respects to her and to her alone, since they wouldn't be paying their respects to her husband, a man they'd never met and knew nothing about.

 Aurora held the door for her as she crossed the threshold between the controlled golden light of the church within and the blinding outdoor light of a tropical afternoon and the noise of convertibles, Jeeps and pick-ups along the beach highway. She glanced back at the two men, who had come to this ritual over a man neither had ever met. They couldn't have come for him. They'd come for her. Finally, she felt moved. "I wish June were here to see," she thought. "I matter."

18

Red tide. Tens of thousands of dead mullets shimmering on the beach, like a jackpot of silver coins flooding the tray of a Las Vegas one-eyed bandit. Warnings were posted on beach entrances to stay away because of the stench that could cause burning eyes and coughing. Where did it come from, Hank wondered as he walked along the beach with a large white handkerchief wrapped around his nose and mouth, which didn't do much to buffer his eyes from whatever was taking place in the air to make them swell and feel hot. Did the construction of condos and the endless dredging of sand to refurbish the ever-eroding beach because of the condos (or so he heard) have something to do with it? Was it global warming? Or was this simply what happened because, as he often concluded, things happen, regardless of what we do or don't do? Humans do make a mess of things. But they're not the only ones.

He bent down to take a closer look at one of the dead mullets, its rigid body curved like a fingernail clipping, in the way that fish shape themselves when their gills are struggling to find oxygen, their lips desperately distended in a death throe and, in this case, the small fins entangled in the elaborate embroidery of seaweed. So sad, so many of them simply going about their simple business and then, wham, finished. Over. Like a head-on collision when one is driving to work on a morning like any other, radio tuned in to the usual station, mind reviewing the pieces of business that will need to be attended to at the office, perhaps a stray thought now and then to considerations more existential or fantastical or silly as the music (or the news) playing on the usual radio station, and then a car comes around the bend too fast and a crush of metal against metal arrives at the soft flesh of the driver and forces an oozing and spurting of internal organs and fluids everywhere—the mangled steering wheel, the upholstery, the windshield, the high-tech dashboard, the femur, the tibia, a piece of intestine, a few key arteries. And just like that, out of nowhere, but potentially anywhere, a life being lived by someone who happens to be alive comes to an end. It happens all the time, out of the thing called "the blue." Blue is such a soothing color. Why blue?

He prodded a dead mullet with his left foot and thought of the sequence of his wife's deterioration that he'd come to expect (but hardly accept) after doing much research in order to elevate her imminent death to something more meaningful than "just like that." He flipped the mullet over and retraced everything that he was supposed to do to help both of them ease into her death, and how when she took her last breath and he could feel her body beginning to cool and petrify in his embrace (he read about that hideous transition, but still), he cursed his devotion to a higher Being, which, despite the research and the painstakingly methodical approach, was supposed to somehow not only keep her alive but make her get better. Except that it didn't. This is what Hell must be like, he thought, although he was certain beyond the shadow of a doubt that Marilyn was not and had never been destined for that place.

He gave the mullet a swift kick and sent it back into the

ocean, where it floated back to the surface in a stiff arc. He waited for a seagull or pelican to spot it, swoop down, clutch it in its beak, and carry it off to devour in peace. That's how it happened, he thought. A living thing serving as an insignificant link in an insignificant food chain. Normally, he would be heading home at this hour, but he lingered on the sand to watch the bird (it was a pelican this time) choreograph its meal and to lay out what he would do once he got home to get through the next part of the day.

* * * *

Seth steered clear of the beach that morning. He read about the red tide and its potential health hazards and wasn't keen on experiencing them in his lungs or eyes, or of having the elixir of his beach walk contaminated by mounds of rotting fish. Yes, he might have a story about it that he could tell one day. But to whom? He tended to recoil whenever someone began a sentence with "I remember when..." or "One time when I..." Invariably he found that the kinds of tales that began with such openers were better left untold. Most people, he thought, have little to say afterward, and even if they have something to say they don't know how to tease out the pertinence of what it is they want to say, which was probably not much at all. More often than not, the need was to simply to say "I" and to then figure out some way to affirm it.

Seth turned to the right, away from the beach and toward the road on the west that paralleled the river. There, the houses were larger, set back by front lawns manicured every other day by Hispanic gardeners who could be seen sweating out their pre-lunch hours pruning and primping lots that never had any human activity carried out on them besides the pruning and primping conducted by these men who shielded themselves from the sun with long-sleeve shirts, loose-fitting pants and floppy straw hats, and who were remunerated at below-minimum wage. Who lived in these houses? What did they do inside these imposing structures with their great rooms and entertainment rooms and who knows how many spare bedrooms and jacuzzied bathrooms? What kind of meals did they prepare in their oversized and over-equipped kitchens? Did their children leave toys scattered in the living room? And if they did, who gathered them up, and where did they put them? Who were these families inside these houses? Where did they earn their high incomes in such a laid-back town?

Winston did his business under a meticulously tessellated configuration of hibiscus, aloe and verbena. Seth pulled a blue plastic poop bag from the pocket of his shorts and scooped up the mass. He spotted a trash bin nearby and deposited it inside. The practical purpose for the walk was now taken care of, but he continued. He hadn't explored this area before, and there was nothing pressing to do once he returned home. In fact, he thought, there's no reason why they shouldn't make a quick stop at the beach, if only to see what this red tide business was all about. And why red?

* * * *

Honey peered into Glen's bedroom. At first she thought to remove the IV pole and oxygen device perched on a small dolly in the corner of the room and return them to the medical supply company for someone who might need them and to not pay for the days when they just sat there without any use to her. Then she thought to purge the room entirely of his existence, oppressive as it was in that final stretch. When did he become anything more than a burden, she asked herself as she stood at the threshold resisting her urge to enter the room to plump up the four pillows whose concavities and inflection points attested to his unimaginable discomfort and seething restlessness and to her unavoidable sentimentality. And his en suite bathroom? The hairs in his comb and on the drain covering of the shower floor? The faint yellow droplets on the rim of the toilet? The toothpaste cap lying on the edge of the sink? The still-damp towel tossed carelessly over the towel rack and emitting that rancid smell of fabric that stays wet too long? So gross. All of it. So utterly him. No more of such things. She shut the door and backed away. Another time, she decided. Not now. I'd rather smell the stench of rotting fish than his towel in the bathroom.

Grabbing her camera bag on the kitchen island, she walked out of the house and headed toward the beach, whatever havoc the red tide may have wreaked.

The red tide disappeared after three days. Seth was the last to arrive at the "Y". As he approached, he could see Honey, ankle-deep in the water, her left hand fiddling with the zoom lens as she faced the horizon. Hank was there too, standing next to the trunk, one hand resting on a smooth branch, his eyes looking at either Honey or beyond her toward the horizon. He was too far away to tell. Seth unleashed Winston, who tore toward them. Seth was relieved that the dog was paving the way for his arrival. He wasn't in the mood to take them by surprise. On this morning, he was more interested in their calculated response than their spontaneous one.

Honey stretched out her arms when he arrived within earshot. "Hugs," she shouted. Seth was embarrassed. She continued. "New rule. Hugs before anything." He glanced at Hank, who raised his shoulders and crumpled his mouth as if to warn him that a hug was the path of least resistance. Seth acquiesced, wrapping his arms loosely around her soft ample frame and letting her determine the degree of squeeze. As he was gauging his embrace, Winston humped his leg.

"Jealous, is he?" she said.

"No. He gets over-excited when the company is more than me."

"What a great way to express over-excitement. I envy dogs. They can be so shameless."

Seth gently pushed Winston off his leg. "I'm so sorry about your loss."

"Thank you. That's very kind of you. Enough said, if you don't mind. I come here to try not to think about politics, physical conditions and death."

"Agreed." They strolled back to the "Y," where Hank released his hand so that he could stoop down and coax Winston to return for another round of raking.

"Hugs. Yes, the two of you now."

Seth and Hank went through the motions of an embrace, although their bodies, from sternum to feet, formed a wishbone-shaped arc that failed to suggest the magic of a wishbone and instead spoke of the discomfort they felt over such a small intersection of their bodies. Nevertheless, in such a confined space of reluctant embrace, Seth was aware of bones more than flesh—so different from what he felt with Honey—and he liked it. He wasn't turned on by too much flesh on a man. It seemed like a cover-up, or a barrier, to intimacy, whereas with a woman it struck him as a comfort zone.

Honey smiled. "Here we are," she said. "The widower, the widow, and..." She looked at Seth. "And?"

He looked out equidistantly between the two of them. "How about none of the above? I'm a bachelor."

"Wow. I haven't heard that word in ages. Maybe since that TV show with John Forsythe. That's probably before your time."

"That's what you think. Niece Kelly. And the so-called 'houseboy' Peter. Do you reckon Game of Thrones will seem as quaint forty years from now?"

"Bachelor Father! The trivia that clogs our brain."

"So I'm a bachelor. Not a father, though. Let's bring the terminology up to date. I'm single."

Honey smiled. "I always think of a bachelor as someone who is suave and who prefers to have lots of brief encounters with women. Kind of a euphemism for Don Juan. Or Lothario. Or John Forsythe. A womanizer. Don't get me wrong. I'm not a disciple of Betty Friedan. I cringe at the concept of radical feminism. There I go again, I'm blathering."

"I've had long relationships. For a long time now, I've had no long-term relationship. I think it will stay that way. At my age, which I think is more or less your age, and Hank's age, I'm not too hopeful about the possibility of such a radical change."

Honey made a semi-circle path in the sand with her foot. "I hear you. But upheaval happens. Despite our intentions, and because of our age."

"It does. But I don't invite it. I'm not into the adrenalin thing."

Hank stood up and wiped his hands on his shorts to remove whatever it was that might have deposited itself there while he was stroking Winston's back. "I should be heading home now. It was good to see you both. I'm so sorry for your loss." He turned and walked away without once looking back, even when Honey called out, "By the way, there's a 'For Sale' sign at the abandoned house."

Honey turned to Seth. "I hope I didn't offend him."

"I hope I didn't either," Seth said. Winston took off toward Hank, who stopped to stoop down and rake the dog. "I'd better get him."

"Of course. Go to him. Don't let him get away."

Seth jogged toward his dog and Hank. Both were looking toward him. He knew that Winston was looking at him for some sort of anchor, or reassurance. He never went far without looking at his master. Dogs do that. As far as Hank was concerned, Seth had no clue.

19

They walked together for the fifteen minutes it took to reach Hank's mailbox at the bottom of his smoothly paved driveway—so unlike Seth's driveway, what with the hairline cracks and tiny weeds running throughout them like a diseased neurovascular system. The two men were mostly silent. Hank wasn't one to talk much and Seth was on uncomfortable terrain when words weren't launched at him to react to.

Hank checked the mailbox, even though it was far too early for the mail to have arrived. As he closed the lid, listening for the click of metal against metal that indicated a tight seal, he asked, "Would you like to come in for some coffee?"

"That would be nice. If it's no trouble."

"No trouble at all. I may have some donuts too. I like glazed, but there might be one cream-filled. The kind without the hole."

"Coffee sounds good." Seth thought better of informing Hank that he didn't eat sweet breakfasts except on the rare occasion when he took himself and his New York Times out for pancakes and syrup at the local diner. He was a yogurt and granola type of guy in the morning. Surely Hank was an eggs and bacon guy, he thought as he looked at Hank's face, waiting for his eyes to meet his. For the instant when they did, Seth broadened his smile, as if to stuff into those two seconds and three words a feeling of pleasant routine among friends who no longer need to prove or demonstrate anything, who have no expectations other than the continued comfort of their history to steer them into their future. He knew this wasn't the case, but he couldn't resist trying to conjure it for those two seconds.

Hank turned the key in the silver doorknob and swung open the front door. "Come in."

Winston pushed between their four legs to enter first, all waggy-tailed and primed to sniff around.

"You can let him off the leash," Hank said. "He's a good boy."

Hank unhooked the leash from Winston's harness. "I haven't figured out if he's the perfect child or the perfect partner. One thing I do know. He is more than what I thought a dog was supposed to be."

Hank smiled. "Well, he does seem like the perfect dog." When they entered the kitchen and Seth saw that the Mr. Coffee pitcher was halfway filled with a dark brew, a silence overcame him despite, or because of, the many questions he wanted to ask. Do you drink that much coffee? Were you anticipating my company? Have you already had coffee? What would you do with all that coffee if I hadn't stopped by? And that Insta-pot on the counter? Did you buy it to make your life as a widower easier, or was it one of your wife's acquisitions? What do you make in it? Or has it just sat there since your wife died? Who are you?

"I can make a fresh batch if you don't like it reheated in the microwave."

"Reheated is fine, thanks." He plucked up his courage. "Was all that coffee for you?"

Hank replied. "I have a second cup when I come back from

the beach, and sometimes I take whatever is left over and make myself some ice coffee after my nap."

"I'm a napper, too. That's another thing I don't remember life without. I took up the habit a long time ago. It seems inhuman to me to not nap."

"I don't sleep very well at night."

"I have no trouble falling asleep. I have trouble staying asleep. After four hours, I start to toss and turn, and I'm not convinced that the remaining couple of hours that I manage to stay in bed are all that restful."

"I'm the same way."

"Have you always been that way? Or is it an old-age thing?"

"I don't know. You?"

"I'm not sure either. I don't remember when I started to think about my sleep patterns. Maybe that in itself is an old-age thing."

Hank smiled. "Milk? Sugar?"

"I take it black."

Hank handed Seth his cup and saucer and reached for the white ramekin dish on the counter. He took two yellow packets of Splenda, gently opened them and poured their snowy contents into his own cup.

"Splenda? What is that?"

"It's a sugar substitute."

"Like Sweet 'n Low?"

"I suppose. I bought it once when it was on sale. It made my coffee sweet so I continue to use it. I don't know the difference, except that Splenda comes in yellow packets and Sweet 'n Low in pink."

Seth was about to ask, "Why not just use sugar?" but he refrained. He didn't want to go down his well-worn road of cynicism and catty superiority about the American way: the powders wrapped in single-dose wrappers whose pastel colors suggested care and safety, the pills perforated at their diameters for full or half doses, the bottled energy and protein drinks, the three-course ready-made meals with compound adjectives like "free-range," "gluten-free" and "non-GMO". The suckers' guide to simple and easy health and longevity. No, he thought. Not this time. Not with Hank.

The kitchen was small, without a table or chairs. Seth stood in the middle of the white tile flooring, waiting to be asked into a more accommodating room where they could sit and chat. He lifted the cup to his lips. "So sad for Honey."

"Yes, it is."

"He couldn't have been more than in his sixties, don't you think?"

"Probably."

"How well do you know her?"

"Not at all, really. Once at the beach and then at the art festival."

"Me neither. Still, I feel I should do something. Offer something. Something. You know?"

Winston settled down by the oven. Hank stooped down to pat him. "Such a sweet dog."

Seth tilted his cup to take in the last bit of coffee. "We should probably be heading home. I don't want to take up too much into your day."

Hank stood up. "My days are pretty uneventful. Monotonous. I have a hard time figuring out how to get through them."

"Retired?"

"Yes. But it's being a widow that makes it hard. My wife and I had lots of plans. She died shortly after I retired. And our two boys aren't nearby. They have their own lives."

"Hank, I'm so sorry."

"Thank you."

He waited for Hank to add something that would signal him to stay on, but Hank seemed comfortable in his silence. He snapped the leash onto Winston's harness. "We'll leave you to your day. Thanks for the coffee."

"Thanks for taking the time to stop by. And God bless."

Seth smiled. "I'm semi-retired. My days are long too. I don't know many people here. By the way, I'm Jewish."

"So was Jesus."

"So he was." He placed his coffee cup in the sink, went toward the front door and opened it to let himself out. He turned and extended his hand. "Thanks again, Hank." Hank took it and placed his other hand firmly around Seth's upper arm.

Hank looked directly into Seth's eyes and smiled as he retracted his hand and tucked it into the pocket of his shorts. The smile was an involuntary one, a genuine one that couldn't help itself, one that pushed through to reveal gratitude and hope. How reserved he was, Seth thought. How effortlessly handsome he must have been a few decades ago.

20

Marilyn would have liked him, Hank thought as he carried the two empty coffee cups to the sink to rinse them and place them in the dish rack. He looked at the pair of cups in the rack, the lip of one cup brushing against the lip of the other in the rack; the coupling of the two objects brought a wave of sorrow over him. She would have liked Seth and, unlike him, would have thought nothing of inviting this amiable neighbor into the living room, where the conversation would have continued far beyond what her dear husband was capable of orchestrating on his own, and this amiable man who was also very pleasing to the eye would have returned, perhaps for dinner, or perhaps the three of them would have gone out together for a burger or pizza and a movie and then, once back in the parking lot of the cinema, gone their separate ways, the evening culminating in a sexual desire on the part of Marilyn that she would make evident by nuzzling up against her husband as soon as they stationed themselves on their respective sides of the bed. She would mold herself against his pajamaed body and tickle his ear with her finger to let him know that she wanted him to have her, and he would oblige, quickly pulling out of her and lying on his back to remind himself that he'd fulfilled his duty as man and husband. He pleasured her, satisfied her. He lay back, spent, content, proud. Before he fell asleep, the same wisp of a doubt made its voice heard: Is this it? I don't get what all the fuss is about.

He dried his hands on the dish towel and draped it over the handle of the oven. Yes, he should have invited Seth into the living room, pointed to the sofa and said, "Make yourself comfortable." That was something Marilyn would have done, with the ease and assurance of a receptionist asking a first-time patient to complete a medical history form prior to the first visit and pointing to a comfortable chair in the corner of the waiting room that seemed reserved for that patient. He wasn't her, he reminded himself. He was someone who had no idea how to steer a neighbor, a potential friend, from a kitchen to a living room.

He went to the living room and paged through his Bible until he found Luke 1. He read:

> In the sixth month, the angel Gabriel was sent from God to a city of Galilee named Nazareth, to a virgin betrothed to a man whose name was Joseph, of the house of David. And the virgin's name was Mary. And he came to her and said, "Greetings, O favored one, the Lord is with you!" But she was greatly troubled at the saying and tried to discern what sort of greeting this might be. And the angel said to her, "Do not be afraid, Mary, for you have found favor with God. And behold, you will conceive in your womb and bear a son, and you shall call his name Jesus. He will be great and will be called the Son of the Most High. And the Lord God will give to him the throne of his father David, and he will reign over the house of Jacob forever, and of his kingdom there will be no end.
>
> And Mary said to the angel, "How will this be, since I am a virgin?"
>
> And the angel answered her, "The Holy Spirit will come upon you, and the power of the Most High will overshadow

you; therefore the child to be born will be called holy—the Son of God. And behold, your relative Elizabeth in her old age has also conceived a son, and this is the sixth month with her who was called barren. For nothing will be impossible with God." And Mary said, "Behold, I am the servant of the Lord; let it be to me according to your word." And the angel departed from her.

Hail Mary, full of Grace? It was a question that perplexed him. God chose to use an average young woman and to announce his intentions in quiet obscurity. Was there something extra special about her that she was chosen to be the mother of Jesus? He believed that God's choice of Mary to bear this child sprang from His grace, not from any inherent merit that she possessed. Mary was not the source of grace. She was merely the recipient of grace, the object of God's unmerited, graciously provided goodness. End of story. When he imagined Mary, one woman always came to mind. A plain woman, neither pretty nor ugly, whose face and facial expressions had little to say to the rest of the human race except, "Here I am, in the world, getting through my days." A woman whose only remarkable quality was her utter lack of anything remarkable. The Jane Doe of the Gospel. If he concentrated long enough, as he was doing while he sat on the sofa with the Bible now closed in his lap, the image would congeal into the one woman who always came to mind: the young woman behind the deli section of the supermarket, whose name tag had "Kayleen" embossed in white on its royal blue surface, which clashed with the green smock and transparent yellow gloves she was obliged to wear whenever she sliced meats, in his case (and as she came to expect) a quarter-pound of honey-cured ham. She seemed to genuinely take her drudgery and blandness in her stride, as though it was her portion. It gave her a strange radiance, like the contestants in the Miss America pageant that Marilyn watched each year as if the pageant were its own religion. Had the deli woman been a contestant, and had the competition been for "Miss Virgin Mary Not Yet Full of Grace," she would have won hands down.

He wondered whether Mary should be worshipped, or at least prayed to, like so many of his faith did. Again, he had his doubts. Yes, she was faithful. She was a model of openness in her dedication to serve God. So many others are as well. And did this really happen? He memorized Luke 1:37 long ago: "Nothing, you see, is impossible with God." How he wanted to believe this—especially this particular version of Luke, what with its two commas shifting the meaning entirely—but he knew that there was only one way he could truly believe the possibility of the impossible once and for all: Marilyn would have to suddenly walk through the house with her airy gait and beaming eyes, as if she'd simply gone to visit relatives in Ohio for a long weekend.

Yes, she would have liked Seth. He would have liked her, too. He could imagine them being great friends. I'd like that very much, he thought. I wouldn't feel threatened.

21

The original owners of the abandoned house on the beach were in their early sixties when they bought the parcel of land and had a friend of theirs who was an architect draw up the design. He knew their tendency for excess, and they trusted him to rein them in if they should stray into dangerous and costly ideas that were inappropriate for the area. "Let's go for banana bread, not a seven-layer cake" was his mantra whenever they suggested some refinement or trend that he knew they would quickly forget about appreciating or using—a jacuzzi, an oversized island kitchen, a second lanai off the side of the house. After much back and forth, they agreed to two bedrooms upstairs and two at ground level. Two stories it had to be, if only to assure them of ample unobstructed views upstairs as the sea oats and sea grapes lining the dunes grew taller. And four bedrooms it had to be as well, to give each of them a separate room (easily convertible into a guest room, if need be) in which to carry out their hobbies, leaving a third bedroom intact as permanent guest room and the fourth as the place that would require them to find their way back to each other by the end of the day, slip onto the queen-size mattress and carve out a space that was intimate or private, depending on the circumstances of the day. With two bedrooms up and two down, they could be assured of two private spaces on each level; until and if the time came when they could no longer do steps, the two bedrooms below could somehow be reconfigured.

Then there was the façade and the landscaping to consider. On this, everyone also saw eye to eye. No Greek- or Roman-style anything; no imported cypress trees lining a winding driveway, their leaves doomed to crisp, die and fall under a grueling sun. Heavens no. A simple form with as much glass as possible, a solid unimposing structure to hold and protect the windows onto this spectacular slice of a sun-drenched world. It had to be right. It deserved to be right. It was their dream. Their architect friend kept the dream in check: a humble dream, one that could be their final dream. So it was. The husband died four years after they moved in. She followed a year later. Their two children had no interest in keeping it. They lived far away in urban settings and thrived on density of people, not grains of sand or beams of sunshine. The house and the area meant little to them other than a place they felt obliged to visit one or two times each year to see their aged and shrinking parents. Still, they felt guilty about selling it. Years passed before they put the house up for sale.

Four bedrooms and three bathrooms, a cut above the standard 3/2, although there wasn't a pool. Asking price two-hundred fifty thousand, slightly above market price. The McCaffreys brought it down to two-hundred sixteen thousand after two rounds of counter-offers. The house had been on the market for three months, which in that prime location could only mean that the price was too high for some reason—a major defect hidden in the plumbing or electric, an insufficient number of hurricane-proof roof strappings, the standard quick-fix cosmetic solutions (the laminate floor tiles and faux-granite kitchen and bathroom countertops.) At that price, in

1980, potential buyers felt entitled to make a fuss over everything down to the towel racks, about which they could become downright belligerent.

At two hundred sixteen, it was still above the McCaffreys' means, but the price was such a deal that they couldn't not buy it. They would find a way to make it work. The McCaffreys were young. There was time. They could have two children instead of three. Mrs. McCaffrey could get a part-time job and cut down on the shoes. Mr. McCaffrey could give up his convertible. A car seat for the children they would eventually have wouldn't fit it in it anyway. It was a dream of theirs to have such a house right on the ocean.

Soon enough the dream shattered with the violence of a fluted goblet dropped onto a marble floor: They'd overlooked the cost of insurance (flood and hurricane) and the continual maintenance owing to the destructive force of the salt air, which found its way to any and all traces of metal in the house—furniture legs, knobs on doors, window trim—causing it to oxidize and deteriorate; the air-conditioning bills that arrived for eight months of the year that were breathtaking. They couldn't keep up. They abandoned the house outright and moved into a nondescript townhouse rental on the mainland. The house went into foreclosure. "How stupid of us," she said. "We're young," he replied, placing a reassuring arm around her sunken shoulders. "There's time."

Several years later, he accepted a job in the northeast. They moved to a posh suburb of a large city and ended up having the three children they'd planned on, and an SUV that accommodated three car seats. Their beach life was reduced to three weeks in Cape Cod each summer. The state took possession of the house, where it remained in limbo, along with the other foreclosures resulting from other people who'd had big eyes, small wallets, and dreams that had less than a toehold in what their lives were really about. There it sat, idle and accumulating useless drifts of flotsam along its foundation as if competing with the foreclosure documentation mounting in a pile in a back office where someone would eventually or never get around to processing it.

* * * *

It was in front of this house that Honey finished her constitutional each morning. She stationed herself there until it was time to go home. The beach was far enough away from the public parking lots, hotels and condos so as not to draw a crowd. Occasionally a shell-collector ambled along, or a jogger with earbuds. But they didn't stop here. For her, it was a secret place, unpeopled and safe, where she could take pictures, talk to herself (even aloud) like a madwoman, dip her feet and thick ankles into the ocean, and not have to concern herself with the quizzical eyes or ears of passersby. Good God, she thought, what would they think?

Glen was usually still asleep when she got home. She was grateful for the quiet in the house at that hour. It felt like an extended grace period before she detected his movements somewhere down the hallway and her day would have to begin in earnest.

"Good morning, dear."
"Morning, honey."
"Sleep well?"
"Not very."
"Breakfast?"
"Sure."
"Did you take your pills?"
"Yes."
"Your stretching?"
"I'll do it after breakfast."
Interrogation over. Breakfast almost ready.

It didn't occur to her to pick up her camera and take pictures of the two of them, even when they did something out of the ordinary like have an afternoon cocktail with friends or spend an hour exploring a nearby nature reserve. When special occasions like these presented themselves, they quickly lost their sheen. He became impatient to go home. She became annoyed at his impatience.

"I'm going to unwind in my room for a while."
"Need anything?"
"No. I'm good."
"Wanna watch a movie in the living room?"
"No. I'm good."

Aside from mealtimes, she learned to not expect to see much of him. She went about her business; he went about his. As long as she kept herself occupied, the question of whether this was how most couples ended up and, if it was, what the point was in coupling, didn't disturb her.

This time was different. When she entered her house after talking with Hank and Seth at the beach, the question didn't present itself. It wasn't so pressing. But then she remembered that Glen was dead. "My God," she thought as she deposited her camera on the kitchen countertop "What do I do now?"

She knew what she would do. She went to the drawer of her night table, pulled out the white envelope, extracted the piece of paper, and read:

> "My love, I don't know why I'm writing this. I think I want you to back off a little. You always make me feel like I'm guilty of something. Everything I say. Everything I do. Even the way I brush my teeth. It's intense. I can't relax when I'm with you, be me. Isn't that why we got married and set up house together? So we could finally let go and just be us? I'm not sure if you like me anymore. I don't think you do. But I think you're amazing. You do all the things you're supposed to do, even though I don't

think you really like doing them. Which isn't good. For you. For us. I'm not so good at this stuff. I guess what I'm trying to say is that I think you're not happy. And I think it's mainly because of me. I'll work on it. I'll try to change. I love you, Honey. I do. You do know, don't you?"

Glen hadn't placed the letter in her night table. She'd found it in the drawer of his night table and transferred it to her night table after she'd read it for a second time. He wouldn't notice, she thought. If he wanted her to notice, he would have placed it somewhere where she would be sure to find it—on top of the stove or the washing machine. He didn't though. He didn't want her to find it, she thought. He was testing intimacy on himself before trying it out on her. The envelope was unmarked and in his night table.

She found it there by accident when she went in the drawer to take inventory of the condoms. If there were fewer than five, she added them to the bottom of her grocery list, leaving a bit of space after the food items before writing only the letter "C," which would be sufficient for her to remember to replenish this particular household item along with the produce, meats, dairy, and canned and paper goods. Had he known this detail of her efficiency in preparing her grocery list, he would have found another place to put the envelope. But he didn't know this detail. It was one of many details about how she went about tending to things—the emotional mechanics of her—that never occurred to him to think about, since he didn't spend much time trying to piece her together or pull her apart.

As she read it this morning, she wiped the moisture in her eyes before it could collect with enough mass to form a tear drop that rolled down her cheek. What he wrote was heartfelt, much like the man she married many years and hopes ago, the romantic surfer dude who was nimble in body and spirit and whose handwriting was rushed and careless, although a few uppercase letters—the L, Q and Z—had an incongruous curl that seemed downright feminine. So slowly had he become overweight and sedentary and bland over the years that she barely noticed it. Neither did she notice the way she accommodated it as it was happening. And he hadn't noticed that she'd moved the envelope to her night table. Time went by with so much not taken stock of; then, just like that, there they were, another middle-age couple who had little do with each other and even less say to each other. An ecosystem gone barren. And now it was too late. She pressed the letter to her sternum. "Why didn't he have the courage to move the envelope?" she asked herself. "Why I didn't I have the courage to tell him I'd found it?"

* * * *

Dear Lord, Hank thought as he inserted the key in his front door. You test me again. What more is it that You think I need to understand? Slipping off his shoes in the foyer, he considered calling Jonathan, his younger son, to tell him about his two new acquaintances; how he did hope to see them again outside of the safe sanctuary and ritual of the beach sunrise; how he was beginning to carve out the afterlife of a widower; and (you see, son?); how there was no longer any need for him to ask so many questions that showed genuine concern for his welfare but that were annoying, sometimes deprecating. Who was the parent here, after all?

He decided against calling him when he remembered that Seth said he was gay. He couldn't not bring it up without feeling a sense of dishonesty toward his youngest boy, the sensitive one, the gay one. They were close and talked about everything. Hank was a deeply religious man. Jonathan was a minister. Hank had been happily married for almost four decades. His son was happily married. To a man. How could he not bring up the topic of Seth? But he didn't want to bring it up. Not yet, anyway. "I'm glad to hear you're getting out and meeting people," he preferred to hear Jonathan tell him, rather than an interrogation about this gay Seth person that his gay married minister of a son would insist on if the gay thing had been mentioned. I'll call him later, he decided.

He welcomed the coolness of the tile flooring as he walked back to the foyer to slip on his plastic sandals. He welcomed the relief he felt about not calling his son, instead returning to the kitchen to stand at its beige- and gray-flecked Formica counter, looking out the window above the sink and (as he often did) pondering what to occupy himself with until lunch. Lunch would certainly be light fare since he'd eaten such a big breakfast. Maybe just a salad and a can of tuna sprinkled on top, and some crackers on the side. Thank goodness for tuna.

* * * *

As soon as Seth arrived home, he gave Winston a Milk Bone and poured himself a cup of coffee. His phone vibrated in his pocket. He looked at the screen. No contact name, but he recognized the number. He didn't need a name to identify the sequence of ten digits separated with two dashes. They were like a tattoo inscribed on the flesh.

"Hey! *Ma nishmah?*"

"*Kol b'seder.* I'm fine." Yoni cleared his throat. "I'm in Miami."

Seth didn't respond.

"Miami. In your state. Can you believe it?"

"What brings you to my state? Work?"

"*Ken.* A conference. Two days. I'm staying on for a few extra days. To check out the scene. Never been to Miami before. And who knows when I'll be back. Are you near Miami?"

Yoni had a full head of red hair. It was kinky and he kept it short. A red Afro on a Jew was out of the question. Then there was the density of hair sprouting on his arms and legs and chest. That hair was longer, slightly darker and less compacted, like nests of spider legs. They reminded Seth of the Neanderthal Man illustrations in his tenth-grade World Cultures textbook that held him spellbound as they provoked desires in him that he didn't understand but couldn't help but succumb to by stroking his penis. Looking at those illustrations in class, he would lose himself in considerations about how those men must have smelled, until his teacher Mr. Anderson would force his return with a sharp "What do you think, Seth?" or something of that sort, as if Mr. Anderson knew that his prize student was heading into perilous waters and needed to be yanked back to safe harbor. Seth returned willingly. Mr. Anderson made him think similar thoughts, what with his short-sleeve shirts that revealed armpits glistening with sweat whenever he raised his arms to write something on the blackboard.

Yoni smelled Neanderthal too, at least what Seth imagined Neanderthal to smell like if those men from the textbooks had been set before him to be smelled. The reality of the smell matched the fantasy of that smell, although he also chuckled at having nabbed an Israeli who shattered his dreamscape of the consummate Middle Eastern man—one with smooth mocha skin, dark hair, mahogany eyes, lithe contours—who could juice him up and hold him. That smell of him. It was the smell, in spite of the geeky Eastern European features, that lured him in and kept him in for more time than he should have remained. A smell that was as evolved as it was primitive. Repugnant and irresistible. Such couplings made sense to him.

"I might pop over for a visit. What do you think? Are you far from Miami?"

"I thought you wanted to check out the scene. I'm hardly a

scene. And I'm not around the corner. Three hours from Miami, if the traffic isn't hideous, which it usually is. Three boring highway hours."

"That's doable. Unless you're not up for it. You're thinking 'no', right?"

Seth held the phone to his ear without saying anything. It sounded like a seduction was in the works. Of all things, after all these years. How tiresome. How played out. He played. "Depends on what you want, what you're looking for."

"I'm not looking for anything, Seth."

He rolled his eyes toward the ceiling and spotted the baby gecko that he saw there yesterday, although it was now a few inches to the left. "We're always looking for something. All of us are. We always are. Why would you want to give up Miami to drive all the way up here? Up here, your only options are me or me."

"Jesus. I'm here. I'm near. It would be nice to see you. It's been a while. If you're not ready..."

Seth grabbed the dish towel draped over the oven handle and swung it in the direction of the gecko. He didn't want to kill it, just stir up a breeze and watch the transparent reptile scurry along the sloped kitchen ceiling, which it did. Each time it paused, an orange flap bloated out from the bottom of its neck to assess risk. It wasn't a gecko after all. It was an anole. "Ready for what?"

"Bad idea. Never mind."

"Idea? What idea did you have?" Now he felt he had the upper hand. "Yoni, did it ever occur to you that I might just be indifferent? That it's possible that you might not have a hold on someone you'd like to keep having a hold on, for whatever reason?"

Before Seth could decide whether to continue, Yoni dropped the call. The scent of red hair lingered on the line. Seth looked up at the ceiling again. The lizard was directly above the garbage disposal. Of all places to stop. Stupid reptile.

*\ *\ *\ *

Honey put the envelope in her night table drawer. I need to get away, she thought. Somewhere that will make me think about things in a different way. A new way. A way that lures me in more than scares me away, so that I can finally start to become a different person. The kind of person who doesn't need to obsess about what kind of person I am. Certain options were at the ready: to her sister and brother-in-law's, or to her long-time girlfriend Stephanie's (divorced five years ago with two grown children) outside of D.C. But no. She didn't want to end up in a place where those around her would oblige her to retrace her steps (how tedious) by asking her questions like "Do you want to talk about it?" or "Why don't you open up?" The people she knew who asked questions like that didn't listen, she understood. They were priming themselves to offer advice and consolation, to make it all about them, when all she wanted was to get away from herself.

There were other options. A planet full of options, in fact. One only needed to think in terms of leaps, not baby steps. Like to Key West. Or further, to Costa Rica. Or even further, to Patagonia. Or even to places that didn't have beaches and palm trees and sticky air. Like Berlin or Prague or Toronto or Stockholm. Places where people couldn't know her situation and wouldn't ask questions like, "How are you feeling?" or "Was it sudden?" or make empathetic remarks like "I'm so sorry for your loss." She was in no mood for decorum, of feeling constrained by the goodwill of others to retrace her steps, misguided as they may have been at various junctures. A jolt was what she wanted, or so she thought as she put down her camera and wondered how to deal with her husband's things, especially the items that could so easily sidetrack her into a sentimental seasickness: the fishing rod that hooked the endless pompano and bluefish that she cleaned, filleted and prepared for dinner, even though he wasn't particularly fond of seafood; the framed photo of them at their senior prom, with his cascade of wavy blond hair and his toned body fitted snugly into a black tuxedo complemented by a ribbed silk cumberbund, red bowtie and, of all things, Nike high-top sneakers (he was captain of the varsity football team and could get away with high-top sneakers—so cool!); and drawers and closets stuffed with other objects: vintage ones that had fed her hopes of what he would be; and more recent ones that fed her disillusionment over what he'd become. What they'd become. She could take care of all of that later after she went away (but where?) and came back. Because she would come back. She had no desire to not come back. She just needed to get away. For a while. And then she would come back and deal with it all, maybe even feeling strong enough to look hard at herself in front of one of the mirrors in one of their 2.5 bathrooms and admit that she too had let herself go, from the gray roots of her dyed and brittle blonde hair down to a waistline that could only be called girth, and ask herself: "What have I become?" But later. She needed to get away. For a while.

    She didn't go away just then. She didn't have it in her. Maybe two or three decades ago she would have. Not now. It was silly to consider radical change at such an age, she thought. Adjusting her bra strap, she found herself searching for a word, which came to her: epiphany. Such a beautiful word. The sound of it. The meaning of it. She laughed. How lovely to have such a word enter her head. And how wise to not take it too seriously. But still. It would be nice. But still. Such craziness, such recklessness. There was a time for all that, once upon a time. She ran her fingers through her hair. It felt thin and dry. She could almost feel the gray. Yes, she thought, that time was long gone.

    She was hungry and remembered that there was some vegetable soup in a Tupperware container in the fridge. And some cottage cheese. That would be enough. She wasn't in the mood to cook, but she wasn't in the mood to feel hunger either.

22

The first summer months after retirement, Hank raised the thermostat to a fixed seventy-nine degrees. He could afford it. His pension and social security checks had kicked in the winter before. "That much?" he asked himself when he saw the figures. "It must be a mistake." But the figures didn't change over the months. All this money coming for the rest of his life and he wouldn't have to lift a finger for it? How he'd looked forward to this day, but on that first day when he went to the mailbox in his bedroom slippers and found the check—proof that it was real—he felt guilty. So accustomed was he to working each day to earn his living (as it should be, he was taught), that this "free" paycheck seemed unethical, almost illegal. He reminded himself that he'd fed into the system the requisite working years and credits in order to reap such a benefit, but he couldn't convince himself that necessarily meant he deserved it. And so his joy was tempered. He deposited the check later that afternoon and checked the transaction online every few hours for two days to make sure it was real. Winter and spring passed. The checks arrived. They continued to be more than he'd calculated. But within a few months they proved to be less than he needed. By

March, he understood that some corners would have to be cut. He encouraged Marilyn to spend more time with coupons, sitting with her at the kitchen table with a pair of scissors he bought at the local Dollar General for the purpose; he filled their car with Regular instead of Premium; and he raised the thermostat. Marilyn was on board with the shift in temperature until she started breaking into regular sweats at night in bed in that first summer. Menopause, she realized. Hardly a subject to broach with her husband as a reason for lowering the thermostat. He might ask why, and then she would have to go through the ordeal of figuring out how to discuss menopause to a man who always took her quickly, dutifully, with the lights out, oblivious to her intimate parts. Besides, it was he who left the house day after day, year after year, to work at whatever it was that he worked at (she knew it had something to do with civil engineering, although for the life of her she couldn't figure out how those two words fit together) and at the expense of who-knew-how-many degrees of happiness he sacrificed in order to keep their material comforts predictable and their children's future cushioned. Who was she to insist on a room temperature that would cure the heat flashes but require the budget to be tightened even more? At night, and with a bit of practice, she could gradually work her half of the blanket off her body, first with her hand and then with her feet, until it was piled up at the foot of her side of the bed. She'd leave the top sheet to cover herself with. And if that wasn't enough, she could rummage through her drawers to see if there was a forgotten nightgown, some thinner and shorter frock, that she might have stowed away. She wasn't one to throw away things. And during the day, well, she would just sweat it out. If there were moments of desperation, there was always the community pool or, if need be, a damp washcloth. The water from the spigots in the bathrooms was always cold if she let it run long enough. She could blot her face with the cloth, return it under the spigot, and bring it behind her ears, which seemed to possess a mystical cooling zone.

Hank wasn't aware of his wife's discomforts and made a point of changing the thermostat exactly one month before the summer solstice. After Marilyn died, he set it to eighty degrees instead of seventy-nine. It was comfortable enough. He could get by.

* * * *

Seth kept at least one window open year-round, regardless of the temperature outside. His house was like a glass box, which was his intention when he renovated it.

"I want as much glass as you can put in," he repeatedly told Eric, his contractor. "The more natural light, the better," he added, as if it were a mantra.

"You snowbirds. A bunch of rookies. Ever think about hurricanes? Flying objects crashing through glass?" Eric replied. "Or passing a wind mitigation inspection, if you even know what that is? Unless you don't care about your insurance premium."

"Fine. Do what you can. But I want light. Gotta have lots of it. That's what I moved here for." Light. Natural light. More light. If it became blinding, which he couldn't imagine it ever becoming, he could block it here and there with curtains and shutters, but if it was consistently attenuated because of a lack of windows, he would be powerless to generate more.

Soon, he came to understand that it wasn't only about light; it was also about air. If all of the many windows were shut, he felt claustrophobic, too sealed in, regardless of the flood of sunlight; at the very least, the window in front of his desk had to stay open so that he could hear and smell what was going on outside, however insignificant it might be—a squirrel scurrying across the telephone wire above his back fence, hamburgers sizzling on his neighbor's barbecue. He liked to be reminded of goings-on that were independent of, and indifferent to, the fact of his existence, however inconsequential they might be. There was something spiritual to be had if he took the time to try to make a calm connection. Other times, especially during the summer months, the open window caused sweat to bead up his body, which led him to think about the sweat on the bodies of other men. He liked that, too.

* * * *

It was never not hot on an afternoon in July. Even the rain in July was hot. When it pounded the streets, sidewalks and lawns, as it often did for twenty minutes or so in summer afternoons, the sizzle and steam rising from the pummeled surfaces mobilized into a thick band of humidity that made the air even more difficult to breathe in. The rising vapors could almost seem healthy, spa-like, if it weren't for the fragrance of asphalt and fertilizer they carried with them. In deep summer, Honey, Hank and Seth, all of them seasoned transplants to the area, couldn't help but wish they were still living in the place from which they'd departed, places that made many people dream of moving here. Deep summer was what separated transplants like them, no matter how seasoned they might be, from the native-born. The three of them couldn't ease into relentless heat the way the locals seemed to do as they went about their business in such impossible weather, mowing their lawns, washing their cars, driving here and there with their convertible tops down, even jogging or bicycling on the wide sidewalks in the neighborhoods or along the river. In mid-afternoon! And so many of them barefoot, clad in the bare minimum (tube tops for the women, topless for the men, gym shorts with no underwear beneath—you could tell). The three of them couldn't fathom slipping into such a careless and slovenly mode of display, even in their own backyard. There was slippage, however. Honey let her gray hair grow long and tied it back with a thick cloth band, where unbrushed strands clung to her back like withered remnants of a happier time, but she chose not to notice; Hank wore a sunhat whose inner rim was stained with sweat the shape of amoebas, but he stopped caring; and Seth gave in to the seductive ease of dime-store flip-flops, no longer caring whether his feet would still stand proud in his suede Birkenstocks. Perhaps the slippage wasn't a function of the torpor of Florida as much as one of aging. They knew in their own way that the year or two that passersby might have subtracted from their age—by the right clothes, the right make-up, the pinching and slapping of cheeks, the sporadic at-home calisthenics and more sporadic visits to the gym—amounted to not so much, as if by taking one step closer to the sun, one could be warmed that much more. They appreciated the wisdom that accrued with age. It spared them a lot of effort made in vain, even as it spread a sadness that was as thick as the humidity in July.

* * * *

"Good morning." Hank waited until Seth was close enough that he wouldn't have to raise his voice. The pre-dawn air was still, the ocean calm and emptied of the colors that the sun would soon dab it with. Winston arrived at Hank well before Seth and worked his head between Hank's thighs. Hank stooped down to rake his extended fingers back and forth along Winston's spine, from collar to tail.

"Good morning." The two men shook hands and continued together toward Honey. They knew it was her; they recognized her stooped shoulders and the zoom lens protruding from her face like some mechanical proboscis.

"Hi y'all," she shouted toward them as soon as she saw

them coming her way. "Did you see the dolphins?"

"I think I saw two fins right before I ran into Seth."

"I must've missed them."

She went to each of them, arms outstretched. They obliged. It was her way. "When the ocean is calm like this, you gotta fix your eyes on a spot out there. Any spot. You also gotta focus on your peripheral vision. Can't lose sight of that. It's hard to explain, but if you can do that, and if you wait long enough, you'll see them. They're almost always out there. They're probably always out there. We just don't know how to look for them. And they could care less about us." She took several steps forward, away from them, to put into practice what she preached. Winston followed her and lay down beside her, looking out toward the ocean as if he too was looking for some abrupt disruption in all that undulation.

"Your dog is so friendly," Hank said.

"He's a trusting soul. He thinks the world is a totally benevolent place. It's a good thing."

"It is."

"It is. For a dog, anyway."

Honey stood up and headed back toward them. "Three minutes, and the sun'll break through."

Winston trotted at Honey's side as they returned to the two men.

Hank glanced at his watch. "I say four minutes."

"I say three," Honey said. "Let's see. The countdown begins."

The three of them turned from the magnificence in front of them to focus on their digital watches. After three minutes precisely, the sun pierced the horizon line.

Hank looked toward Honey. "I'm impressed. Which app do you use?"

"I don't."

"Then I'm *really* impressed."

She laughed. "It's nothing to be impressed by. I've been coming here for years, so I know. Nothing I can take credit for. I mean, it's just nice to know something. Just like that. Don't you think?"

The three of them were positioned in the irrefutable triangle that any three stationary objects placed anywhere must form, but theirs somehow resembled an arc more than a triangle. They returned to their silence, watching the sun until it broke through in its entirety, as they knew it would, sending its message of a certainty among uncertainties, as they knew it would. The wind picked up and the water broke into small units of choppiness, as it usually did after Nature completed her phase of Labor and once again, as with each morning, gave birth to and delivered the orb that made Life possible. The show was over. The period of reverence lost its target and with it the comfort of their silence.

Seth was first. "Beautiful."

Honey smiled at him. "When isn't it?"

"Never, come to think of it." He felt trite.

"Are you a widow too?" she asked him as she glanced at Hank. "Should we let you into our club?"

He looked down at Winston. "No, I'm not. I'm separated. Amicably separated. Permanently separated. After twenty-five good years."

Hank was confused but landed on something he could contribute. "I'm sorry to hear that."

"Thanks, but no need for that. If we'd hung in there when there was little reason to, maybe you could feel sorrow. It wasn't like that. We were good. Solid. Until the last couple of years of hanging in there when it wasn't so good and we couldn't find our way back and we decided that it was probably better to not be together than to stay together. Stay together for the sake of what? You know what I mean?"

Hank had no idea what Seth meant. He didn't say anything. It struck him as a travesty of some sort, although he couldn't pinpoint it. Anyway, who was he to judge? He looked up at the sky. Yes, the show was over. The sun made its grand entrance and had subdued itself to something far more modest; the sky was vast and blue; the clouds white, scattered and without any particularly dramatic offering. The pinks and purples and oranges peeled off, and the inevitable heat of a day in July was gathering momentum. Soon it would be time to head indoors until sunset, another indoor day to get through. He wasn't keen on returning home to face another twelve hours in his own company, but he wasn't thrilled about the way the conversation was going. He took a deep breath. "Why don't we walk for a bit."

"I'm game," Seth said.

Honey unscrewed the zoom lens and put it in her camera bag. "Sure. Why not?"

The distraction of preparing themselves to walk, and to walk beyond where they usually stopped, and to do all of that in company, caused a pause in their conversation until they set off in a line, with Honey in the center, and a walking rhythm established itself—brisk but not requiring much exertion for any of them.

"I do know what you mean," she said. "I thought about it a lot over the years. Separating. Divorcing. Having done with what I was used to having. Why we persist in some things that don't work anymore and don't seem to be able to be repaired. But then he died and that took care of all that."

The three of them continued along the beach, oblivious to the pipers that skirted out of their path sensing the perilous activity of humans coursing through the sand.

Seth looked toward her. "Why do you think we do stuff like that?"

"Like what?"

"Persisting in things that don't give us pleasure anymore."

"Who knows? Maybe something to do with faith in something. Or clinging to the old-school way of things. Or maybe out of fear. Or lack of imagination. Or some or all of the above. Beats the hell outa me. It doesn't matter now. For me. He's gone. I'm getting out of the habit of thinking about those things. They're not relevant for me anymore. No need to turn them around in my head."

"The game is over?" Seth ventured.

"Right," she replied.

"I should probably be heading back now," Hank said.

"Oh dear. I'm so sorry," she said.

"About what?" Seth asked. He was about to continue but Winston dashed to the water line, tempted by a lazing heron, his favorite prey. "Did you see how he took off? I love when he reminds me that he's a dog."

"Such a sweet one." Hank turned away from them. "See you soon."

"I can head back too, if you'd like some company."

Hank smiled. "That's okay. I have things to do."

"See you tomorrow?" Honey asked.

"Weather permitting." Hank headed toward his home. Winston stopped dead in his tracks, unsure as to which direction to go. He preferred traveling in zones where the smells were familiar, the zones where Hank was now traveling as he made his way home. His master was heading the other way, with Honey.

"Here boy!" Seth called out. Winston obeyed.

"My gosh, what a sweet man," she said.

"He is. A sweet man." He wanted to add that he could almost taste his sweetness but instead said, "Fragile, too. I think we put him off."

"You think? Shit. I'm like a leaky valve. We'll find out tomorrow morning. Will he or won't he be here?"

They were approaching a stretch of beach that was attached to a large public-access parking lot. Here the band of sand was more populated, mostly by non-locals—those who needed a car to get to the ocean and who consequently made a morning or afternoon out of their trek to the beach, filling up their trunks and back seats with blankets and food and radios and sunscreen and every other accoutrement that they could possibly need for an outing. There were many of them, and many accoutrements, and they claimed large spaces of sand. It felt different there, what with all that clutter and density of objects.

"Yuck," Honey said.

"Fuck."

"Sacrilege."

"Lemming ledge."

"Strip mall."

"Human squall."

They laughed. "You must have teenagers in your life. Kids? Grandkids?" he asked.

"Both. And all of them are wired. You?"

"Nope. None."

"Really?"

"Really."

"That surprises me."

"And it surprises me that you don't remember the part of my story I told you about at the diner. But it's a long story. For another time."

"Okay. What do you say we turn back?"

"I was about to say the same thing." They reversed direction, toward the empty stretch where they'd come from, and continued walking. "Ah, much better," he said.

"Suicide is something I think about. How about you?" she asked.

"Jesus, that's a bit much."

"Don't get me wrong. I don't have a gun or a noose in my bag. Don't you think about it sometimes?"

Seth slowed his pace. "I don't think so. Maybe. I don't know."

"I do. Not that I really want to do it, but it crosses my mind sometimes. It's not like I decide to think about it. It just makes itself thought. Just like that. Out of the blue."

"Like a theme song from some old movie that works its way into a dream at three in the morning?" he said.

She laughed. "You could say that. Maybe a bit heavier, but not much."

"That's good to hear." Winston was between them. They both bent down to pat him. When their hands touched, she said "Sorry" as they retracted their arms.

"I should probably head back home," he said.

"I'm sorry."

"There we go again. Nothing to be sorry for. I enjoyed myself." He angled left, away from her and toward a beach access point that saddled a condominium.

"Wait. You forgot. A hug."

"Right. A hug." He wrapped his arms around her. He kept his legs at a distance from hers but could feel her breasts against his chest as that distance narrowed upward starting at the waist. Winston mounted his left leg and started humping him.

"Such a sweet dog," she said. Seth smiled at her as they parted company.

23

Hank placed his index finger where the band of maroon ribbon met the top of the Book. Bending the top half of his finger into a hook, he pried the Book open to the pages where the marker nested itself tightly against the inner spine: Luke 17, verse 33. *"Whoever seeks to keep his life shall lose it, and whoever loses his life shall preserve it."* Honey. A strange creature she was, he thought. So was Seth. Not as much as she was. He didn't know why he thought about them just then. Neither of them had lost their life, but they didn't seem desperate to hang onto it either. No matter. Who was he to try to figure them out? No need to read into them. Reading the Bible was enough for him. His life was enough. They had their own lives to live out and contemplate, if contemplation was something they did. He had his life to live, intertwined with the Book like a double helix, which was as it should be, he thought. For him.

He carried his cup of tea to the living room, curling his toes upward to avoid tripping where the kitchen floor gave way to the living room carpeting. Luke 1, verse 50; his confusion about the difference between mercy and grace. He lowered his toes and raised the teacup to his lips. The rising steam sent a signal that he would need to inhale deeply as he took small sips if he didn't want to burn his mouth. He didn't mind taking his time. He wasn't in any hurry to drink his tea, let alone finish it. He wasn't all that thirsty.

He sipped slowly, taking in more air than tea, batting mercy and grace about like two athletic teams vying for the championship. Mercy, he decided, was God not punishing us as our sins deserved. Grace, he decided, was God blessing us even if we didn't deserve it. He was pleased with his decisions. Neat and clean. Tidy enough to keep going. Mercy, he decided, was deliverance from judgement. Grace, he decided, was extending kindness to the unworthy. The teacup was still three-quarters full when he also came to decide that Honey didn't seem to be as happy as she let on, and that Seth seemed to be waiting to pounce on him with something to shake him up. The two of them made him curious in a way that he wasn't used to.

Marilyn was good at contemplating God, too. She steered him along the path of God, even when he was entering her in the night darkness. She wasn't there now to keep it simple. God's other people populated the setting now; people like him, who walked along beaches but, unlike him, still went to work and came home to their family and provided for them and presided over them with an overwhelming sense of responsibility as if their very lives depended on a domestic breadwinner such as he had been, and not on God. He no longer figured among such people. His children were grown and had lives of their own. His working days were over. His skin was dry and crenellated. His life with Marilyn was over. Oh the plans they'd made when Jonathan accepted his first real job and moved away, emptying the contents of his bedroom to take with him, just as Matthew had done. They'd been warned about the disquiet of the empty nest. They'd prepared themselves with a medley of hobbies and day trips and cruises.

They were ready. But she was taken away shortly after. He wasn't ready for that. As much as he tried to acquiesce to His design in what he knew to be a test of submission or blind faith, he couldn't shake off the unfairness of it. How cruel a test. Grace? Mercy? Where were they to be found? He finished his tea and put his cup and saucer in the sink without so much as a rattle. He would leave them there and rinse them out and place them in the upper rack of the dishwasher after dinner. He was feeling rebellious.

* * * *

The following morning it was foggy. Or was it mist? The shrouded vista wasn't new to him, but on this morning the question posed itself for the first time. Seth realized he didn't know the difference between the two. He started to pull his cell phone from his pocket to Google it but released the phone and let nestle back into his pocket. The beach was a place for questions and suggestions, not for instant answers. Winston vanished into the opaque air twenty feet ahead of him. Seth trusted him not to venture off too far.

The landmarks that he took for granted and that gave him his bearings were shrouded in the fog (or was it mist?): the condominium that had a slender, needle-point tower on the roof with a dot of red light at the top (for airplanes? pelicans?), a fishing rod or two stabbed diagonally in the sand several yards beyond the prison-like structure of the condominium, and, further ahead, Honey stooped or standing at the water's edge with her camera hugging her face. Seth could hear the waves as he walked in a kind of white-gray myopia, secure that he was headed in the general direction that habit took him but unable to pinpoint precisely where he was.

The blinking red light finally came into view, as did three fishing rods after. The figure of Honey wasn't taking shape further down. Only a vague outline of a broad-rimmed hat sitting on the head of a man. Seth didn't discount the possibility of the man being someone new at this place and hour. Winston tugged at the leash to arrive at him. He knew. It was Hank.

"Good morning."

"Good morning."

They hugged each other, even though Honey wasn't present to goad them on to the touchy-feely greeting that she insisted on. Strange woman.

"She's not here again. She must be going through a difficult time," Hank said.

Seth stooped down to pat Winston. As he rose, he looked at Hank directly in the eyes. "I remember when my partner left."

"I was thinking the same thing about Marilyn. Forty-five years together before she died."

"Twenty-five years for me. Mutual separation, which is an entirely different thing. The other person is still out there, somewhere, living a life, maybe even being happier for it." A blue heron was lolling at the water's edge. Winston tugged at his harness to have at the slender, winged creature. Seth unhooked the leash from the black mesh harness, and the dog made a mad dash toward the bird, which took flight as soon as Winston's front paws made their first mark in the sand toward it. He circled back toward the two men, satisfied. Mission accomplished. It was all about the chase.

"I wish I knew her better. I'd like to help in some way if I could. I wonder if she has children nearby."

"How many children do you have?"

"Two. Boys."

"That must help."

"They have their own lives, in different states. We talk once a week, sometimes with a webcam. Sometimes for fifteen minutes. Sometimes for an hour. It depends on how busy there are. I'm never too busy." The sun broke through the horizon and burned away the white veil. The expanses revealed themselves. They retreated back into their silence together. How could their talk, small or otherwise, compete in front of all this?

* * * *

Honey didn't show up that morning. The afternoon before, she wandered through her home as if she was being led through a series of Escape Rooms. Along the way, she scooped up items that could serve her for both the short and long terms in the event she managed to escape. She found her way back to the front door, arms full, threw everything into the back seat of her car and drove to Iowa. Her sister and brother-in-law lived there. She loved her sister and was hopeful that Ray could be loveable one day soon. On her visits, she didn't spend much time with him. A long weekend here and there, but in those short intervals Ray demonstrated a kind and tactile affection to June—an arm around her shoulder, a finger hooked around her finger, a hand clasping her hand or sweeping a wisp of dirty brown hair away from her face, whatever a body part of hers could be latched onto by him, lest she get away. He was sweet, she thought, but cloying, which could mean trouble down the road.

When Honey arrived at their home in Iowa and again witnessed the unending number of moments Ray latched onto his wife (she stopped counting at twenty-six), she realized it wasn't a performance for her benefit. Neither of them was putting their best foot forward. They were simply being who they were when they were together. It didn't matter that she was there. He would do it, and she would welcome it, anyway. How lovely, she thought. She ended up staying on; and when it seemed to her that staying on might lead to brighter things for her as well, she made a quick visit back home to arrange to have her belongings shipped to a modest home she found in a suburb of Des Moines, close enough to her sister and brother-in-law's downtown condo that she'd be able to drop in from time to time and ingratiate herself into the smooth dailiness of their life together as man and wife, in sickness and in health, and all the rest. She and her sister had a history of closeness, even though their thoughts about things that mattered most to them didn't converge all that much. It was a kind of meta-closeness. She needed closeness, meta- or otherwise. Especially now. It was one thing to eke out moments of aloneness when one had a spouse in the house who made your eyes perpetually roll in exasperation; it was quite another to find connection amid a perpetual state of aloneness. That kind of aloneness was unbearable to her. She signed a six-month renewable lease on the house she'd found, figuring that half a year should be enough time for the radical change to calm down, take root, and let her see whether it had made a difference or whether she was simply riding another wave of intoxication. Six months. At her age, it shouldn't take longer than that.

* * * *

It was just the two of them and Winston then, on the lookout for Honey to save them from their discomfort at finding themselves alone together. Hank the eternally grieving widower; Seth the newly single and randy homosexual. Honey was a stabilizing force. She didn't arrive. They carried on nonetheless, as two people who were not unfamiliar with each other and who found themselves face to face in a special place would feel obliged to. It was awkward. Seth asked questions that Hank answered in single sentences, eyes cast downward. Hank didn't return questions in kind. He looked outward or downward. He bent over to run his fingers through Winston's disheveled pompadour, where he hoped to find some release and relief from his agitation at having to navigate this without cues from Honey.

It was laughter that saved them, prompted by a simple question that Hank struggled to finally get out: "What do you think about grace and mercy?"

"Who are they?"

"I'm not following you."

"I'm not following you either. My memory isn't terrific. I don't remember us talking about a Grace and Murphy."

Hank was the first to laugh. It started as something confined to his throat but soon extended throughout his body, which abandoned its tautness and began to quiver. It was contagious. Seth followed suit: throat-body-eyes.

Seth caught his breath. "Wow. That felt great. Amazing. I don't remember the last time I laughed like that. And over something that I don't get at all. What was that about? Did I miss something?"

Hank tried to regulate his breath as he reintroduced the topic of grace and mercy, but bouts of laughter broke in, insisting not to be over with. Grace and Murphy! When he finished explaining, Seth looked and him quizzically and laughed again. Hank laughed at the laughing. When their laughter finally subsided, they were breathless and tears were streaming down their cheeks. Silence came back to them. A brief silence, just long enough for them to understood that they'd taken a short-cut to establishing something solid and to be trusted. Seth put his arm around Hank's shoulder. "Of all things to ask a nice Jewish man. Grace to me is a woman's name, like Grace Slick. You know of her? Or some dowdy lady who forgets to take off her apron after she's pulled the cornbread out of the oven. And mercy? Mercy is a word that someone with a name like Grace would say instead of a crass alternative. Kind of a synonym for 'Land sakes.' Or 'fuck.'

Forgive my French."

Hank wasn't following. He cringed at the word "fuck" but didn't pull away from the arm around his shoulder. "Should we go for breakfast?"

"Sure."

"Do you eat bacon?"

Seth squeezed the tendon at the top of Hank's shoulder. "Take a guess."

He thought for a moment. "Yes? But aren't you Jewish?"

"Correct on both counts. Well done. The bacon, that is. Not for religious reasons. I just have problems with undercooked pork. Undercooked chicken, too."

The two men headed toward the beach exit that would bring them closest to the diner. Winston distanced himself from them, preferring to sniff further inland, along the dunes. Warnings had been posted recently of coyote sightings, but Winston couldn't read. He nosed around with abandon. He preferred green areas like the dunes, with their endless variety of leaves and branches and blossoms where he could pause to take in a particular scent, make an assessment, and, conditions permitting, lift a hind leg to let out a drop or two of pee.

By the time they arrived at the exit, Seth's arm had long receded from Hank's shoulder and he was several steps ahead of him.

"It's a shame Honey wasn't at the beach. We could have invited her," Hank said.

"We have Grace and Murphy."

Hank could feel the laughter inside him gathering force. How good it felt. He restrained himself.

Seth ordered pancakes, one of his favorite breakfast meals. He didn't prepare them at home. They were too much trouble to make from scratch for one person, what with all the precise sequences of stirrings and foldings and rising-times required to get the batter just right. He didn't trust the lumps of flour that he wasn't supposed to whisk away to smoothness. "Could you bring the butter pats out right away?" he asked the server when she took their order. "And could you throw in some extras?" He turned to Hank. "I like the butter to get soft so it melts between each layer and oozes out when I cut in. I'm usually a pretty clean eater. But every once in a while I let go."

Hank squinted his eyes to read the server's name tag. "I'll have the Classic, Pam," he said with a smile on his face. He wanted her to know that he appreciated her. What she must have to put up with, he thought. People she didn't know calling out to her all morning because it was taking too long, or they dropped their teaspoon, or there wasn't enough ice in their water glass. He imagined her going home at the end of her shift. She seemed to be in her early thirties and probably had at least one young child. Maybe more. He hoped she was married if that was the case.

He spared her the litany of questions that she was obliged to ask each of her customers: "How would you like your eggs? Bacon or sausage? Hash browns or home fries? White, whole wheat or rye?" Before she could begin, he told her, "I'll have Eggs scrambled. Bacon. Hash browns. Rye toast." He added, "Please, Pam." She seemed grateful.

As Pam turned away, Seth called out to her, "Oh miss, can I also have a side of sausage? Extremely well-done?" Turning back to Hank, he said, "May as well go for broke."

"Sure thing," she called back, interrupting her brisk walk away from him while she stuffed her order pad into the pocket of her apron and veered toward the kitchen.

Everyone around them was engaged in conversation between mouthfuls of breakfast. And here they were, having just closed their laminated menus and facing each other across a table that was empty except for a plastic bottle of ketchup with a maroon crust on its outer rim, a sugar-flecked white condiment holder, and two sets of utensils tightly wrapped in a paper napkin. The rest would arrive soon. For the time being, they had to do with these accoutrements. Neither man knew what to say or to ask.

Seth fiddled with the condiment holder and ventured first. He opted for something safe and expected. "Tell me about your children."

"There's Matthew. The oldest. Just turned forty-one. He lives outside of Chicago. He's in construction. Manager of a large firm. Maybe director. I don't remember. Not sure what the difference is anyway. Very successful but overworked. He's married to Julie. A fine woman. They just moved into a beautiful house. At least four bedrooms. I can only imagine what their mortgage payments must be. I worry about him sometimes. He has a long commute and he works long hours. The school district is supposed to be the best in the area. They have two children. Boys. My two grandsons."

"That must be nice. Grandchildren."

"It is. I wish I could see them more often. They're up there in their lives. I'm down here in mine. Matthew asks me to move to the area. He says that because it's the right thing to say. Such a good man. I don't want to be a burden. I'm self-sufficient. If I move near them, they'll insist I'm not self-sufficient, even if I am in my own way. But they won't understand that and they'll worry too much."

"And the other?"

"The younger boy. Jonathan. He's thirty-six. His birthday is coming up next month. He's a minister. He lives in California."

"So he's not married? Or maybe he is. I don't know how those things work in Christianity. Vows of celibacy and such."

Hank unrolled the napkin, placed it in his lap, and laid out his utensils.

"Is he married?" Seth asked again.

"No, he's not."

Pam arrived and hastily deposited a small ramekin dish

piled high with pats of butter, each pat sealed in a white plastic casing topped with an aluminum cover that could be removed at the corner lip. Seth busied himself prying open the flaps with his knife. "Gotta get them ready. I have this thing about lots of butter on pancakes. Soft butter. Nothing worse than trying to spread hard butter on pancakes and shredding them in the process. I don't know why, but it really upsets me. Like when I end up with a middle seat on an airplane. The only two times I'm capable of throwing a tantrum. Center seats and mangled pancakes. There are probably other times, but they don't come to mind."

Hank smiled. "Do you have kids?"

"Me? Oh no." He struggled with the last nested butter pat, whose aluminum flap refused to be pried open at the corner and peeled back. "Not that I didn't want them. Let's just say that it wasn't really a possibility at the time I could have had children."

"What do you mean?"

Seth saw the server coming toward them again. He couldn't remember her name. Her left arm was extended like a narrow shelf for the plates and side plates she was balancing on it. "I could make that a long story or a short one. I thought I gave you the short one before. Maybe it was too short. Maybe it deserves the long one. Let's save it for another time. Kind of delicate. Not something I can give justice to when I'm trying to distribute all this butter."

"Okay."

After Seth emptied each butter holder of its butter pat, he inserted it into the previous one, creating a precarious tower in the base of the ramekin dish. He emptied all of them, placing the last holder on top and gently pushing down with his knife to compress the teetering structure into something he hoped wouldn't come tumbling down. He hadn't registered Pam's name but he did want to make it easier for the server to clear the table once they had finished eating.

Hank gave a short blessing. They ate. Hank was slow in every movement—the slicing of his food, the lifting up to his mouth of the modest portion he'd sliced, the chewing of the portion before he swallowed it down. So much abundance with so little effort. It could be the last. One never knew, after all. Life should be carried out like that, no? he thought. Yoga. Buddha. Jesus. It amounted to the same thing, didn't it? The miracle of life, second by second.

Seth was less reverential. "On the rubbery side," he said after one bite of his pancakes. "But the butter and syrup make up for it." The drippy stack felt as forbidden and seductive as when he used to filch a cigarette from his mother's pack, hide behind the wall of Lombardy poplar logs in the back yard that were used for the fireplace in winter, and puff away, thinking how delicious it felt to be not such a good boy as everyone thought.

They concentrated on their food, each in his own way, the pressure of having to converse diminished by the presence of something else to attend to. Seth glanced at Hank, who seemed unperturbed by the bout of silence. He reached for the plastic container of syrup and squeezed another tic-tac-toe grid onto the top of his pancakes, thinking about Jonathan as he waited for it to soak in. A minster. In California. Not married. A curious offering of facts about the younger son. He wanted to ask Hank more but didn't want to seem pushy or intrusive. He sliced into a sausage link. No grease spurted out, thank goodness. His foot accidentally brushed against Hank's under the table. "Oops. Sorry."

"Sorry?"
"My foot."
"Your foot?"
"Nothing." He eased his foot away. "How are your eggs?"
"Fine. Your pancakes?"

"Saturated in butter and syrup. Just the way I like them."

As they continued eating their breakfast and until they went to the cashier, to whom Seth insisted on one check that he would pay ("You can do the honors next time," he promised), they didn't return to the subject of family or Honey. Topics of conservation were brief, light, pleasant, of no particular consequence. Seth settled up with cash. They walked toward the exit.

"I'll have you over for pizza one night," Hank said. "I make it from scratch. I haven't perfected it yet, especially the crust."

"It would be an honor. Count me in."

"Do you have a favorite topping?"

"Pepperoni."

"Me too."

"Let me know when. I don't do much in the evenings."

"Me either. How about Wednesday?"

"This Wednesday? Sure. What time? And what should I bring?"

"Would six o'clock be too early? I eat on the early side. If you drink wine, you can bring some. I don't. And Winston is more than welcome."

They parted company in the parking lot. Honey should have been there, but she wasn't. They hugged. Winston squeezed between them.

"See you on Wednesday. Or maybe before at the beach." Seth watched as Hank walked in the direction of his house. Hank didn't turn back. He was more light-footed than usual.

* * * *

"jonathan bauer minister california." Seth typed the four keywords onto the search bar of Google, then Facebook, then LinkedIn. Photos appeared on each site of a man who was attractive but didn't fall within the flexible parameters of Seth's type. "Is that him?" he asked himself. It had to be. This particular Jonathan Bauer shared enough lineaments of Hank Bauer—angular facial features, steely blue eyes, similar contour of hairline—that it had to be the son of Hank, even if he found Hank physically appealing and Jonathan not so much. It didn't make sense to him. Hank was attractive. He exuded no scent of sex. Jonathan was far less attractive, but his photos emitted a scent of sex and sensuality as pungent as the odor of a skunk crushed under the tires of a truck on the highway. How could this man, this minister, not have considered such drives when he chose these photos to post? But maybe it's just me. Seth studied the photos carefully. He could feel the subtle sensual preening in each and every one; he delighted in the ministerial collar in each and every one. The double-message was a masterpiece. The man was a genius. But still, he thought, returning to one photo in particular, where several spidery chest-hairs escaped out of the collar and worked their way around a bulging Adam's apple that begged to be lightly bitten into. He laughed at himself for thinking such things and at being aroused by a photo on Facebook of a reasonably attractive son of a friend who happened to be a minister.

He scrolled down to the brief bio. Jonathan was the minister of a small congregation. Before that, he was minister of.... Before that, he studied...His published work included... He was married. Five years. The name of his betrothed was Adam. Before Seth turned off his computer and went to bed, he sent Jonathan a friend request. In the morning, the request was accepted.

24

"If you read Jonathan's posts, I'm sure you'll discover some interesting things about him."

Hank's email was a quick response to one that Seth had sent to him after much thought and five iterations and whose final version read: *"Just wanted to let you know that your son and I are now Facebook friends."* Reading Hank's reply, which arrived a half hour later, he understood that a door had been opened. He answered: *"I see that Jonathan is about to get a dog. He's been posting the countdown on Facebook with the eagerness of an expectant father. His husband must be excited too. I wouldn't be surprised if that's why he friended me. He has a husband. Not that I have a husband. I did have a partner for 25 years who was a man. A good man. We're still friends. I remember asking you at one point whether your children were married and you said yes about one and no about the other. I wonder why you responded in that way. They're both married, no? Heading out now. Winston needs his evening walk."* He pushed the "click" button and went out for a long walk with the dog. Before he went to bed, he checked his inbox. There was a reply from Hank.

"I consider myself a very honest person and perhaps even pride myself on telling the truth. One of the things that I stressed most to my two boys growing up was that they be men of their word. I always tried to be a model for that for Matthew and his younger brother.

I told you that Jonathan was not married and that was not the truth. I could say that he was not married in the traditional sense of the word, but that would only be my trying to justify my untruth. Many years ago, my son had a beautiful girlfriend named Eleanor (we called her Ellie) that his mother and I thought he was going to marry. He even told us so, and his mother and I gave them our blessing. Exactly what transpired during the time of their relationship I don't know, but one day he called us and said that he broke up with her and was moving to another city. A number of months later he called us from there and announced to us that he was gay. You can imagine the shock (at least I hope you can imagine it) to his mother and me that this caused, as well as the strain it put upon our relationship with him. To make a long story short, his mother and I came to the point where we accepted his gayness, even though we wished it were otherwise. Rather than disown our son, we decided to love him regardless.

You may not fully know this, but his mother and I come from very conservative, evangelical Christian backgrounds. Gayness was something considered outside the realm of Christian experience. Although I now have a great relationship with Jonathan, I still feel uncomfortable telling others that he is gay, especially because he is a minister. He is unique. Let me say that he couldn't have chosen a better man as his life partner than Kelly. I have a great relationship with Kelly. Kelly's father essentially disowned him and never accepted his relationship with my son to his dying day.

My lengthy email is my attempt to try and explain why I responded the way I did when you asked me if my son was married. I accept their marriage, but I'm not yet to the point where I feel comfortable sharing this with others. Jonathan has tried to explain what it was like to 'come out.' Maybe I'm figuring out how to come out too. Please forgive me for not being totally truthful with you.

I treasure your friendship and hope my equivocation has not harmed it. Perhaps we will have occasion to explore this area more. I'm sure that you could be of help to me.

As always,

Hank."

If Seth had been thirty years young, or even younger, the email plus the color of Hank's eyes would have jettisoned him into love. He wasn't thirty years young or even younger. At more than twice that age, he still gave in to stirrings that were mild and playful, but he steered clear of upheaval. Leave that to the young, he thought. He struggled to hold onto that thought through a sleepless night. As the next day began to show evidence of coming through once again (the sky was lightening and giving respite to the stars; a chirp or croak could be heard coming from the back yard), he got out of bed, turned on his computer, and went to the kitchen to get the Mr. Coffee going while he waited for the laptop to boot up.

"I can't say how much I appreciate the time and the care you took to write what you wrote to me. I'm sure it wasn't easy. It also wasn't necessary.

One of the things I've always admired about you was how your Christian faith leads you to try to understand how to embrace people rather than disparage, exclude or condemn them. I can easily imagine how difficult it was when your son told you he was gay—a kind of ultimate challenge of your faith, if I may. I say that I can imagine this because I had to come to terms with this myself, and then I had to go through it again when I told my parents that I was gay when I was all of 16. Even at that age, it took time, but fortunately within a year they embraced who I was and my desire to love and to be loved. And during that year, they didn't disown me or even diminish me. They just tried not to believe me.

I don't consider what you didn't tell me to be an untruth. I think of it as a truth that you weren't yet ready to tell me. And this too is something that I understand. I have to make this decision every single time I meet someone. Sometimes I feel the person is ready for this truth. Sometimes I don't. Sometimes I feel the person will never be ready (in which case I usually wean that person off my life; gently, I hope, but decisively).

So in short, there is nothing for me to forgive, Hank. In fact, I'm sure that our friendship has been enriched. And I'd be more than happy to talk to you about 'this area.' If you think I'm a guru on the subject, you're mistaken. Our perspectives and experiences about 'this area' are so different. I'm gay. You're not. We could probably both learn a lot from each other."

* * * *

The following Tuesday and Wednesday morning, Hank and Seth took different beach routes, ones that wouldn't lead them to each other. At six o'clock on Wednesday evening, Seth pulled into Hank's driveway and rang the doorbell. Winston was sitting by his left side, tail sweeping the pavement of the front patio in anticipation.

Seth didn't recognize Hank when he answered the door. It wasn't the button-down shirt or the slacks. It was his hair, which was always hidden under a hat and which Seth had assumed was the gray/white, filmy, fly-away hair of men of a certain age. Liberated from a hat, Hank's medium-length hair was mostly black (gray at the temples), perfectly parted on the right side, and slicked back. When the smell of the gel that kept it all in place reached Seth's nostrils, he lost his sense of place entirely. It was the exact sexual-awakening smell of his ninth-grade gym teacher, whom he had a crush on that was so secret that not even he himself dared to let himself know about it at the time, even though he lived for the few seconds each day of his fourteenth year when his gym teacher might pass by him, all burly and sweaty and stern, and send a waft of that scent as he passed by. There was something irresistibly repugnant about that smell; he couldn't get enough of it.

"Come in."

The kitchen counter featured an orderly line-up of small transparent glass bowls heaped with doses of sliced pepperoni, dried oregano flakes, shredded mozzarella, slivers of onions that resembled nail clippings, and halved and pitted black olives. Each bowl had a teaspoon in it, and the handles of each teaspoon were uniformly angled at the ten o'clock position. The larger matching bowl at the head of the line contained the chunky tomato sauce and a spoon that was larger than a tablespoon but lacked the depth of a ladle. In front of the row of glass bowls lay what looked like a weathered oar whose enlarged paddle dangled off the counter's edge.

"You said you liked pepperoni, but I thought I'd add a couple of other ingredients in case you like them too. The crust is baking in the oven. It should be ready in a few minutes. I'll pull it out with this paddle. I made it out of a piece of driftwood I found. We can sprinkle whatever we want on top." He indicated the perfectly aligned glass bowls. "And wherever we want to."

Seth looked at Hank with a half-smile and then lowered his glance. "What do you think, Winston?" He was embarrassed by the amount of thought and the preparation that Hank had put into a pizza dinner and regretted having bought a pre-made packaged salad that he'd transferred into a Tupperware container and placed in a plastic shopping bag for easy carrying.

Hank coaxed the paddle under the crust so that he could pull it out of the oven "Looks ready. What do you think?"

"I leave it to the expert."

Hank maneuvered the paddle to the stove top, his hands tightly gripped around the long slender handle. Nice nails, Seth noticed. Unridged and meticulously clipped.

"There. Now help yourself to the toppings. This should go first." He pointed to the tomato sauce. "Then we can add whatever else we want and however much we want."

"You said you were an engineer, right?"

They started the process of assembling the pizza together, like two buddies playing with Lego for the first time. Seth ladled sauce onto the middle of the crust while Hank distributed it evenly with a rubber spatula. They took turns extracting fingerfuls of pepperoni, which they doled out on top, leaving as little space as possible between each disc and sometimes overlapping the discs. Three handfuls of mozzarella followed (Seth sprinkled two handfuls and Hank topped it off with another in order to bury the pepperoni); as a final stage, they took turns dipping their fingers into the bowls of olives and onions at the end of the row. It was Seth who suggested that they sprinkle one third of the pie with the olives and one third with the onions, leaving the remaining third with just the pepperoni.

"How will we slice it if it's divided by thirds with toppings?" Hank asked.

"We can slice each third in half, so we have six slices. Three slices each."

"Six?"

"Why not? Who says it has to be eight? Let's make a rebellious pizza."

They finished the toppings. Hank slid the pizza back into the oven. "About a minute. Until the cheese starts to bubble. That's all it takes."

"I brought this." Seth pulled out the container of salad from the bag. "No dressing, though. I usually just use oil and vinegar. Sometimes a little salt and pepper. I hope that's okay."

"I have a bottle of Ranch in the fridge. I usually use Ranch. I have some olive oil and a bottle of vinegar somewhere, I'm sure."

"Ranch sounds great." Seth reached back into the bag. "And this. A bottle of wine. I know you don't wine. I can go either way."

"I don't but go right ahead."

"I'm good with water. Hang onto it for when you have other company."

"No. Please. Have some, or take it back with you." He opened a kitchen drawer and pulled out a corkscrew. "See? I even have one of these. Help yourself. Please." Seth obliged.

The table was already set. They sat down to eat. Hank said Grace. It was all so uncomfortable, this dance between strangers who had the desire to be past the stage of being strangers (each in his own way and for his own reasons), although at their age, with its calcifying routines, these things took more time and effort than their tired emotional muscles were willing or able to endure for long. During dinner, Seth had fleeting urges to be impulsive, to ask provocative questions, to make unexpected gestures or facial expressions, as he did when he was much younger and hungered for awe or desire, or at least confirmation. With Hank, though, he wasn't sure. The last thing he wanted to do was to put off, to offend. The last thing he also wanted to do was to get through the evening solely by decorum and then get in his car with Winston and think, "That was nice. I'm glad it's over."

Between his first and second and slices of pizza, he let the orange oil from the pepperoni and mozzarella drip down to his elbow twice so that he could proceed to lick it off, his tongue starting at the elbow and working its way toward his wrist. That was as much as he could do in the way of provocation. Hank was unfazed. He knew that grease was inevitable with pepperoni pizza. A wipe with a napkin might have been better, but still.

A pizza dinner. How simple, Seth thought. How classic. How what American men did when the wives weren't about. It was new to him, since he didn't have a wife. It wasn't rowdy, as he'd expected. There was no Sports Channel in the background. It felt intimate, delicate even. A rite of passage. The wine helped him. He offered some to Hank three times during dinner: "Would you like some"? "Are you sure?" "C'mon, just a little." As Hank was reaching for his second slice, he relented on the third time. "Okay. Just a tiny sip though." He went to the cupboard to get a wine glass, dusting it off with the kitchen towel as he brought it to the table.

Seth took the bottle and brought it toward Seth's empty glass. No sooner had the first drops poured out of the bottle than Hank said, "That's enough. Thank you." Seth pulled back.

Seth raised his glass and brought it halfway across the table. "God bless this wine," he said. "There's a Hebrew blessing for the wine but I don't know it." He tapped the rim of Hank's glass. Pieces of glass fell on the table and to the floor. Winston lifted his head to see what had happened and then placed it back between his paws.

"I'm so sorry. You probably think I'm drunk. I'm not, I promise you. Getting drunk isn't my thing. It's just that..."

"No worries." Hank went to the kitchen and returned to the dining area with a red plastic dustpan and brush. He stooped down and passed the brush along the floor, stopping when no traces of glass gathered in the dustpan. As he rose, he patted Winston's back. "There. No harm done."

He returned to the kitchen to empty the contents of the dustpan into the trash bin. "Don't forget to bring another glass with you," Seth called to him. "I'll be more careful this time."

Hank came back empty-handed. "That's okay. I'll pass after all." He sat down and placed the paper napkin back on his lap. The two men reached for a third slice. They could have easily done without, but it was the most comfortable thing to do if they were to somehow steer back into a semblance of fluid conversation and perhaps even arrive at a source of their discomfort and curiosity, which, Seth was sure, had something to with the subject that they'd emailed each other about but hadn't spoken about, eye to eye. Hank was sure of this too, but they kept circling around it, waiting for the right conditions, whatever they might be, that would announce to one or both of them: Do it. Do it now. Take it forward.

They didn't that evening. On his way out, Seth noticed a bowl of hard candy on the foyer table. He picked through them and chose a butterscotch and a peppermint. "Do you mind?"

"Of course not. That's what they're there for."

He tried to release the peppermint candy but it was stuck to the wrapper. When he picked at it, pieces of cellophane chipped off. He slipped the two candies into his pocket. "A nice treat for the drive back." He tossed them into his console, wondering how many years they'd been sitting in the bowl.

* * * *

Seth woke up three times that night to pee. It couldn't have been the wine, he thought. He remembered only drinking two glasses and not taking any water during or after the meal. But there it was, an urge so strong that it stopped his dream in its tracks. His bladder was giving way. It started about five years ago, on an evening out with Yoni and friends at a pizzeria when the combination of pepperoni and baked mozzarella caught his throat on fire and forced him out of bed to guzzle down fistfuls of water from the bathroom spigot down the hall. By the time he arrived back at his bed, he could feel the fire again. He trudged to the kitchen and brought back a pitcher of water and a glass to his night table. During the night he drank all of it. During the night, he woke up to pee four times. He swore off pepperoni pizza for dinner, but the need to pee continued regardless of what he ate or drank. The sensitive bladder, the classic symptom of aging men, the rising from the still of the night to empty the vesicle (where did all that liquid come from?), the struggling to work himself back into bed and pick up on where his dream had left off, the dread of not being able to fall back asleep. He got used to it, worked it into his routine. He eliminated baked cheese from his diet, except on special occasions, such as this dinner with Hank. He wasn't sure whether the pepperoni had anything to do with it.

He attributed the first pee of the night to the sex he'd had and the fact that, as hard as he got and as often as he got hard during the hour or so of sex that he tried to have regularly and managed to have that night, he didn't reach orgasm. It wasn't unusual to not climax, especially at his age, and especially with Mason, a regular Grindr hook-up whose libido was driven more by the desire to affirm his body as an object of carnal desire than by a desire to explore the body of another. Seth didn't mind playing the role of the worshiper from time to time, especially when the male to be worshipped was young, beautiful and fragrant, and when the youthful efforts at bravado were undermined by a shimmering nervousness that could be felt as Seth navigated the terrain with delicious unsteadiness. Better than nothing. Much better. He didn't mind stroking himself to stoke himself as he did what he did to Mason, timing his movements to arrive at mutual and simultaneous orgasm. This time, like many other times at his age and with Mason, it wasn't mutual. The constant stimulation without the release was a pee-provoker. Without a doubt.

He realized that he hadn't thought about sex that night until the double-ding of the Grindr notification sounded after he discarded the candy and was backing out of Hank's driveway. Winston was lying in the passenger seat next to him, his head resting on the console between them. "Shit. I forgot the plastic container for the salad." He stopped his car and read the message. "Free tonight? I can stop by. I'm horny." The container could wait. In all probability, Hank would bring it with him to the beach in the morning. And if he didn't, did it matter? Jesus. One plastic container less in a kitchen cabinet was a victory in the crusade against the household accretions of old age: the used gift wrap, the magazine and newspaper clippings, the plastic bags, twist'ems, Styrofoam trays, socks with holes in the heels kept for possible use as dust cloths, and on and on. Oh the curse of ample drawers and cabinets and closets. "In fifteen minutes?" he responded. He lingered in the driveway for a minute. The double-ding arrived. "Sounds good. C U soon."

He'd seen Mason about a dozen times. Never at Mason's house. The idea of going to a virtual stranger's house to have sex made him uneasy in a way that snuffed out the flame fed by the prospect of quick and unexpected sex. It was risky enough to strip down with a stranger and go at his body, but to travel in order to do so was out of the question for him. He knew what would happen. On his way to the unknown house in the unknown neighborhood, he'd have second thoughts, think "What the hell am I doing?" and turn back. Another age thing, but still. Mason didn't give a second thought about getting in his car and driving the fifteen minutes it took to arrive at Seth's. No big deal. It worked for him. It was ideal for Seth. Home delivery. No main course, no pizza. Just dessert.

Mason rang the bell. Seth opened the door and saw the hunger in Mason's eyes as the young man hunched over to pat Winston, revealing the uppermost part of the crease between his buttocks. Pure hunger, stripped of the need for preliminary niceties (the offering of a drink, a finger pointing toward the sofa where they could sit on for a while to chat). Seth had satisfied Mason's appetite enough times to know that he need only lead him directly down the hallway to his bedroom, but each time he found it more of an effort to get hard and stay hard, let alone to shoot. Perhaps the routine of their brief and direct encounters was starting to feed into something too narrow and predictable. He wasn't convinced that Mason was his real name. There was no reason to believe it wasn't, but there was no reason to believe it was. Nevertheless, he looked more like a Dylan or a Connor. It didn't matter. Whatever his name and however spontaneous and pleasurable the encounter, the gyrations and secretions played out predictably in the end. Each of them rolled onto their back to return to who they were. They were uncomfortable. They dressed. Mason left. Seth was determined to stop seeing him but deep down knew he wouldn't. Maybe the next time would be different.

Their encounter lasted forty-five minutes. They did what by now each expected of the other to do, to have done, and to be done. He watched Mason back out of the driveway to head home. Or maybe not to head home. What did he know of this lad?

The second pee was annoying. The urge was strong enough to stir him to wakefulness, but there was barely a trickle when he stood above the toilet concentrating on relaxing his pee muscles. What the fuck, he thought as he got himself out of bed, stepped over Winston, and staggered down the small stretch of hall to the bathroom, keeping his eyes closed as much as he could in order to prevent certain waking thoughts—a stock-taking of the dinner with Hank and the sex with Mason and then on to a list-making of things to do tomorrow—from snapping the filament of the dream he was in the middle of when the need to pee a second time woke him up. Dreams. He didn't remember them often, but he believed in them. Their contents needed as much time to unfold as those of wakefulness. Who could argue that they didn't hold equal claim to the making up of a life, minute by minute, day by day, every day?

To be sure, dreams were harder to hold onto, harder to make sense of. And so? Should they be devalued on the grounds that the dreamers lacked the ability or desire to give them their due? Standing over the bowl, he could feel the trickle of pee being released from his weary member. He kept his eyes closed as he felt around for the flusher. He kept them closed as he lingered in the bathroom. He didn't want to wake up too much. He wanted to get back to his dream.

Winston is there. Hank is there too, dressed in a pair of royal blue bathing trunks and a floppy-rimmed hat that isn't the one he usually wears when he goes to the beach. His body is tanner, more toned; his face less lined. He is a younger or idealized version of who he is during wakeful hours. The beach is there, surrounding them, but not the beach of sunrise walks. There are two suns, and the dunes are lined with abandoned buildings whose window frames are empty and whose roofs are collapsing. Not quite apocalyptic though: the sky is free of clouds, a brilliant blue is in the making. Pelicans are gliding overhead in chevron formation. Their necks are stooped, beaks aimed downward, on the ready to swoop down and snatch whatever object is moving, even if it is land-based. Hank's hat, Seth's backpack, Winston—everything seems to be potential prey for such graceful hunters.

He is looking up at the birds. "How do they decide who's at the front?"

"I don't know. If I did and I told you, would it make any difference?"

"What do you mean?"

"Think about it."

"I still don't understand."

"Is the point to know as much as we can? Then what? Look!"

The pelican that has been relegated to caboose position darts down, grabs something jutting out of the sand and returns to formation. The object glistens in the pelican's beak as it's being carried off into the sky but is soon released and falls back into the sand further ahead. Seth runs toward it in order not to lose sight of it: a shard of glass surrounded in the sand by drops of blood.

"My wife is home ironing my shirts, bless her heart. We're going on vacation tonight. Ten days. To Jerusalem. Some wadis in the desert. And Saint Catherine in the Sinai. Like a dream."

"I never iron my shirts."

"I don't either. She does, bless her heart."

"Do you need ironed shirts in wadis?"

"Do we need to visit wadis?"

He looks at the clean stretch of sand in front of them. "I never thought about it."

Hank adjusts the crotch of his bathing trunks, or maybe he is scratching down there. Winston sniffs the piece of glass that Seth is holding.

"Take this with you," he says to Hank.

"Thank you. It will come in handy."

"I agree. It will."

Seth hands Hank the shard. He studies Hank's fingernails. They are slender, unridged, freshly trimmed. He brings Hank's hand toward his mouth. It looks young. He resists the urge to smell it, kiss it. He lets it drop and gazes out toward the sky. The ocean is no longer below. In its place is a wilderness. Winston has disappeared. The war-torn people strolling on the boardwalk carrying boxes of caramel popcorn, sticks holding candied apples, bags of salted peanuts.

"I have to find my dog!" He tries to run toward the boardwalk but his body rebels, as if it was stuck in molasses muck, a classic dream impediment.

"I'll go home and check the shirts." Hank strolls away with ease. He turns for a moment. "You can tell me you love me. I don't have a problem with that."

He cracked open one eye to watch the water in the toilet

bowl make its clockwise swirl down the hole and slowly be replenished to the tune of the gurgling of the tank being refilled. He went back to bed, even though so little time was left before the time arrived when he usually woke up to venture to the beach to watch the sun rise on the other side of the ocean and begin his day. He propped up his two pillows and lay back, not to fall back asleep but to relax for a few minutes before getting up to make his way through the day that was about to call him. No orgasm and two pees. His dick felt exhausted. He wondered what Hank did before he went to bed at night. No. Don't. Not there. He switched on the night table lamp. Winston was fast asleep at the side of the bed and didn't budge at the invasion of light. Such a lucky beast. Seth moved to the floor, curled himself around the dog and rubbed his belly. He kept his eyes open until he could see the faintest light coming in through the window. Winston kept his eyes closed.

25

June's house wasn't all that different from her older sister's. One less bedroom and a décor that was a tad frillier around the windows (lavender fleur-de-lis peel-and-stick strips), on the beds (embroidered toss pillows behind lacey toss pillows) and on top of the many end and side tables (porcelain and crystal figurines whose thematic coherence was elusive). Honey considered all of these differences between her and her little sister to be girly and oh-so stereotypical of a type of domestic division of labor whose time had passed. For her anyway. Not that Honey's husband ever prepared a meal or kept golf clubs on the ready in the garage, but still. Glen did know how to run the vacuum and the dishwasher, if pressed to do so.

Honey and June looked enough alike for passersby to assume they were sisters, what with their triangular nostrils and chins, their low hairlines that dipped into widows' peaks, their eyebrows so thick and straight that no amount of tweezing could pluck the suggestion of an arch into them—and further down to their knock-knees and finally to the heels of their feet, which barely touched the ground when they walked in flats. There were differences, too. Honey was heavy, June wasn't; Honey had blue-gray eyes (from their father), June had brown (from their mother); Honey kept her hair long and unkempt, June had hers bobbed and conditioned twice a month, and occasionally gave in to restoring most of the gray to auburn. Any passerby could tell they were of the same clan—if not sisters, then no more distant than first cousins.

A third bedroom proved unnecessary. In the end, June and Mike had only one child. A boy. Wayne. After him, two miscarriages and they called it quits. The heartbreak of two dead babies almost ruined their marriage. She harbored a molten resentment over what had to be his faulty sperm; he, a disdain for her inhospitable uterus. Like Honey, June was brought up Christian, but try as she might, she couldn't find the divine signs of appeasement that her miscarriages should have led her to if she were the devout Christian woman that she tried to be. Where to look for signs? In the puddle of dead baby between her legs? Somewhere along her ravaged body? "Can we stop trying?" she asked Mike several months after the second miscarriage when she was able to pull up her 29-inch-waist jeans and button them without having to breathe in. Mike didn't put up a fight. He arrived easily at their fate of having an only child. They cost so much nowadays, what with all the pricey gadgets and toys, the private schools. And at least the one child, Wayne, was a boy. Had he been a girl instead, they would have named her Mandy and he would have insisted that they keep plugging away, regardless of the cost and the heartbreaks, until a male sprang forth. And once a male sprang forth, they would have argued again about the need to circumcise, as they did with Wayne. ("You don't have a penis. You don't call the shots on this one," he told her as she was breastfeeding their newborn. Wayne was circumcised.) And they would have probably upgraded to a three-bedroom house, like his sister-in-law did. It made sense. He made a decent living. The cost of real estate in that neighborhood in that part of that town in Iowa was manageable. It was a pleasant but altogether nondescript location that didn't carry a hefty price tag, and probably never would. They could have afforded an upgrade. But it didn't unfold this way. After the second episode of excruciating pain that came far too soon, and the dark ponds of blood floating in an abundance of effluvia in which nothing resembling a baby was evident, Mike and June had only to sit through one silent dinner of crab imperial (her specialty), accompanied by a bottle of upscale pinot grigio that they kept on hand for those special moments that were never special enough until then, to understand, without speaking of it beyond the one question June asked herself, and then him, and then both of them—"Can we stop trying?"—that the dream of enlarging the house to accommodate an enlarging brood was dead in the water. There would be no more water to break.

* * * *

"You can take Wayne's room," June said to her sister as soon as they entered the house. "Do whatever you like in it to make yourself at home. And if you want to take down his posters, you'd be doing me a great favor. They're hideous. I can roll them up and stick them in the garage. He's trying his luck in California, sweet boy. I can't imagine he'll come back here after a taste of LA. I've heard things about that place and I'll tell you something. If I were his age, I'd high-tail it out of here for LA in the blink of an eye. I'd high-tail it out of here for anywhere but here, and I wouldn't be surprised if I didn't come back either. Do whatever you want with the room, posters included." She pointed to the bed. "The mattress is new. Untouched. I bought it after he left. Who knows what he did on the other one? Fumigate or eliminate. No other way. The closet and chest of drawers are empty. Go to town, if you can call this place a town." She reined in her rant. "My poor big sister. A widow. What a label to have stuck on you at such a young age." She walked over to her older, larger sister and hugged her.

"Thanks, Junie girl." She thought of her brother-in-law, with his tobacco reek and stained shirts. "Things could be worse for me." She extracted herself from her sister's heartfelt embrace as soon as it seemed natural. "Where's Mike?"

"He's away on business. Maybe it's not business, but it works. I like having him around as much as I like when he's not around. I should feel guilty about that, but I don't."

"When is he coming back?"

"I forget."

Honey took in the room. The natural light was muted, even though the thick, burlap-like curtains were wide open and the windows unobstructed by the lush green of palm, ficus and other vegetation that grew like weeds in Florida. The struggling light felt sad and was made sadder by the heavy oak furnishings positioned randomly along the mocha-colored walls. To embark on sleep and wake up in such blandness. How could her nephew's testosterone survive in such a place? Did he bring girls in here? Could heat be generated here? Maybe the posters of rock bands and sports figures were enough. He must have found a way. God knows how many times she'd done it in ugly rooms, she reminded herself. Without a doubt, Junie did well to throw out the mattress, which had to be funky. One thing was certain: The small cross hanging on the otherwise empty wall above the bed (had it always been there?) would need to be shoved into a drawer, even if she stayed for only a few nights. Don't want that hovering over me, she thought.

As she bent over to unzip her suitcases, the tinge of pain in her lower spine was activated. Damn it, she thought. Serves me right for forgetting to stoop down with my back upright.

June didn't know whether to stay in the bedroom with her sister or withdraw to give her breathing space. "How about I make us some tea? I can bring it in for you while I get dinner going."

"How about a glass of red wine?"

"I think I have some somewhere." June left the room relieved. Honey was relieved too. She gently removed the cross from the picture hook. It left a brilliant white shadow on the wall. She replaced it. No getting away from the sign of the cross.

She loved her Junie. The cross notwithstanding, there wasn't anything she felt she had to hide from her or rehearse saying before saying it to her, she thought. Just like June felt. "A widow," she'd said outright just a minute ago. Yes, her husband was dead. She was a widow. Hard and indisputable facts. "Thanks, Junie girl," she'd replied. She would have liked her sister to ask for details, but she knew better. June preferred simple decorum and a hug. She understood this. They were cut from the same cloth. Even so, she thought, she would have welcomed a word or two of sympathy. Who wouldn't? In a situation like this, the death of her husband, she was entitled to hold court. Red wine should be delivered to her room and automatically refilled when she carried the emptied glass to the dinner table after June's shrill cry "Dinner's ready!" And then sipping wine at a table across from dear sis while they nibbled and talked about this and that. Like old times, the many mini-milestones between, during and after boyfriends when the two of them sipped wine or beer and jabbered about past men, present men, future men, and occasionally about men in other tenses—the ideal ones, the would've, could've, should've men.

She smelled good things being whipped up in the kitchen as she placed the items in her suitcases into the unfamiliar drawers and shelves and hung other items in the closet on the pole holding dozens of white plastic hangers. Twenty minutes later, the call came: "Dinner's ready!" She dropped everything and went to the kitchen. June hated when food got cold. If it didn't sear the tongue, it was compromised. Their mother had insisted on this fact, and June believed her.

"Cheers." They clinked their glasses above the roast beef and quartered rosemary potatoes. Honey brought her glass to meet her sister's. She was careful not to clink too hard. The glass was thin and adorned with a painted inlay of leaves under the rim. Clearly delicate but on the tacky side, like everything else about the house. "It's sad, you know," she said. "Not in a surprising way. In a predictable way, which is sad in itself."

"Now don't get all brainy and cryptic on me. I don't go for that crap. Just spill."

Honey took a sip of wine and opted for a second more ample sip before setting her glass down while June brought slabs of rare roast beef to her sister's plate and spooned some flour-thickened gravy on top that had gathered at the corner of the platter.

"Say when."

"When."

She stopped the spoon in its tracks. "There you go. Now tell me."

"Tell you what?"

June slapped the spoon back down onto the platter. "For Pete's sake, just tell me what you want to say to me. Or maybe to yourself. But none of the fancy words. Speak your mind, sis. Out loud. To me. Remember? Me. June."

Honey set her glass down carefully, making sure the bottom was nestled securely on the doily coaster at the upper-right-hand corner of her doily placemat before releasing her hand. "Okay. Promise you'll keep quiet until I finish? Not just quiet from your mouth. Quiet everywhere. Quiet in your eyes, your neck, your shoulders. Play dumb. Pretend your body is one big ear and all it knows how to do is listen." She picked up a forkful of roast beef. "Can you do that? I wouldn't ask you to if I didn't think you could."

"Promise." June took a generous swig of wine. "You're a hoot. I love you. Go. I'm all ears. The rest of me is dumb, just the way you like me."

"Perfect." Honey rested her hands in her lap after she sliced through another piece of the roast beef and put it in her mouth, sat upright and looked directly into her sister's eyes as she chewed the second bite. "This is great, by the way. So tender." She swallowed. "So. It has to do with suicide." Her eyes darted to her sister's mouth. "Not a peep, mind you. You promised."

June held back whatever it was she was about to say.

"So. It has to do with the course of things, the natural order of things. The order of those things that we call natural because they've ended up happening that way so often that we assume it must be the natural order of things. It makes us feel secure. We can predict probable outcomes and prepare for them. But there are other outcomes too. The ones that throw us completely off guard and seem unfair because they upset our order of things. The light that they transmit, the hope, are unrecognizable to us."

"Can I just say that so far I'm with you? Kind of. Maybe."

"Good. Now shut up and hear me out. Between us siblings. Us girls. You, the dumb one. Me, the dumber one. Where do I begin? Near the beginning. When our legs are still shaped like sticks and we don't have to shave them. When we still dream dreams that have a purity about them. Dreams filled with desire, but not burdened by the mess of sex. Then the baby hair grows on our legs, and then thicker hair on our cunt, which becomes the new center of our universe because the guys around us know that this is when things like this start to happen. Maybe they smell it, they can pick up the scent. Like curs. They know what's going on down there and they want it. And we want nothing more out of life than for them to want it. You find someone who lets you know he does, and you convince yourself that you're in love with that guy, and then another guy, and then another. Each time the resolve lasts a little longer. Because that's what you want. Love. And you think that Love feeds off of that hairy spot between your legs. At some point you convince yourself about one of those guys, the one who has the *cajones* to ask you to marry him before you've had enough time to figure out how to leave him because he really isn't enough and will never be enough. Even though he's nice enough and he's cute enough. You think the sex is amazing because you never felt such sensations like the ones he's been able to produce down there for you. Or was it for him? You spend a couple of milliseconds thinking about his future and are pretty sure he'll have a string of decent jobs. So you say yes when he asks you. You marry him and think that finally the whole Love issue has been taken care of. After not too much time, you start to feel that it's not all you thought it would be, so you have a child, to make it better, to right it, you think. To set it back on course. Or maybe more than one child, if things still keep being nowhere near what you thought they were supposed to be. Taking care of the little ones distracts you from thinking about certain things that you used to take so seriously and with a passion that made you believe that everything was about to make sense. Twenty years go by like that. Years that are okay. Nothing more, nothing less. Flat, if you plotted them on a graph. Then you get to that stage when the last of however many kids you ended up having by design or by accident is ready to be launched up and out and away from you and this man, this husband, that you've been with for thirty-odd years. The kids have flown the coop. It's only natural. And there you are. Back where you started from, more or less. Mostly less. You did what was expected of you. You followed the instruction manual, written by Anonymous. If you're lucky, people pat you on the back and say what a great job you did, especially if your kids made it through university and land good jobs. You smile and thank them. Something is wildly off kilter. You feel like a shell. And you realize you've always felt like a shell, waiting for something to fill you up, but it hasn't come. And it probably won't." She pushed back several strands of long gray hair that strayed from beyond her shoulders to her face and took a gulp of wine.

"Jesus, sis..."

"Not another word. You promised. I might be almost finished."

June obeyed.

"So. I think of boredom, of weariness. I don't think of desperation. I don't want people to feel sorry for me. I'm not miserable, I swear. I'm just bored and weary. I imagine this endless stretch of flat highway, like in Kansas or something. It's felt that way since the first time I shaved my legs. I was so thrilled when I took that razor to my legs. I didn't even need to that first time. I felt like I'd arrived. That everything that needed to matter would finally start to happen. Love. Husband. Family. And they happened. And they went away. The love, the kids, the husband. The natural order of things, in a different order."

June continued eating, even though she didn't taste anything.

"I guess I'm done. You can talk now."

"What can I say? You're not serious about this, are you? Jesus, sis. Have some more potatoes."

"Serious about what?"

"You know. Suicide."

Honey laughed. "Are you afraid I'm gonna hang myself in my dear nephew's bedroom or take every pill I can find in your medicine cabinet? Please. I want to move on. Move away. From all this, whatever this is. Something having to do with life, I guess."

"Jesus, sis..."

"You said that already."

"Have some more meat." She scooped the serving fork under the slice at the corner. "You like the end, don't you?"

"It's really delicious, but no thanks. I've had enough."

June continued to negotiate the end piece for her sister. Honey reached over to intercept her and knocked her wine glass to the floor with her elbow. The stem broke off, and a few small pieces of the rim shot across the floor. "Jesus!"

"No big deal. They're cheap glasses. Jesus won't mind." They laughed. June steered the slice of meat toward her sister. Honey rose from her chair.

"Really. I had enough. I'll clean up the mess. It's the least I can do."

26

When Seth installed his battery-operated doorbell, he selected the "Chimes" option after testing the five sounds offered. The chimes were soothing, he thought. They wouldn't become annoying if it took him a while to answer the door. He was not one to run to the door.

Hank walked up the driveway past Seth's car and pushed the button. The chimes went off. Winston's barking went off. He waited. No answer. Maybe he wasn't home, he thought. Strange, though. The car was there. So was the dog. Where would he be without one of those essentials? He tightened the knot on the plastic bag filled with ocean water that held a freshly caught pompano he brought to give Seth. No answer. He turned away to head down the driveway and backtrack home. What a stupid idea to just show up like this, he thought. Serves me right that he's not home. The price one pays for imprudence. Passing Seth's car, he considered putting the bag in the freezer once he arrived home and bringing it to Seth another time. Or just eating it himself and chiding himself for his lapse into impulsiveness.

"Hank?"

He turned around. Seth was at the screen door. Before he

could say "Hi," Seth opened the door and Winston scurried outside to greet him, squeezing his muzzle between Hank's thighs.

"Winston, that's enough!" Seth said, even though he saw the pleasure Hank took at such a loving reception. "What a nice surprise. What brings you to this neck of the woods?"

Hank held out the bag. "I caught this an hour ago and thought you might like it. A pompano."

"Wow. You thought right." Winston worked his way through the open door and entered the house. "You too. Come in."

Hank walked slowly toward the door and stopped midway. "Thanks, but I should be heading home."

"Nonsense. I won't accept the pompano unless you come in."

"Okay. Just for a few minutes."

Seth opened the door wider. "Come. I was making dinner."

"I'm sorry. I didn't mean to disturb you."

"Disturb me? Please. If you leave, I have the joy of sitting down and staring out the window while I eat. If you stay, I get to have company. Please. Stay. I have more than enough of my own company."

"Okay."

"Besides, I was thinking about you. Not this second, but in general."

"Maybe I should go."

Seth squeezed Hank's shoulder as if testing a melon for ripeness. "Too late. You're in. Stay. I want you to."

"Are you sure?"

"Yes, I'm sure. Keep me company in the kitchen while I dish out dinner. Do you want some? There's plenty."

"No thanks. I've already eaten."

"Can I at least get you something to drink? Juice? Tea? Water?"

"I'm fine, thanks." How he wished he hadn't responded this way. It's what people said before they went on to talk about why they weren't so fine. Another incident at home. Arthritis acting up. Too much rain or not enough rain. He wasn't one to find reason to complain or to reveal himself. But he wasn't fine. He was nervous. He stood there, thinking how he should have stuffed the pompano in his freezer and stayed home.

"Come." Seth led him to the dining room table and pulled out the chair that faced the picture window looking out onto the pool, the chair where he normally took his meals. "Have a seat. Let me throw my dinner on a plate and put the pompano in the fridge for tomorrow. It would be a sin to freeze it. Be right back."

Hank sat down. Winston navigated table and chair legs to find a spot where he could lie down on top of the feet of this person whose scent was familiar and safe but new in this house. Seth arrived with a plate of food in one hand and a goblet of white wine and a glass of water nested between the fingers of his other hand. He took a seat perpendicular to Hank.

"Can't I get you anything besides a glass of water?"

"Really, I'm fine."

"How about you giving a blessing?"

Hank closed his eyes, lowered his head, and clasped his hands above his empty table setting. "Dear Lord, we thank you for the bounty which you have set before us. You provide with love. You nourish with love. Amen." Seth kept his eyes open, watching Hank's face. He closed them only when Hank began to open his to say "Amen."

"Amen." He lifted his glass and brought it to a spot midway between him and Hank, where he clinked his glass into the air like one hand clapping. "Thanks for the pompano."

"Not at all." Hank positioned his index finger above a

crumb near his empty table setting. He pressed down on it and stared at his finger to see if the crumb managed to stick to the clammy tip. It had stuck, but he didn't know where to put it. "Do you believe in God?"

"Wow. Going for the jugular." Seth took a sip of wine. "Let's say I don't discount the possibility." He took another more sizeable gulp. "My turn. Do you believe that being gay is a choice and that the choice is the work of the devil?"

Hank lowered his head toward his empty place setting.

"Sorry about that, but you started. Let's keep going." He picked up his wine glass again and made another toast in midair. "In the name of friendship. Yes, to friendship."

"I don't know what to say."

"I don't either. Let's agree that it's okay to not have a response at the ready sometimes. That some questions aren't asked in order to be answered on the spot. That they're asked more for the other person to turn inward and do a bit of exploring." He took a forkful of the pasta. The fusilli were slightly overcooked because the doorbell rang unexpectedly, right when he was about to test the consistency of the pasta, but the sauce was one of the best he'd ever made. Diced tomatoes were definitely better than the finely chopped ones he normally used, and the few seeds that he coaxed out of the dried pepperoncini and sprinkled into the bubbling sauce gave it a zing without being too severe on the throat or nasal passages. A nice touch.

The light outside the kitchen and dining area windows was beginning to fade, and with it the sense of defined edges brought to bear by harsh illumination. The recessed spotlights in the sloped ceiling were already turned on at a low setting. Hank didn't notice their illumination until the soft yellow of the bulbs overtook the pink hue that the setting sun had cast into the living room. He wondered whether the switching on of the lights at a low setting was something Seth did every evening before he carried his dinner to the table to eat by himself. He thought about the 175-watt bulb over his own table where he took his meals. He couldn't regulate it except to turn it on or off. The wrapper called it "Cool White." It was harsh.

He didn't know what to say. He left it up to Seth to continue. Seth was a talker, and he trusted him to pick up the thread and to then listen to what he hoped he would be able to say about the weight of his Christian devotion and the episodes that tested that devotion, like those that had to do with his minister son who found glory in God despite being married to a man. He longed for male camaraderie based on some shared interest, like fishing or watching a ball game on television. How strange that it had never happened. Maybe God was getting in the way. Marilyn invited her women friends to the house to play canasta or bridge. What did these women friends, all of them housewives in the neighborhood, talk about as they manipulated their cards? Was it merely to pass the time or was it to enrich the time they were passing through? Whatever the reason, Marilyn was such a cheerful soul, while he, on the other hand, was usually dour, even in his boundless gentleness and patience with her and the boys. He could feel it, at that moment, in the downward pull of his facial muscles that wasn't so much a function of gravity as it was the natural pull of a man who was vexed and melancholy. How he missed her, he thought again. Her way of casting a lighter touch onto everything. God, he thought. Maybe He had something else in mind for him.

He looked at his glass of water, then at Seth, and spoke first. He talked about how he knew that his son was gay, and how he knew that Marilyn also knew, and how she probably knew that he also knew, and how they didn't speak about it. And how, when Jonathan told them ("I'm gay," he said), they looked at each other as if they'd talked about it a million times and were just waiting for their son to bring it up in order to then look at each other and realize that they would now have to figure out what to do now that their son had made official what they had known about all along but hadn't given words to. "I'm gay," he repeated, as if to make sure that he'd said it. They were gentle in their initial individual rejections of what their son just told them. They were Christian and felt obliged to be gentle. They were Christian and also felt obliged to reject. (Seth took small bites of pasta.) They tried to believe, and to make him understand, that it was a choice that he'd made somewhere along the way. A choice that could be forsaken, that had to be forsaken in the name of Jesus. Marilyn made a heroic effort to convey this in words. Hank buttressed her with his silence. They were a potent team, as gentle as they were determined, even if they suspected that their implicit collaboration would be too facile for their sophisticated son, who would have expected and prepared himself for such a reaction by listening to it, feeling it, and not responding, and then letting it go to see where it would go. Both of them, without talking to each other about it, understood that it could go one of two ways: he would see their light; or they would see his light. Both of them allowed for either possibility. He talked to Seth about these things, hoping he would understand.

Seth took the last sip of wine in his glass and poured himself some more, filling the glass only halfway. "And?"

Hank finished his glass of water and said that in time they were able to fit their son's desire for men, and his marriage to a man, into the way they thought a life was supposed to be for one of the Christian faith. They talked about Jonathan's choice a lot, less so when once they came to understand that "choice" didn't come into play and that Jonathan was their beloved son. They came to terms with it, made their peace with it. Their final effort—to accept—came about with much pain and intimacy. He couldn't have done it without her. "Jonathan's husband is a good man." He looked down at his glass. "Could I get myself some more water?"

Hank was about to ask his guest if he was sure he didn't want some wine when a loud explosion went off in the distance, accompanied by a rattling of pictures hanging on walls and of knick-knacks stationed on tables and shelves. Winston scurried under the sofa.

Seth jumped up. "What in God's name was that?"

"The space launch. I forgot. If we hurry into the back yard, we might see it."

Seth dropped his fork and headed toward the back door. Hank followed him. Winston didn't budge from under the sofa. A steady, low-decibel rumbling persisted.

"Over there." Hank pointed his index finger toward the sky in the north. "See the smoke?"

Seth saw a curled billow of white and a pinprick of blinding light at its tip that etched a slow and gentle arc in the night sky.

"Keep looking," Hank said. "Don't lose sight of the light. It'll break in two. The bottom part will fall back to Earth and the top part will keep going until it reaches the space station way out there in outer space. See the stars? One of them isn't a star. It's the space station. The light will disappear before we know which one it is."

Outer space, the real thing. Here in plain view from a back yard. So huge. So vast. So above and beyond what the contents of his thoughts revolved around. Seth felt dizzy and small as he looked up into the sky, desperately trying not to lose sight of the ever-diminishing dot of man-made light veering toward the troposphere and possibly the stratosphere, mesosphere, thermosphere and exosphere. Outer space. If the spaceship was manned, it would almost be enough for him to believe in God, he thought. And then he would have to talk about what he thought about God. Thank God it wasn't manned. He looked at Hank, whose focus was steadfast, and then into the sky again. He couldn't locate the light. It was gone, lost, finished for him. He thought of his pasta. It would probably be cold by now.

They returned to the dinner table. Winston got up from under the sofa and transferred himself to the floor under the table. Hank picked up the pitcher of water and went to the kitchen to fill it up even though it was two-thirds full. He needed to have a moment alone. The launch was something huge and unprecedented for him. It didn't matter whether the spaceship was manned or unmanned. That tiny pinprick of light, followed by its slow and graceful arc into the deep darkness beyond, spoke of the possibility of infinite possibilities. He was no longer hungry.

At the table, they touched upon other, smaller topics. Standard entry points. The weather. The beach replenishment project. The abandoned house on the beach. The local drug and petty-theft problems and the sightings of coyotes that had recently been reported in the area.

When they parted company a half-hour later, Hank had drunk three glasses of water but didn't ask where the bathroom was before he left. Seth and Winston watched him walk down the driveway and fade into the darkness toward his house. Did he leave so that he could pee at home? Seth asked himself. And if he couldn't wait? What would he call the place where he needed to pee after so much accumulation of water and nervousness? Bathroom? Restroom? Powder room? Toilet? The choice would have helped him to decode Hank by another strand. Three glasses of water and no need to go to the bathroom. Remarkable, he thought as his friend vanished into the night, under the stars and the space station somewhere amidst them, to arrive home as soon as possible, in order to take stock of the evening and have himself a nice long, luxuriating piss.

27

Honey thought about turtle season as she settled into her nephew's room, which June didn't get around to redecorating after Wayne left for university, got his B.A. in information technology, took a good job in North Carolina, met and married a colleague, and purchased a home just outside of Charlotte. She'd removed a few items that she always found objectionable: black-light posters of rock groups that produced nothing but "noise," the framed photo of Wayne and his senior prom date (she didn't like her; her eyeliner was too thick and ended in tapered curves like dirty fingernail clippings at the side of her eyes, a presentation that was in keeping with the stories about her loose ways she'd heard from some of the other mothers), the mass of Gameboys, Nintendos and other black and gray boxes of different sizes, along with their snake pit of wires with multi-colored nibs designed to fit into only one orifice like one half of a monogamous relationship. For her sister's stay, June also consolidated the contents of the chest of drawers, relocating her son's socks and underpants into the t-shirt drawer, and his sweatpants into the sweatshirt drawer, thus freeing up the two deeper drawers at the bottom for her sister. In Wayne's closet, she yanked some of his rattier clothes off their hangers, folded them neatly into plastic storage bins and stacked the bins on a shelf in the garage where one day, in a next phase of her life that might also involve arranging photographs into albums, she would drive them somewhere where used clothing was accepted sight-unseen.

Despite her forays into purging and transforming the space, it remained a boy's room, what with its trophies and pennants (varsity football), its ochre walls, its burlap drapes and the navy green bedspread with matching dust ruffle whose square manly pleats grazed the floor. The nondescript furniture was not a set, per se, although the main pieces happened to be of oak. The floor was the only one among the bedrooms that wasn't covered by accent-colored wall-to-wall carpeting, although it was the one most in need of protection from the nicks and scratches of a rough-and-tumble boy who couldn't give a shit about décor and its upkeep and would have preferred being grounded for life than have his private sanctuary muffled with baby-blue high-pile shag. Oh, the field day his friends would have over that.

Honey felt more at home in this room than anywhere else in her sister's house. Its only connective tissue with the other rooms and hallways was the smell of lavender Glade that June sprayed generously above her head after she did the cleaning. The macramé sachets of potpourri nestled in the front corners of each drawer were yellowed on the outside and had long lost ability to emanate fragrance. Without the scent of Glade in her nephew's room (which was now her room), Honey could have easily pretended to be in an economy-fare motel room. Away somewhere and alone, which was the point.

June opened the two empty drawers. "These are for you," she said. "Let me know if you need more." The nauseating scent of lavender was superseded by cedar and camphor. Honey didn't know which was more repulsive. The two drawers and one-third of a closet were all she needed.

"This'll do just fine," she said to her sister as she turned her gaze toward the single bed.

She settled in. As she made her rounds of the house trying to make it familiar enough feel like a neutral place, she lay in wait for her sister to once again broach the overall topic of Glen or nose-dive directly into any number of subtopics: how she put up with him when he was alive; how she was feeling now that he wasn't; what she would do now that he wasn't; was she okay. Every time she heard June call out "Honey", whether it was softly from across the dinner table or loudly from a room that Honey wasn't in, she tensed up, expecting it to be the one-word inroad to The Talk that was surely at the front of the line waiting to happen. They were close. They were sisters. They'd shared a bedroom growing up. They'd covered each other's backs during the antics of their adolescence; June's veered toward boys and alcohol, Honey's toward boys and rebellion against The Establishment and Society, although she would have been hard pressed to explain what she meant by either if anyone asked her, which, lucky for her, they didn't. Above all, they colluded in their hatred of their father over his disinterest in them because they didn't happen to be born boys. In this, they were inseparable.

A week of calling out "Honey" from different places in the house didn't lead them to continue The Talk. "Honey" ended up being a call to something much smaller and of the moment. "Honey, do you want to run errands with me?" "Honey, where did you get that dress?" "Honey, when you have a chance, take a look at the article about craft beer in the newspaper. It's on the coffee table."

One day, it almost came. They were out in the yard weeding the flowerbeds lining the front porch. It was Honey who started the name-calling. "June," she said.

"You need the other spade?"

"No, I'm good. Let's talk more."

"Sure. What's on your mind?"

Honey let her spade fall from her hand. The yellow firma-grip handle fell on top of a thick stem of violet coleus, pushing it to the ground. Where to begin, she thought, when it's about life. All of it. My husband. This poor coleus. She pulled the stem out from under the handle and watched it spring upward like an obstreperous erection. "There's a wasp about to land on your head."

"I ignore them and they go away." June shook the earth off a clump of crabgrass that she yanked out by digging her fingers under the root mass and tugging at it until she could pry it from the ground without the help of her spade. She could feel the dirt pushing way under her fingernails as she pried. So satisfying. She looked up at her sister. "Love is incomprehension, and you failed. Death is incomprehension, and you're not acing that either. How's that for a start?" She shook the crabgrass until as much dirt could loosen itself from the clump without her having to dig her free hand back into it. She tossed the clump into the plastic bucket by her side. "Let's go in and make some lunch. Something light. We're going out for Italian tonight, and pasta tends to bloat. We've had enough bloating, don't you think?" she said. "We can talk about all this later. We'll get around to it. We always do."

They got around to it at dinner, after Honey was halfway through her second glass of wine and June asked, "Glen and you?"

Honey took a sip of wine. "I didn't know him very well. We had math and history class together. I always made sure to sit right behind him so I could study the back of him without him or anyone else catching me." Another sip as her eyes glazed over. "He had such a broad neck and shoulders, his spine was so upright. His feet were usually crossed at the ankles under the desk. Sometimes his pant legs were raised. If he was wearing a pair of ankle-high socks I could see the individual dark hairs at the bottom of his calves. My, the way he looked from the back, so grown-up and self-assured. If I held my position long enough, he would eventually turn his head to the side and I could study half his face too. He was so cute and didn't have much acne. Just a whitehead or two on the puffy part of his cheeks. Him in front of me in class made every day worth waking up for. Funny thing was I didn't know him. I mostly made up who he was when I was alone, which was a lot of the time. You were busy. I was afraid of telling you these things. I created a version of him that would keep this feeling I had going strong." Another sip. "Half the school year went by like that until I got the courage to accidentally bump into him in the cafeteria. I saw him walking toward me and I turned my head to the left, like I was looking for a girlfriend. I made sure we collided. My fruit cup dropped to the floor. He got all flustered. We talked as we tried to clean up the mess. I got to see the front-view of him up close. I got to hear his voice from so close that I could feel and smell his breath. We got married."

"I know," June said. "I was the bridesmaid."

Another sip. "After a few years, my version of him started getting chipped away at and I wasn't liking him all that much anymore. His ankles were thick. He watched too much television. He didn't fawn over me. His only hunger was for the meals he expected me to prepare. I felt like a background prop. He was a habit for me. We were a habit for each other." Her eyes came back into focus. "Routines give comfort. We all want that, don't we? Comfort?" She took another sip of wine and wiped a tear from her eye with her free hand.

"Eat before it gets cold," June said. She hijacked the conversation and went on and on about Wayne, leaving Honey to work through her plate of linguine and mussels without so much as a splatter on the tablecloth or her blouse.

The next morning, after the dew had evaporated, Honey took a bunch of selfies—in the house, the yard, the neighborhood, in town. She studied them carefully, looking to find one or more where her smile didn't seem forced, one or more for which the caption could be a variation on the theme of "See how happy I am? It's all good." She chose two. One was of her about to dig into a Belgian waffle at the diner in town, where she'd gone with June one morning before accompanying her on a round of errands. The other was of her on her sister's narrow front porch sitting on one of two wrought-iron straight-back chairs that looked out onto the quiet residential street. She often sat there when June was doing certain household chores with an efficiency that could only be comprised if she were to offer to help her. She'd retreat to the front porch, hoping to see one or more residents pass by on a walk or step out to fetch the mail at the end of their driveway. She liked looking at trees and shrubbery, but she had a preference for people, especially when they were engaged in an activity that kept them bustling about with an unflinching sense of purpose. Like ants, she thought, the masters of enterprise. How fortunate they were. On the day she took the selfie on the front porch (June was inside hand-washing delicates), not a soul appeared. She worked her face until she could produce what could pass as a genuine smile. No small feat, she thought.

She was satisfied with her selection of the two photos. The smiles expressed a sense of well-being that was the main criterion for her selection, even if she wasn't thrilled about her smile in general. Her teeth were cream-colored and irregular, and the top two front ones had a gap between them created by a tiny band of gumline that her parents had refused to pay an oral surgeon to remove in order to close up the space before it was too late. In the two photos, her smile was sufficient to suggest that the well of happiness hadn't run dry. She was happy enough of the time, she thought, certainly happier than most of the people she spoke with. It was enough to ask them "How are you?" to open the floodgates to woeful tales of family, job, medical conditions, and the minor infractions that certified their sense of injustice and consequential unhappiness ("I found dog poop in my yard!" "She tried to double-charge me!" "I was put on hold for fifteen minutes!" "They were late and didn't apologize!").

"Who am I kidding?" she asked herself after she chose the two selfies whose smiles seemed just right. "I'm no different from those other people, except that I don't open the floodgates. When they ask me 'How are you?' I say 'Fine, thanks' and leave it at that." Happiness? Is that the point? One's quotient of happiness? Or is fullness the point, whether through happiness, tragedy, drama of any kind? These waves arrived, each in its turn and often unpredictably. She had little control over them, she knew. Happiness was welcome. She longed for it. But the pursuit of it, like the pursuit of anything else, made her weary. I need to keep paring down, she reminded herself.

She deleted the waffle selfie and posted only the front-porch selfie on Facebook. The choice was difficult, but in the spirit of paring down, she chose only one. She was smiling in both, but the smile in front of the porch struck her as less insistent, a smile caught off guard, a smile not intended to gloat about her mastery of life's pleasures but rather to hint at defiance in the face of life's cruelties. The wry smile of a warrior woman. Nice, she thought. It captured what she wasn't but what she aspired to be. If she were to put an end to a smile such as that and to the possibility of a life such as that, some people looking at that photo might think she was sad at her core. Sad in that large and fecund place where death incubates, waiting to have its moment. No no, she thought. She didn't want people to think of her like that. She didn't want to think of herself like that. "Having an AWESOME time with my sis!" was the caption.

28

The High Trestle Trail Bridge was a place she meant to visit each time she made the trip by car or plane to spend a few days with June and Mike. It was a dissonant piece of architecture that she came upon by accident some years back during an aimless drive, which she did from time to time to take a breather from her sister and brother-in-law. Street signs with strange announcements led her there: Madrid, Hindu Temple, Sky Zone Trampolines, Let's Talk Café, Absolute Concrete. No advertisements for the 13-story bridge, though. She wouldn't have known that it was in her path if she hadn't spotted a series of towering rectangular steel frames in the distance that were placed one behind the other, each at a different angle. They gave a dizzying effect, something alien, too, as if they'd been conceptualized and executed by extraterrestrial visitors long before the human species had appeared. Wouldn't that be something? The flight of fancy made her feel the way she felt when as a child she lay down in the back yard at night, looking upward, trying to figure out which one of the infinite lights glittering in the quilt of the night sky would reveal itself to her, and to her alone, as a spaceship searching for a suitable place to land; and, once she determined which one it would be, willing it to land in the large space between the oleander and the crescent of rhododendrons in the yard. If that were to happen, she promised herself, she wouldn't run away. She'd get up slowly, approach it and enter inside once the door at its base slid open without a sound. She was sure she would do it. She'd be afraid, of course, but she would muster the courage. How could she not? If she went inside and eventually was able to get back out alive, go back into her house, and wake up the next day for school—oh the stories she'd have to tell, or the secrets she'd be able to keep all to herself, to set her apart. On the other hand, if she went inside and was swept off and away into outer space, life would continue in a very different way. Either possibility was fine by her. She watched and waited. Nothing happened. She went back inside.

She parked her car by the side of the road a few yards before the bridge's entrance. There were no signs indicating that parking was not permitted along the shoulder, but there was a placard with a photograph of the bridge during its initial stages of construction. Underneath was a caption explaining that the execution of the bridge had greatly benefited from a grant provided by the Municipal Arts Council and from the voluntary services of a local art studio for the commission of its design. So much for alien presences. She was disappointed.

She walked to the bridge's midpoint and leaned over to look down where the river threaded its course thirteen stories below through a vastness of indiscriminate greenery. So different from her lookout point at the beach, she thought, where it was the indiscriminate vastness of the ocean that prevailed over threads of greenery. Just like a photograph and its negative: How was one to determine the focal point among such stark contrasts? And just like Glen too, she supposed: How was she to determine whether to love him or to leave him? But then she remembered that he was dead, which was why she was here on an unknown bridge in Iowa. She tried to miss him, but she wasn't arriving at missing him nearly as much as feeling relieved about no longer having to negotiate him.

The heat of the day was tempered by a light breeze that brushed against her skin as she continued across the bridge to the first of the rectangular frames, which was positioned at a thirty-degree angle and had random blotches of rust on its surfaced like some outbreak of a disease. She ran her hand over one of the beams and looked at her fingers. They had powdery stripes the color of turmeric.

She looked down again. The river was still in view far below her, unremarkable. In fact, she thought, it resembled nothing more than an annoying leak coming from somewhere important but hidden. The vista hardly seemed worthy of being crowned by this bridge, whose tunnel of unruly rectangles she didn't understand and made her hands dirty when she touched their parts. What the hell? She asked herself again. She proceeded to the next rectangle and looked down. The perspective offered nothing new. The river continued to be an insubstantial filament of water threading its way through a blurry ecosystem. This second rectangle was set at a ninety-degree angle; its five-foot base beam extended in a straight line into the open air, not unlike a gangplank on the prow of a pirate's ship. A breeze rose from the valley and cooled the beads of sweat forming on her temples and under her arms. She took her phone out of the pocket of her shorts and snapped several photos to capture the contrast of industrial beams above and wild scrub below. An interesting compositional premise, she thought. She continued taking photos, hoping that when she scrolled through all of them later she would find one or two keepers. Oh dear, she said to herself as she slipped the phone back in her pocket, how could Glen possibly understand what goes on in my head? "The nonsense that goes on in the mind of this woman," she pictured him thinking as he waited for her to bring dinner to the table while he opened his bottle of beer that he'd taken out of the fridge all by himself.

At this, she laughed. Her man, her partner, her husband. Her one and only Glen. She knew him in and out. He gave her the comfort of predictability. And the frustration. That's how it was. For better or for worse, like a steadfast habit, an addiction. Yes, he was that for her, she realized. But now he was dead and she was free. Free to fly; free to suffer the pangs of withdrawal because she missed him terribly. For better or for worse. At this, her laughter subsided. Why was I laughing in the first place? she asked herself as she tried to locate a salient feature among all the gray-green mass below her. Nothing presented itself. Dull. Her knees and lower back were beginning to ache. She needed to sit. She'd overextended herself. It didn't take much these days, what with all the extra weight she had to carry around. Ever since the children left home, she moved less and ate more. Much more. She adopted the habit of eating until she felt full. Fullness has to come from somewhere, she thought to herself whenever she looked at Glen at the far end of the dining room table and tried to think of something to say that might rekindle the kind of banter or conversation that used to feed them so heartily before the dessert of their lovemaking.

Yes, she needed to sit. Her body was giving her signals. She should return to the car and drive back to June's. And then? They'd have meals together, run errands together, pass time together, until she felt ready (or until her sister insisted she was ready, if only to get rid of her and get back to her own life) to get in the car and make the long drive home to be greeted by all the objects and smells that had taken root there and were proof that she had a life and that her life, such as it was (and what was it?), wasn't over.

Or she could push her body further, slowly work it onto the beam extending over the river and make her way on all fours until the drop was directly below her. How ridiculous she'd look, she knew, but who was there to see her? And if someone should happen to pass by? What did it matter what they thought? As long as they didn't try to intervene when she started to teeter and then to fall off the narrow solid surface of the beam, which was the whole point of her balancing act. Not a spaceship taking her up and away, but the weight of herself dropping her down and away. Very away. The violent rush of air as she plummeted would be as terrifying as the nimble landing of the spaceship, she knew, but it would last only a few seconds before she smacked against the surface of the river and sank through its murk, legs splayed like a frog, arms outstretched as if she welcoming a long-awaited friend she'd been expecting at her front door and who finally showed up on the other side of the peephole with a gift-wrapped box that the friend had been thoughtful enough to have slid a scissor blade through along the ribbons to make long curly-cues that dripped down the side of the box like an embarrassing spillover of something long desired. But what if the gift-bearer down below was Glen? It could very well be, she thought. How many times had he presented her with a gift just as she was on the verge of standing up to him and accusing him of her unhappiness? How well she knew him. How well he knew her, even if those hand-curled ribbons on his gift boxes infuriated her. No, she realized, the risk of finding him at the bottom of the river waiting for her with a fancy box was too great. Silly too. She walked back to her car and drove to June's. I'll stay for a day or two. It's always nice to visit with June, especially when Wayne isn't around. Then I'll escape home. Don't want to miss turtle season.

29

Hank and Seth sought each other out on the beach at sunrise almost every morning. As each of them took their solitary walk and spotted a male figure in the distance, they scrutinized the way he swung his arms, the position of the feet as they hit the sand, the tempo of each step, to determine whether it might be the person they were hoping to arrive at.

Those first times when they made each other out in the mist on the beach, they drew in closer, but with caution, unsure as to how things would fare without Honey's gravitational pull and her way of getting the chatter going. But her absence proved to be a trigger in its own right.

"Have you heard anything?"

"How strange that she's disappeared like this."

"I hope she's okay."

After several encounters, they found other triggers. They continued to imagine what might have happened to her, but the steady lack of news about her made the subject of her wear thin of content. She receded further and further as they came up with other things to talk about, other ways of being together. The awkward moments were many, but the two men were drawn to getting through those moments in order to establish a new system of language, gesture and affinity that could be codified into a comfortable and comforting intimacy. It was just the two of them now, after all. How much did they know about Honey anyway? She took pictures, Glen died, she insisted on hugs and joyfulness, she had no difficulties talking. They found subjects other than Honey to hold them in each other's company. They'd become accustomed to managing their days alone for quite some time. They didn't mind being alone for most of the time; being lonely was quite another state of affairs. A dangerous one. No, they didn't want that.

Hank hugged Seth as he looked out toward the horizon. "God's work."

Seth waited for him to pull back. "Quite the masterpiece."

Hank drew away and held his gaze toward the horizon. "Why do you come here?"

"I could ask you the same thing."

"Yes, you could."

Seth dug his toes into the sand. It was cool and damp. As he focused on his toes, he considered a number of safe responses—What better thing to do when one wakes up too early and knows that turning over in bed to try and fall back asleep is an exercise in torment? What better thing to do than to walk a block to arrive at primordial things like sand and sunrises in order to remind us that our need for recognition or confirmation is kind of silly and that all of the things that we think we are involved in and have influence over amount to less than a fistful of sand? He joined Hank in his gaze toward the horizon. "I enjoy running into you and spending time with you," he said.

"Why would you say something like that? I'm so boring."

"I'm not sure what that means."

Hank bent over to pet Winston's back and reached further to Winston's belly. "You're so smart. How could you care what I have to say?"

"What do you mean by smart?"
"You know so much."
"Really? What do I know?"
"You know a lot. About a lot of things."
"Like what?"
Hank's fingers dug into the white spot on Winston's belly. "That's his favorite spot. You know a lot too."
"Not like you. You're educated. You went to university. You bring up articles you read in the Wall Street Journal. Or is it the New York Times? You have a way of saying things."
"Interesting. A way of saying things. What is it that I have to say?"
"I don't know what to say. You know a lot."
Seth let silence interrupt them. "Smart. Intelligent. Knowledgeable. Wise. I never did understand the difference. Even if I did, I'm not so sure I'm any of them." He looked out. "Here I am. On the beach at this god-awful hour staring at the sun coming up like it does every morning and will keep doing long after we're gone. Here you are, too. Doing the same thing. We leave our houses in darkness to come here every morning to see the birth of the light of day. A simple common denominator. Maybe not so simple. What do I do it for?" He looked directly into Hank's eyes. "What do *you* do it for?" He made a sweeping motion with his arms toward the sun, whose violent rays had disappeared completely. Those golden tentacles knew the score. They'd served their purpose and promptly vanished into the ether. "Look at it. Dependable. Silent. Huge. Eternal. The great equalizer."

"God's work."

"See. You have a way of saying things, too."

Winston took off for a blue heron at the water's edge and looped back after the bird had taken flight. Mission accomplished.

"Good job!" Seth said, patting him on the head. He turned

to Hank. "He wouldn't hurt a flea."

"No, he wouldn't."

"I should get going. I haven't eaten breakfast yet."

"I'll stay on for a bit."

Seth walked to him, arms outstretched. A Honey-habit taken root. Hank reciprocated and they fit themselves together tentatively, like the first two pieces of a difficult puzzle that would have many false starts and take a great deal of time to snap in place. That was the point of puzzles.

* * * *

Since Honey's unannounced disappearance, they'd spent enough time together, whether by circumstance or design, to relax into each other's company, lazing on each other's front porches and learning to derive equal comfort from whatever chatter or silence spilled out. Their encounters took place when the sun was low in the sky, its light too weak to delineate sharp outlines; times of day and frames of mind when the boundaries between what was happening and what could be imagined as an alternative to what was happening were perforated; when what was going to happen hadn't yet happened; and what had happened and couldn't be unhappened hadn't yet been fully digested. Sometimes the two men brushed surfaces, at other times they dug underneath. Then there were the long intervals when they sat quietly, grateful for the presence of the other regardless of the wealth or poverty of tangible interaction, which seemed to be haphazard, although surely it had something do their mood, the humidity and, above all, the feeble light.

It was Seth who invited Hank to go out to dinner on one such evening. He proposed a steakhouse chain with senior citizen discounts on Tuesdays. How could Hank refuse such a package? He assumed that Hank, like most people, liked steak and that he was of the type to be on the lookout to save a buck or two. Hank agreed to go. "Sure," he said, adding that he and Marilyn used to go there regularly, especially when family was visiting. "We all loved when the server brought a metal bucket of unshelled peanuts to the table for us to munch on while we waited for our steaks to arrive," he said. "And we could just toss the peanut shells on the floor because that's the way it was done there. In a restaurant of all places. Do they still do that?"

"Follow me." The hostess seated them at a booth toward the back, near the kitchen, where the noise of servers entering and exiting the swinging saloon-type doors was less distracting than the general din of the main dining area, which had large round tables that were flexible enough to accommodate a dozen or so people. Every table was fully occupied, and Seth observed these boisterous groupings as he and Hank were led to their booth on the outskirts. He was especially drawn to the men, what with their sloppy guzzling from beer mugs and the peanut-shell crumbs on their wife-beater shirts as they laughed heartily at what was being said, or as they recounted something themselves that they hoped would produce belly laughs among the others. He watched them as he was led down the narrow aisle to their booth, feeling the crunch of peanut shells underfoot. The men in this place. Their foreheads releasing beads of sweat, their cheeks flushing to the color of a beet, their beer bellies keeping them at an awkward distance from the table. Anthropologically they were a fascinating species. Almost repulsive, except that most of them were laughing, and laughing was sexy.

Hank passed his laminated menu to the server after placing his order (New York strip steak with a side of garlic mashed potatoes and steamed broccoli, the daily special whose ten percent discount would be deducted in addition to the senior discount). As he did, his arm struck Seth's thick-stemmed goblet of the house Chardonnay, which tipped over, rolled to the table's edge and dropped to the floor, sending most of the pieces of glass under their table. No one looked up. No one heard it. Even so, he was mortified. He hadn't gone out for dinner since Marilyn died, he realized. And here he was, dining with a man who knew so much about so much. It served him right.

Seth shrugged his shoulders and smiled. "No big deal. I'll ask for another. I'm sure there's more." He couldn't tell whether his foot was brushing against Hank's foot, or whether it was just a table leg. "Maybe you could use one too."

"Maybe I could."

Seth couldn't believe his ears. "Really?"

"Maybe. Okay. Why not? Just this once."

Seth felt rise inside a vaguely familiar substance and power that was beginning to break through. Evidence of the presence of connection. Perhaps love. He felt it here, now, after so long an absence. He felt it coming from Hank, and he felt it going from him to Hank. He felt it extending beyond him and Hank, as if the two of them were mere capillaries toward a larger drive. He wasn't bowled over by Hank accepting his invitation to dine out; that was within the realm of the possible. But how was it possible that this God-fearing abstemious man could decide, just like that, to imbibe? It took his breath away long enough that he had to wait for the server to pass by twice before he was ready to gesture to her to come to their table so that he could ask for two glasses of the house Chardonnay, which was sweeter than he preferred but would probably go down easier on Hank.

"Cheers?"

Seth raised his glass. "Yep. That's what we say. Cheers." He took a sip of the wine. "Who knows why we say that. Any idea?"

"Not the faintest. How about you?"

"Same. Cheers? It makes me think of laundry detergent." He pulled out his cell phone. "Let's find out. Do you mind? I normally don't Google on my cell phone but..."

"No, go right ahead. I'm curious too."

His screen displayed two Facebook notifications. He couldn't resist. The origin of "cheers" would have to wait. He'd be super-quick. Hank wouldn't know what he was doing anyway, what with his clamshell cellphone that didn't have internet. He probably doesn't know what Facebook is, he thought as he opened the first notification, a posting from a high school classmate, B.J. Their friendship, based on pranks and smirks, was confined to the two twenty-minute intervals of homeroom they shared at the beginning and end of each school day; Seth's crush on B.J. consumed many more hours outside of homeroom. The friendship ended after the final bell of the final homeroom of the final day in their four-year life as high school students rang on an unseasonably cool summer afternoon in mid-June. Over, he thought. High school and B.J. The senior students in every homeroom pushed back their wooden chairs and stormed out of the building past the parking lot reserved for staff, where not one car was new or impressive except for the red MG convertible owned by Mr. Rafferty, the English teacher, about whom rumors circulated that he liked to invite select varsity athletes to his home, offer them a beer or two, and proceed to blow them. Seth tried to have a crush on Mr. Rafferty, thinking it would have resolved so much, but Mr. Rafferty was too short and slender, too soft-spoken. He didn't correspond to Seth's secret erotic imaginarium. And obviously, Seth realized, he himself wasn't the type of boy Mr. Rafferty was looking to lure to his house. He didn't play any sports.

The destination of the graduating class was the main parking lot, which was full. Some of the seniors had their own cars; others had begged their parents to let them use the family car for the occasion. The main parking lot was as large as the adjacent baseball field. The freshly graduated boys converged in small clusters, pushing the hair from their foreheads toward the vastness behind them, feeling oh-so pleased that the world was finally ready for what they had to bowl it over with.

The girls were slower to arrive at the parking lot. They moved in small girl clusters toward the boy clusters. They too swept the hair from their forehead as they made their way. Some were indifferent to the destination, while others steered themselves toward a particular boy in one of the cliques whom they'd fantasized about talking to, getting whiffs and tastes of, maybe even feeling inside them (a prospect of competing terror and delight). Most of them had kissed one or more of these boys at some point during their four years as high school students; many of them had even let one or more of these boys slip his unruly tongue into her mouth; some had advanced to second base (whether over or under their training or legitimate bra); fewer had dared to go to third base. Then there were those who were naïve or brazen enough to go all the way, if only to get it over with and gloat that they'd done it. How they bragged to the other inquiring girls about what they'd done, knowing all the while that they were not only not done with it, they'd only just begun.

Here, in the parking lot after the final bell rang, the girls felt raucous, each and every one of them, down to the homeliest and most solitary of the bunch, the ones who didn't end up near a car festooned with boys but found themselves once again relegated to the sidelines standing alone by a lamppost or access point to the playing field and watching those boys, all of them revved up as they flung their mortarboards high into the air. Liberation! Fuck the Establishment! It wasn't the moment to consider what lay ahead once the brouhaha died down.

Those girls, from homecoming queen to "easy lay" to librarian's assistant, obsessively pushed their hair back from their foreheads and watched. Not one of them had bangs; not one of them wore a hairband or barrettes. They preferred the continual back-raking of undulating hair obstructing their face. The gesture felt so cool, so loose, so inviting as they hung around the boys hoping to hear one of them ask, "Wanna ride?" They wanted a ride. They wanted to be in one of those cars with one of those boys. Once inside, they would laugh, argue, take a few swigs from a bottle, get buzzed, and fuck. That was the point of high school, of graduation, of the parking lot.

Gradually the cars dispersed, some turning to the exit on the left, others to the exit on the right; some were crammed with as many as nine graduates, others had only two. None was empty of passengers, regardless of who they might be. Driving out of the parking lot toward the future of liberation that they were certain they were finally bound for because it was owed to them required company. Everyone sought it out, but there were those few who'd failed to gain entrance to a car. Heads down, mortarboards still on, they made their way to the school entrance, where one of the school buses lined up would take them home. They avoided speaking to each other or looking at each other as they boarded the bus. Any hope of connection, of fitting in, of belonging, had disappeared with the exodus of cars. They knew that once again they'd been handed another raw deal. Life sucked. Liberation indeed.

Seth was about to step onto the bus when he saw B.J's signature Camaro approaching. The car slowed down. The window unrolled. B.J. poked his head and elbow out. Brushing his hair away from his forehead, he looked at Seth and said, "Wanna ride?"

* * * *

The posting read "Having an AWESOME time in Cancun!" Three Likes, one Love, no comments. Seth couldn't have cared less. The only reason he friended B.J. on Facebook in the first place was to gain access to a glimpse of him, to see if this beautiful adolescent who'd held him captive for four years and was crowned Homecoming King had managed to hold onto his beauty so many decades after his coronation. The Cancun photo indicated otherwise: B.J.'s blond unruly hair was reduced to thin gray strands on the sides of his head that were pulled back into a ponytail that looked like a dying thing; his body, intensely tanned from the Caribbean vacation sun, was pear-shaped, its flesh loose and wandering under the upper arms and lower breasts. He had the audacity to be wearing a baseball hat backward. As if. His exaggerated smile ("Having an AWESOME time in Cancun!") revealed a set of teeth so white and flawless that they shouted implants. Funny, Seth thought, how B.J. would have chosen his teeth as the one and only part of his neglected body to pay a professional to restore to a semblance of youthfulness.

B.J.'s two front teeth. They were crooked from the time Seth first knew him, and then they chipped during junior varsity football practice in second year. He remembered those crooked chipped teeth and how they fueled his fantasies as he lay in bed at night trying to go to sleep, along with his fantasies along other zones of attraction, like B.J.'s hairy armpits that were dew-drop moist, his hairy arms and legs, his long feminine lashes, the outstanding bulge putting pressure at the crotch of his jeans and gym shorts. He remembered when the high school parking lot was draining itself of cars and seniors and he was searching for B.J. was among them. From behind, a Camaro slowed down. It was B.J. "Wanna ride?" Before he could figure out how to say, "Sure," B.J. laughed and sped off.

He never saw him again and forgot about him soon enough. After the post-graduation summer lolling about within the familiar parameters of his suburb, he went off to an urban university. His turf became larger and looser. He came across other men, many of whom he was able to do more with than jerk off; some of whom, because the sex was amazing, he tried to be in love with. Sometimes the bite of love took hold for a few weeks, sometimes for a few months, twice even for a year. Ultimately all of them ended up ending because the sex stopped feeling essential and forbidding. As soon as these men gave signs of settling into a pattern that suggested the limits as to what he could expect them to deliver (perhaps a bit less at times, perhaps a tad more), he knew that the days of the relationship were numbered and that he'd been a fool for love, or a greater fool for not yet knowing anything about love. He kept asking himself whether the strength of love was in direct proportion to the inability to comprehend it.

Yoni was impetuous and had a large dick, a formula kept the flame ignited for twenty-five years. Then it didn't. Was this a gay phenomenon, Seth asked himself over and over as he tried to understand what it was that could put an end to a relationship that was easy for so many years. What was struggling for air during those decades? Even their separation was easy. As they divided up the spoils of their time together, they had their episodes of bickering—who would get certain coveted knickknacks and the cat (who died shortly after their decision to have joint custody of her). They got through it, though. Sometimes they laughed through it. They remained friends. When they saw each other, they had no qualms about hugging. Seth went so far as to hold the hugs and nest his nose behind Yoni's earlobe. Its familiar animal scent broke through whatever hint of soap fragrance he was using. The odor of Yoni through herby soap. It made him want to try and love him all over again. It was no small feat for him, and maybe for Yoni too, to resist the need or desire to end up in bed, even if it meant looking at each other afterward and thinking, "What now?" He resisted, a meager redeeming factor of growing older and wiser.

"Did you find it?" Hank asked.

Focusing on B.J.'s teeth in Cancun, he forgot entirely that he was supposed to be searching for the reason why people said "Cheers" whenever they raised a glass to acknowledge an event (graduation, wedding) or a feel-good sentiment (friendship, life). He was losing his way, another factor of growing older.

He looked around him and snapped back. He was in a steakhouse with another man who was drawing him closer for reasons he didn't understand and who was raising a glass of wine for the first time—unbelievable! —hoping to make a toast.

"Just about," he replied as he quickly scrolled to the second notification. It was the posting from Honey. ""Having an AWESOME time with my sis!", followed by photos of unfamiliar flowers and a bridge. Underneath was the caption. "Enjoyed my much-needed getaway with my sister in Iowa. Time to head home." He didn't remember when or why he friended Honey.

The server arrived with a large tray propped on her open palm at chest height. She shifted the condiment holder to the edge of the table to make room for their oversized oval platters. "I'll be back to check on you," she said. "Enjoy your dinner!"

Seth raised his glass. "To Honey."

"Honey?"

"Yes. She posted on Facebook. She's coming back."

Their thick-stemmed goblets met above the basket of garlic rolls and clinked softly. Nothing broke.

"Cheers," Hank said. "Whatever it means."

"*L'chaim.*" Seth replied.

"What does that mean?"

Seth sliced into his steak and took a bite. "To life."

30

Seth and Hank shadowed the steps of a greenback turtle dragging her body back to the ocean after laying her one-hundred-odd eggs in the dunes. "What a shame Honey is missing this," Seth said. The sun was struggling to be radiant as it pierced the horizon line. A thin haze strafed the gray sky and the air had a warmth and humidity that felt like that of a low-grade celestial 'flu about to settle in for a day or two of unhealth, as 'flus do. The spectacle of indefatigable turtle drudgery came to an end when the curl of a wave lifted her up and away into an easier zone in which to go about the rest of her life. "What a shame Honey is missing this," Seth said.

"Have you heard anything?"

Seth kept his gaze on the turtle, whose head poked out of the shallow waves from time to time with an expression that he couldn't see but could only imagine as having to be one of exaltation over the newfound weightlessness and liberation. "Nothing. She's probably somewhere in the belly of America on her way home. Let's go for breakfast." At the diner, he persuaded Hank to try eggs Benedict.

"What's hollandaise sauce?" Hank asked after he closed his laminated menu and handed it to the server. Seth explained what classic hollandaise was, although he assumed that the diner version would have been poured out of a packet of powder, to which water would have been added slowly and blended violently with a whisk to prevent telltale lumps. It was a diner after all. Who knew who lurked behind the swinging door leading to the kitchen? The so-called cooks were probably as clueless to hollandaise as Hank was.

"English muffins at the bottom. Look at that!" He thought the idea of using English muffins in this way was ingenious. He studied the multi-textured layers—the ragged-edged muffin tops, the disks of Canadian bacon, the cupolas of egg, the thick yellow varnish of pale yellow—before taking his fork and knife to it. Such a fancy breakfast.

"What do you think?"

"I like it. Yes. Very much," he said as he reached for his cup of coffee after taking a trial bite. "It's good. Very good." He took a sip. "Did you ever think Honey disappeared because she'd died?"

"It crossed my mind."

"Me too. We didn't really know much about her. And things happen regardless of what we think we know."

Seth offered to pay.

"No. You did the honors last time. It's not right." He pulled his wallet from his back pocket and handed the cashier a twenty and a five. He studied the bill and said to her, "Just give me a dollar back, please."

"Wow," Seth said. "Cash. I haven't seen bills in ages."

"You sound like my boys," he replied. "They make fun of me too. But I prefer cash. I don't want to wait until a credit card statement arrives at the end of the month to know where I really stand. Cash keeps me from the temptation of overindulgence."

Seth struggled to respond with a snappy retort. Instead he said, "I admire you."

They walked together until they reached the corner where their paths needed to diverge in order for each of them to arrive home. They stood there for a moment under a Bismarck palm. Hank extended his hand. "Today is my day to do the wash."

His hand was soft, the fingernails freshly clipped. Seth withdrew his hand and wondered whether Hank ever let anything in his home become soiled. He was always so put together, even at sunrise trudging through sand. Of course he would have to do "the wash" at a designated hour. He smiled. Doing the wash, he thought. It wasn't an unfamiliar expression, but he hadn't actually heard anyone use it, like certain first names that weren't particularly exotic but which he didn't know anyone who was branded with: Jeanette. Wilbur. Madge. Brent. Or like using cash instead of plastic. Seth didn't do the wash. He did laundry.

* * * *

"Drive safely," June called to her sister as Honey backed out of the driveway. "Don't overdo. You'll get there when you get there. But call me when you do."

Day one. Iowa, Missouri, Illinois, a corner of Kentucky, stopover in a motel in Tennessee. Day two. Tennessee, the long stretch through Georgia, and the crossing-over to her state and the final stretch of highway with its view of ocean and its fragrance of home. Most of the way she drove above the speed limit. It was turtle season. Can't miss them, she thought as she maintained pressure on the gas pedal and kept her eyes straight ahead as she drove. She didn't want to miss these creatures. Their agony, their trudging, their drudgery. And all of them females. Where were the males? She selected radio stations with soft music. Each song was announced by the velvety voice of a man. Where were the females?

She arrived home late at night on the second day. She knew she wouldn't be able to sleep, but she set her alarm for five o'clock just in case.

In the waning darkness, she stumbled upon the first set of tracks almost immediately. They were wide and deep. Three other sets, narrower and less pronounced, were visible before she arrived at her spot. In that small window when night merged into day, the greenbacks and leathernecks relinquished the ease of their weightlessness in the ocean to drag themselves to the dunes and deposit their scores of eggs in wide sand pits they carved out by scooping their fins like oars rowing through molasses. Then they went into reverse, covering the pits and dragging themselves back to the ocean, where they swam away. Each turtle went about her slow-motion drudgery alone, like a chain gang of one; none would ever witness their newly hatched babies scurrying toward the water two months later while clouds of ravenous birds hovered above savoring the prospect of such an imminent and abundant meal just a swoop away. Where were the males?

Like the other sparse beachgoers at that hour, Hank and Seth were fixated on the possibility of happening upon one of these brief seasonal splendors as they strolled along their routine stretch of sand in expectation of ultimately finding one another. Their quest to witness such primordial acts gave them a sense of intimacy that was quieter but stronger than the intimacy Seth tried to manufacture with all of his questions and probings.

"Did you see anything?"

"I gave up counting the track paths after seven."

"I broke my record. On the way here, three mother turtles heading back to the ocean. None of them took more than five steps before they had to stop and rest. Poor things. What a life."

"And the babies. So many of them scurrying in the wrong

direction. I was tempted to scoop them up, take them to the ocean, and drop them in. Make it easier for them."

The subject of turtles replaced the weather forecast as their way of slipping into comfortable conversation after they pulled back from the hug that had become a habit, thanks to Honey. The subject of turtles segued to other subjects, most of them easy-going and good-natured, some more prickly, until one of them said, "I should be heading home now." Sometimes Seth offered to accompany Hank to his house, sometimes not; sometimes Hank accepted the offer, sometimes not. They danced around each other during the start of the turtle season, which was particularly fertile that year.

31

Whenever the doorbell rang, Winston let out a low, robust bark until he could discern whether the visitor at the screen door was someone he knew or whether the human form beyond the mesh was a stranger. To those who didn't know him, the bark suggested a menacing and warning unleashed by a dog who was clearly protective of its owner, although if the visitor could see Winston's tail pointed toward the ceiling and wagging in sheer delight, he or she could have easily entered the premises with a knife in hand or an M-15 slung over a shoulder and browsed the household items with the relaxed and carefree pace of a customer window-shopping.

Seth jumped when the bell rang and Winston grumbled. The mail had already been delivered. He wasn't expecting any packages. As he headed toward the door, Winston pushed into him, tail gyrating upward in propeller mode. Green light. Friend, not foe. He looked out the glass window of the front door and through the screen of the porch door. Ah. He smiled.

"I never heard that sound coming from Winston before," Hank said, taking off his hat to wipe his brow.

"He does it when the doorbell rings. It's a good thing.

Helps me feel safe. You never know. Scares off any bad eggs." It took him a few seconds to recognize the hatless Hank. He hadn't seen the mostly black and slicked back hair since their create-a-pizza night. Hank was holding a plastic bag filled with water and two squirming pompano. "What a surprise. And you brought guests. Come in."

"Thank you. I can't stay long."

"You know what I say to that. You don't stay, the fish don't stay." He held the door wide open. Winston escaped and orbited the driveway, returning to rub against Hank's legs and finishing off with his muzzle between Hank's thighs. From their encounters on the beach, Hank came to know Winston's cue—rake my back, rub my belly—and gladly obliged as he removed his sneakers by prying the heels of one sneaker off with the free toe-end of his other sneakered foot. "You can keep them on if you want," Seth said to him. "I like to walk around barefoot, but that's just me."

"It's fine."

"By the way, you don't have to bring me something in order to stop by."

"I caught four pompano today. I wouldn't know what to do with so many."

"Freeze them."

"My freezer is stocked."

Seth smiled at him. "Still."

Still. The word gave Hank pause. It was a word he didn't expect Seth to resort to. Seth wasn't one to fill silence with lazy words the way most people did. The absence of words like "like," "I mean," and "so" gave Seth's speech a crispness and sense of intention. He enjoyed that. "Still" was a crossover word. Said with a lilt at the end, it suggested something provocative that was to follow; stated as a complete thought with a full stop, it conferred authority, not unlike that of a master giving a command to his dog: Heel. Stay. Come. Still. He replayed the way Seth said it and couldn't find his way to any lilt. Was it an order of some kind? As he stood there with his bag of pompano, the agitation rose to that spot below the sternum that made it feel like a case of heartburn. It had landed there an hour ago, when he was considering stopping by Seth's for a visit, pompano in hand, and had intensified when Seth opened the door and he realized he couldn't turn back.

Seth stretched his arms out to the man standing in front of him holding a bag of fish. Such a sweet, sweet man, he thought, arms levitating from his sides as if they were wings preparing for flight. Hank followed suit and approached him. Their embrace was tentative but longer than the ones Honey had insisted on whenever they converged on the beach. Their stomachs touched.

"Let's make them now. Ocean to table. No refrigerators, no freezers. Come. Help me."

Hank couldn't feel himself into his reservoir of phrases that served him well when he wanted to decline invitations without offense so that he could scuttle back to where he'd left off in his daily routine, the routine without Marilyn, the routine that kept him away from others' pain, his own pain. He stayed for dinner. They wrapped the pompano in foil after Seth indoctrinated him in the art of sprinkling the fish with white wine, chopped parsley, a few pats of butter, and freshly ground salt and pepper. After they put them in the oven to bake, Seth made a small pot of herbed rice while Hank busied himself assembling a salad that Seth told him to rummage through the refrigerator to find the ingredients for. "There's a bunch of salad fixings in there on the bottom shelf," he said. "Help yourself. Surprise me." He poured one cup of jasmine rice into a measuring cup. "Don't bother looking for bottled dressings. Remember, I only do olive oil and balsamic vinegar and they're already on the table."

Hank assembled a salad composed of butter leaf and arugula, sliced beets, tangerines, cilantro and goat cheese. He had no idea what he was doing. Most of the ingredients in Seth's refrigerator were unknown to him, like foreign countries he perused in the travel and adventure magazines laid out in the waiting offices of doctors' offices. He was acquainted with sliced beets, which he didn't eat unless they were put in front of him, and tangerines, although it never occurred to him to do anything with them but peel and eat them segment by segment, spitting the seeds into a napkin. How many tangerines he and Marilyn peeled for their boys when they stormed into the house after their baseball practice. Marilyn had a talent for peeling tangerines in one unbroken coil. Maybe it was her long unpolished nails. Hank did his peeling over the open garbage bin, where the many bits of skin could break off and fall into without making a mess. And then there were the rind threads. Marilyn didn't fuss so much over them; he did.

He enjoyed the meal, especially the salad. Its daring combination of ingredients perked him up, excited him about the rewards to be had by venturing into something new. They cleared the table together.

"Let's take a dip in the pool. You can use one of my bathing suits. We're more or less the same size, to judge. The suits have elastic tops and inner strings. They should work."

Hank paused.

"You won't get cramps. That's an old wives' tale."

"Where should I change?"

"Come with me."

"Okay. One thing, though. I can't swim."

Seth led Hank to his bedroom, where he pulled out three pairs of bathing trunks from a drawer and flung them on the bed. "You don't have to swim. Just a dip. Submerge. Water. Dark sky. No clouds tonight. Stars overhead. Slice of moon. It's the tropics, remember? You'll feel like you're on vacation. Pick a pair of trunks and I'll meet you on the deck."

When Hank appeared in Seth's navy-blue baggy trunks cut above the knee, Seth scrutinized his body in the various lights being offered at the moment: the dim light of the low-hanging moon, the pool light under the surface of the water, and the two spots at the side of the house that he put on Low as he himself headed to the deck with two towels. It was the body of a man in his later years, but it was slender, with more hair than he expected (especially on the chest), and with some slight sagging under his armpits and chin, around his pectorals and neck. Still, he thought, he's fit. I should only look so good at his age.

He dove in at the deep end. Hank worked his way down the three steps. The water was at the top of his stomach when his feet reached bottom.

"Keep going. No sudden dips. It's a gradual slope."

Hank worked his way toward the deep end until the water reached his sternum. "That's as far as I go."

Seth swam to him. "You've got to at least wet your head and your shoulders. That's what makes the difference in this heat and humidity."

"I can't swim. I can't even float."

"News flash. Nobody can't float." He faced Hank, brought his arms to the surface of the water, outstretched as though he were serving a large tray of hors d'oeuvres to guests. "Now, I'm going to fit you in here. Trust me."

Hank looked down at the surface of the water. He wished he were home.

"Trust me. Let me just slip my right arm under your knees and my left arm under your neck. Then, all you need to do is let go."

"Easy for you to say." He yielded. Parts of his body (nipples, stomach, kneecaps, toes) broke the surface of the water and caught the chill in the air as Seth cradled him.

"Take a deep breath. Fill your belly with it."

His body didn't sink. It remained undulating on the surface, like some kind of offering. "Oh my."

"See. You can float."

"I'm not sure..."

"I won't let you go."

Seth walked Hank's supine form around the shallow end of the pool.

Hank closed his eyes. "*After being baptized, Jesus came up immediately from the water; and behold, the heavens were opened, and he saw the Spirit of God descending as a dove and lighting on Him, and behold, a voice from the heavens said, 'This is My beloved Son.'*"

"Keep your eyes open. Look at all the stars. You're doing it. You're floating. I won't let you go. There's Orion's Belt. Can you see it out up there?"

Hank motioned to be released.

"Still," Seth said. "Be still."

32

The next evening was starless. The crescent moon occasionally sabered through a continuum of black cloud cover as if to warn those below, "Stay indoors. The heavens are about to open. You'll get drenched." Seth looked at Winston. "Sorry, buddy. No walk tonight. Too risky." He turned back to his book.

Hank stepped outside his front door and noticed the absence of moon shadows outlining his mailbox at the bottom of the driveway and the neighbor's vintage Impala always parked in the driveway across the street. He glanced up at the sky. It was featureless, a dark tabula rasa. He remembered the clean blackboards of his school years, and the smelting of anxiety and excitement he felt as the teacher approached the board, chalk in hand. Something new to learn; something new to be tested and graded on. He looked at his umbrella-stand by the front door. No. Best to stay in tonight. No constitutional. No airing out. He summoned up the list of what he did on those dreaded nights when he didn't go out for a walk to break up the taut stretch of empty time that lay ahead of him after dinner and eased up only when he could justify calling it a day and go to bed. The list was slender: television (the main go-to); a book (occasionally); tidying up (the last resort).

As he considered the possibilities, he knew what he would end up doing. It had been a while, so he allowed himself to do it: Facebook, but with a measure of discipline kept in check by a mission. No catching up on posts only to discover when he looked up from the screen that it was after midnight. No, not that. He'd hold steady to his mission, resist temptation.

A distant thunder split the silence as he headed down the hall toward the spare bedroom, where his computer emitted a soft blue light onto the white tile floor of the hallway. After five minutes on the keyboard, he found what he was hoping to find against the odds: a selfie of her. She was holding a bunch of geraniums upside-down by the roots, like an obstetrician dangling a newborn. "Should be home tomorrow. Miss the palm trees, the beach, the ocean. The tropics!" the caption read.

Without looking at his watch to see if it might be too late, he called Seth. "Hi. Guess what. She's on her way."

"May I ask who's calling?"

He realized with shame that he'd fallen prey to a state of exhilaration without censure or modulation. How could he not even identify himself? He was about to hang up the phone but found it in him to forgive himself. "I'm new at these things," he thought. He put the phone back to his face. "Sorry. It's Hank."

"Hang on a sec." Seth logged out of Grindr. "On her way?"

"Sorry. I found her on Facebook. Honey. She'll be back tomorrow or the day after."

Seth wondered whether Honey could swim, and if he could solicit her help in teaching Hank. "That's great news. I guess we should expect her on the beach one morning soon."

"Should I write a comment or something?"

"That's between you and you."

"I'll have to think about it."

"If you did, what would you say?"

"I need to think about it."

"Sounds like you have some thinking to do."

There was a silence. "I just thought you'd want to know."

Seth drew a long deep breath. "Thank you, Hank. I appreciate it. It's good news. Surprising news. Welcome news." The three of them again. Triangles floated in his head: isosceles, equilateral, scalene. He remembered the terms from geometry class. Miss O'Connor was his teacher (or was it O'Connell? He couldn't remember). The battle-axe of his junior year. She was stern and bored and gave too many suprise quiz-zes. He remembered nothing of geometry except the names of triangles and one fact that Miss O'Connor (or was it O'Connell?) had stated as an afterthought: A table with three legs can't wobble. Then he remembered going to see *Jules et Jim* when it hit the cinematheque at university. He was first in line. He had to see whether the three of them—Jules, Jim and Catherine—fit themselves together into a new kind of paradigm that could last. "Do you think you'll reply?" he asked Hank.

"I think so."

"Let me know what happens. And thanks for calling to let me know." As he put down his phone, he questioned his sincerity. Did he really want to know? He wasn't so sure.

* * * *

Hi. It's Hank. From the beach. I bought one of your photographs. I'm glad to hear you're almost back. He back-spaced over "back" and replaced it with "home". *I hope you are well.* He thought about adding an emoticon. He never used one before. He scrolled through the offerings. Amusing but childish, like variations on the colored stars that teachers put at the top of homework assignments way back when. He couldn't feel sentiment coming through any of them. He scrapped the idea of emoticons and added *It will be nice to see you soon.*

Seth logged on to Facebook. He read Honey's posting and Hank's comment. He considered replying with an emoticon as well and chose the light-skinned thumbs-up gesture. It felt direct, bold and hip. Everything that he knew he wasn't.

* * * *

Quarter moon giving way to sunlight. Clear sky emerging. Light breeze. Calm ocean. Low tide. Wide beach. Perfection of breadth and illumination. Suggestive, safe. Reassuring to walk along. Promising.

> *O Lord,*
> *The safe light falls, heralding a new day*
> *The warm blush carries your everlasting promise*
> *I soak in the grace you give*
> *At the dawn of each morning.*
> *With the sun, hope also rises*
> *To cast light into the darkness.*
> *Sweet songs flow from skies*
> *Emerging in the hazy glow.*
> *Sounds of comfort*
> *That lead us to wonder again at the beauty all around.*
> *A taste of Heaven is poured into each new dawn.*
> *We are reminded of new birth,*
> *Of your redeeming love*
> *And with this wake-up call,*
> *Each and every one can trust in*
> *The promise of eternity*
> *And carry its gentle presence into*
> *The day anew.*

Try as he might to inhabit the blessing, there was interference in the form of images of the many times she'd appeared at the water's edge, camera perched on her belly as she gazed out looking for a visual to capture of a slice of the world's soul. She meshed with his sense of religion. That's what it was, he thought. She came here too, dressed in shabby beachwear and always looking out and up for things far bigger. Like God. He knew that any day she would be standing there for real as he took his daily constitutional along the beach at dawn. She would draw him into an embrace with outstretched arms, and he would feel the presence of the ineffable in a modest and humanly possible way. He couldn't help but look straight ahead, away from the immensity of sea and sky, to see if he could see her in the distance. Was she there?

The morning after he sent the emoticon, Seth went to the beach earlier than usual. She'll show up one day, he thought. Will I find her first? On her own? Or will she already be with Hank and have traveled a certain distance with him that will leave me forever behind by the time I arrive at them? It was still completely dark when he and Winston set out. Winston resisted, creature of habit that he was. At that hour, Seth had to lure him with a Milk Bone into an upright position in order to place the harness around his neck and hook the leash onto the metal ring. Winston didn't like walking in the dark. Outdoor darkness made him tense. His tail hung down until the creeping light gathered enough force to define the familiar shapes around him.

Until that morning, the two men ran into each other almost every sunrise. As soon as the distance between them narrowed to a couple of feet, Winston would tuck his head between Hank's legs, expecting Hank to bend over and satisfy his need to have his neck scratched. Until that morning, Honey wasn't a subject of conversation. She didn't need to be talked about. Her absence on the beach was presence enough. Words weren't necessary. They knew that. And they knew that the other knew that. They talked about other things, topics that would hold them together for a while longer even if what they had to say wasn't compelling. They felt the limbo but didn't speak about the limbo. They knew it would pass as soon as she appeared one morning on the beach.

And she did, that morning, as they knew she eventually would. Each of them spotted her from different points of equal distance. They didn't rush to get there first. A few paces slower or quicker didn't matter so much. Ultimately, they'd find themselves reunited.

"Welcome back."

"Yes. Welcome back."

Honey extended her arms to each of them as they approached her. "It's good to be back."

They could feel her thick flesh as they wrapped their arms around her sides and back, which were already damp from sweat. They wanted to know so much. They also didn't care. Here they were. That was the most important thing. They said nothing. The sound and sight of the waves beginning to stretch and swell made their silence feel like a private language. All that had happened to each of them since the last time they were together now compressed itself into a tiny space with little power to interfere with the present instant. Here they were again, in triangle formation before the rising sun.

It was Honey who broke the silence. "Steady as she goes."

Hank provided a refrain. "Steady as she goes."

"So reliable," Seth said.

Honey looked at him. "That's a good thing, isn't it?"

"Yes. A good thing."

"Good. I'm glad you said that."

"It IS a good thing, reliability. Isn't it?"

She smiled.

They rejoined Hank in his silence. Seth could hear Honey take in deep breaths, as if she were catching up on all the salt air she'd been deprived of while she was away. He tried breathing to the rhythm of her breathing. It took effort, but he could feel certain zones of his body being quenched and expanded as if for the first time. He would have to remember to do this more often, he thought. Another good thing.

Hank's face was lifted toward the rising sun, which was still too feeble to envelop him in the comfort of its heat; his upper eyelids rested, unquivering, on the lower lids. It was a position that came naturally to him after years of preparing himself for prayer.

> *Dear heavenly father,*
> *I know there is more. My vision is limited.*
> *Give me the eyes of the eagle. Let me see.*
> *By your Spirit may I rise up over the darkness, even*
> *when there is light from the sun.*
> *May I journey past my wounds,*
> *Past the sadness and injustice,*
> *Above the highest mountain.*
> *A greater plan, a secret place evolved over the ages.*
> *Lift me up to your greatness and glory poured out all*
> *over creation.*
> *What answer reveals a deeper truth?*
> *What answer lives forever?*

He opened his eyes slowly, stopping halfway. The sun was too bright for a fully open human eye to gaze at directly. Crows' feet inscribed themselves on the sides of his lids. They were long and deep, like the mapping out of a difficult itinerary whose destination had yet to be reached.

"I'm glad you're back," he said.

Honey looked at first at him, then at Seth. "I'm glad I'm back. I'm glad you're here with me again in front of all this." She raised her arm and made a loose fist, as if toasting with an invisible glass. "To the reliability of the sun. To the reliability of its witnesses. To us."

Hank raised his arm. "Praise the Lord."

Seth raised his arm. "*L'chaim.*"

33

They saw the signs alone. "Tender loving care and the dream can be yours." The larger signage was fastened onto two wooden posts hammered into the sand on the beach in front of the house; a second, smaller one with the same slogan was fastened to the mailbox at the bottom of the driveway where the property intersected with the road. The real estate agency details were located under an above-the-shoulder photograph of the agent, a middle-aged woman seated on the diagonal like she probably did for her high school yearbook picture: one shoulder dipping into the foreground, a cascade of hair with the sheen and smoothness of liquid mahogany, a Pepsident smile, and an expression of caring that few teenagers were capable of feeling other than towards themselves. The only missing item in the standard heartfelt photo was a string of pearls around the neck.

Honey came upon the signage on the beach side, with its thick red "For sale" letters prominent at the top and impossible not to see from a distance. "Wow!" she thought as she took note of the realtor's name—Dawn Salmon—and the name of the agency—Upstream Realty. She stepped inside the dilapidated structure to inspect the remnants of its carcass: fragments of artisanal and assembly-line tiles, genuine and faux wood floorboards, concrete block and sheetrock walls. The guts—pipes, wires, ducts, insulation—were exposed by gaping holes here and there. "Wow," she thought again. "Look at this mess. Look at this possibility." Fuel for dreams.

Hank and Seth saw the posting but neither of them was curious enough to step into the remains of the house to take a closer look. In their area, "For Sale" signs cropped up like weeds: homeowners upgrading because of job promotions and higher salaries; downgrading because of grown children flying the coop or because of retirement and the modest Social Security income it would give them; scrambling to return to the Northeast or the Midwest, having realized that the tropical life wasn't all they thought it would be, especially in summer with its four months of suffocating humidity and non-stop hurricane warnings. Hank and Seth took note of all the "For Sale" signs and imagined the various perturbations of circumstances that might have caused them to be posted. Whatever the story behind the two-word signs, the outcome seemed inevitable to both of them: dreams and hopes of better times ahead that ended up being waystations toward a progression of futures that, time and time again, proved themselves to be lacking. Even so, the signs persisted. For sale. For rent. For change.

* * * *

Onset of evening. Seth arrived at the coffee shop at five minutes past seven. He'd suggested that they meet at seven, before the sun set completely, and at a venue that didn't serve alcohol. The man, who'd identified himself as "Daniel," agreed. They'd chatted online three times. Each time, the topic of sex didn't surface. How refreshing, Seth thought, especially since the man's photo was sufficient in itself to arouse him: mid to late forties, fit but not ripped, tousled brown hair with unapologetic streaks of gray, slapped-on jeans and t-shirt; nothing suggesting a catwalk pose or attitude, no hint of a dark or kinky crux as the prize for tapping at the keyboard for more time than one had wished. A regular-kind-of-guy snapshot that suggested a simple desire to meet someone decent and nice, and to let whatever happened happen. The new Sexy, Seth thought. He was growing weary of the selfies taken by men who'd mastered the art of inhaling to pull their stomachs in while tensing their arms to bloat their biceps out for the few seconds it took them to snap a photo and then subtract ten years and 30 pounds from their profile stats, after which they might be rewarded by a meeting someone like him at some dank and dingy bar nearby where, after a drink or two guzzled down under the poor lighting of a few bare bulbs, the desired altered state of fuzziness and sloppiness would be strong enough for him to take such a man (and there were many of them) home, where he'd yield to an hour of abandon with this disappointing hunk of male flesh until orgasm was reached (or not) and the desire kicked in to have this momentary accomplice (who was by now loose, flaccid and pot-bellied) disappear as soon as the panting began to subside. This man, Daniel, seemed different. Not averse to sex, to be sure. On this site, who was? But without that pungent animal scent on and around him. Genuinely amenable to other possibilities.

Seven o' five on the dot, as Seth had planned. The man was already seated, as Seth had hoped, so that he could study him for a minute or two before deciding whether to approach him and say "Daniel?" or slip out and go home. Seth recognized him right away, not because of any salient features but simply because he was exactly how he'd portrayed himself in the photo. He was at a window table with a mug of something in one hand and a magazine being leafed through with the other. Seth watched him from a safe distance for a minute before beginning the approach. In that minute, the man didn't raise an eye to look around, as Seth would have done if he was sitting in a coffee shop waiting to meet someone he'd never met and who should have already arrived if he wasn't playing games. Daniel seemed to be perfectly content to be doing what he was doing: reading his magazine and sipping his beverage. Seth could imagine him going on like that until an employee of the coffee shop stopped by to say to him, "Sir we're getting ready to close now," having forgotten entirely that he'd come to this place to meet a man. It was a good sign.

"Daniel?"

"That's me."

"Hi. I'm Seth."

Daniel extended his hand without rising. Seth grasped it and left it to Daniel to determine the strength of the grip and the amount of up and down before the release. The grip was strong but not competitive. Daniel was the one to pull back before the handshake became evidence of awkwardness.

They talked through their one drink each (Daniel, ordered a tonic water with lemon; Seth a Virgin Mary with extra ice). Afterward, they ambled along the main street of the downtown area and didn't spend the night together. The conversation was filled with an easy intelligence and humor. The attraction was strong. The desire to resist it was stronger. First-time sex was a game they both knew. It could wait. When it was time to time to part company, they gave each other a peck on the cheek.

"I really enjoyed meeting you," Seth said.

"Me too."

"Let's get together again."

"Sounds good to me."

Seth pulled out his phone. "Can I have your number? I can text you."

"Why don't you just call me right now? I'll answer and we can talk more."

Seth called him. They talked into their phones while they stood next to each other. Nervous giggles. The phones got in the way. Daniel ended the call in the middle of a sentence and put it back into the right-hand pocket of his jeans. "I should head home. We have each other's number. Call me. Or I'll call you. Not now, but soon." He brushed Seth's wrist with his index finger.

Here was a man with experience, Seth thought. Someone who studied each step of the dance and had worked out the degree of measuredness required for either party to decide whether to proceed or pull away. Game on. It was efficient and would take them where they were supposed to be quickly, and without too many bumps along the way. Had their trajectory been plotted on a graph, it would have displayed itself as a straight line with a gentle upward slope. Date one finale: a kiss on the check; date two finale: a kiss on the lips with a hint of tongue on the part of Seth that Daniel accepted but didn't ante up; date three finale: a tenuous exploration of clothed bodies, from the waist up, with tremulous hands; date four finale: the plunge. Date four took place at Seth's house. After it did, and as their heavy breathing was subsiding, Seth's spirit sank: He wanted Daniel to vanish. They ended up spending the night together locked in an embrace that Seth wasn't aware of until he woke up the next morning to the sound of Daniel's soft snoring. He turned, looked at Daniel's full lips, and still wanted him to vanish. That's it, he thought. It won't happen again. I don't have it in me for it to happen again. Please please please remember this. Remember it this time, with him, so that I don't have to try to remember it again with anyone else who might spend the night. Remember how the delicious arm wrapped around my torso becomes a weight, an impediment to getting a good night's sleep; remember the bathroom in the morning, with its yellow drips of urine on the toilet rim that aren't mine because I would have blotted my drips away with a sheet of toilet paper, and maybe even have put the toilet rim down afterward; remember the glorious pre-waking silence being shattered by the soft shuffling of someone else's feet going down the hallway. He thought these things as he stirred at the usual hour of five o'clock and was startled to see that he was sharing a bed with a man who, only hours before, he was longing to taste and smell and had gone so far as to fantasize about possibly living with one day; and who now was just another man who'd been tasted and smelled and was now to be... discarded. How cruel and narrow, he thought. But maybe I'm just sleep-deprived from Daniel's snoring.

He shook Daniel gently on the shoulder. "Good morning."

Daniel rolled onto his back and stretched his arms and legs. "Hey you."

"I need to get my day started."

Daniel's long lashes fluttered as he unsealed his eyes. His lips arced upward into a smile when his eyes opened enough for him to understand where he was and who was responsible for him being where he was. "So soon?"

"Yep."

"It's still dark. There's no day yet to get started."

"There is."

"Stay here. It's still dark." He made a scooping gesture with his left arm. "C'mon. Come over here. Fit inside here." His armpits were exposed. They were hairy. Seth remembered what they smelled like just a few hours ago in the epicenter of the darkness. Tempting.

"I really need to get a move on."

Daniel brought both arms to his side. His smile receded. "Okay. Got it." He rose from the bed, gathered up his clothing from the floor and got dressed.

Seth showed mercy. "Would you like some coffee?"

"That's okay. I'll be heading out. I'll get my day started, too." He turned to Seth as he was opening the front door. "Call me." Before closing the door behind him, he took three paces toward Seth, gave him a peck on the forehead and added, "If you want." He retraced his steps and was gone.

Seth stood in the empty hallway. He could have bolted to the front door, opened it, leaned out and cried out something to not make him vanish, but he didn't. He could have called him a day or two later, when the aftertaste was diminishing but could have been brought back to full flavor, but he didn't. He'd been through this too many times to hope that this time would be different, even if he was hoping that this time it could be different. It was time for a different hope, or no hope. In the days to come, he checked his phone. There were no messages from Daniel. Yes, he was right. Daniel was also a man with experience in these matters. That was a good thing. A promising thing, even if it meant that he wouldn't see or hear from Daniel again. He changed the sheets.

* * * *

Onset of evening. Hank looked out the window and watched his neighbor Donna walk down the street with three of her grandchildren behind her holding hands. The paisley-patterned curtains that Marilyn had selected and Hank mounted in the living room window weren't meant to be drawn open or shut. "Perfect," Marilyn said when Hank stepped off the ladder. He started to test the pulley to see if they closed. "No no," she said. "They'll be staying to the side."

"I don't understand."

"Don't you see? The window is like a picture that changes. That's why it's called a picture window. The curtains are just the frame. For decoration."

Donna's grandchildren ranged in age from four to nine, he figured, and the hand-holding was most likely the result of their grandmother's firm instructions to not stray off separately unless they wanted to be whisked back into the house to do chores. Donna was bossy. "Your grass is looking awfully high," she called out to him on innumerous occasions, arms folded across her bosom like the prudish schoolmarms of his youth. What does she make her grandchildren for breakfast? An array of cereal boxes laid out on the table like dominos? Or something requiring a grandmotherly touch—platters of eggs and bacon, or stacks of pancakes or French toast? Marilyn would have pulled out the skillets and set the kitchen into a frenzy of activity. "What'll it be this morning, young men?" But they only had two grandchildren, and they lived far away and only visited one or two times each year. When they did visit, Marilyn had to make it special, memorable. Donna told him that she had thirty-eight grandchildren. All of them lived within two hours of her. He believed her. Why shouldn't he? She, like him, was a good Christian woman. She had eight grown children, all of them married off, and with children of their own, many of them. Donna cleaned other people's houses to supplement her Social Security. Her used SUV had decals on all four of its doors: "DUST-FREE FOR YOUR HOUSEKEEPING NEEDS! Call for a free estimate NOW!" How could he not believe her?

"How do you keep track of all those birthdays?" he asked her once when he reached the bottom of his driveway to wheel in his emptied garbage bin and saw her doing the same.

"Keep track? You must be kidding." she replied. "I don't. I can't. Who could? You?" She opened the bin to see if all of the contents had been emptied. "I keep a lot of ready-made desserts in the second freezer, the one in the garage. It comes in handy. I pull out some sweet gunk, nuke it in the microwave, and they think I never stopped thinking about them. Especially if there are M&Ms on top of whatever I pull out."

He hadn't seen this particular trio of grandchildren before. Then again, he realized, maybe he had, but in a different grouping. Thirty-eight of them! He couldn't imagine how she managed the comings and goings of so many grandchildren. Such a profusion of fertility and clamor for attention. Such messy joy. To be sure, he and Marilyn could have risen to the occasion. They wanted to, in fact. They assumed that it would be the natural outpouring of their way of life according to His Word. They didn't speak much about actual numbers, but they'd taken for granted that a family teeming with the constant activity and demands of waist-high or arm-cradled youth was to be had, put up with, cherished. Their life was to be about that. They wanted at least six children, and they tried to conceive them before, between and after the birth of their two surviving sons. Two years after the birth of their second son, they gave up trying by giving up sex altogether, since its purpose—procreation—seemed to have run its course with them. They had two wonderful sons. When they went to bed at night, each of them covered most of their body in flannel nightwear, kissed each other on the cheek, and retreated to their respective side of the bed; he on the left, she on the right. It gave them a sense of relief that was far greater than the animal urges they felt from time to time but avoided understanding by always keeping the lights off. Occasionally he rubbed her shoulder with his hand before turning over to sleep. In the morning, she rose before he did and got breakfast going. He woke up to the familiar clattering of skillets and spatulas being positioned to prepare the morning meal. Like his two sons, he didn't make a move toward the kitchen until she called out, "Breakfast is ready. Don't wannit to get cold!" That lovely morning refrain.

 Watching them from the living room window, he shifted his location to the front door, thinking to open it and wave to Donna and the three of her thirty-eight grandchildren she had in tow. Donna moved slowly and had a gait and pallor that suggested chronic health issues lurking beneath the vigilance with which she kept these three grandchildren in check. Such an abundance of issue, and with thirty-five others constantly streaming in and out of her life. How does she do it? He refrained from signaling her. He knew what he was after as he watched this woman infused with family. His two boys had wives and children far away. They didn't enter and exit his life in a steady stream. They paid visits once or twice a year, dictated by school breaks. They were occasional sons to him. Then there was Marilyn. She was dead and didn't pay visits. Maybe it wasn't possible to. If it was, she hadn't found her way to him yet. He didn't open the door. He turned around and leaned his back against it, as he closed his eyes and folded his hands.

And when are you going to see them again? When will the day break and the shadows flee away? My child, that day is nearer than you think! In heaven above, the souls of your dear departed may be preparing for your reception even now... for you. Yes... yes, the procession that is to receive you is forming even now... The days and the weeks pass so swiftly, you know. A little more patience, My child... Yet a little while upon the cross of your earthly exile... and then... then ...

Listen! Do you not already hear the familiar accents, O the sweet voice that so long was as music to you, until death caused it to die away? Hark! It is calling you... It is pleading that you be pious and true ... Today it is but a clear sweet voice...And tomorrow? ... Ah! Tomorrow will bring a dear sweet voice... and a loving heart... and two welcoming arms stretched out to embrace you?

Yes, tomorrow... there will be happy homecoming of the dear ones in the eternal courts of heaven! Forever!

He opened his eyes, unclasped his hands and peered out the front door just as Donna and her grandchildren were turning the corner and he heard her yell out to them, "Pick up the pace if you want some ice cream!" Yes, she was bossy. The children released their hands, sprinted in front of her as if in a race, and disappeared behind the rhododendron hedge bordering her front yard.

He opened the door and waved his hand. "Evening, Donna."

"Hi, Hank. Lawn's looking good."

"I'm trying to keep on top of it. But all those weeds."

"Looks nice."

"Thanks. I do my best." He knew it wasn't true, and Donna would realize it if she studied his yard more closely. The overall effect of his yard was lush and green. But all those weeds. He wondered whether Honey had grandchildren. Surely she did. He would have to remember to ask her.

* * * *

Onset of evening. Before Honey entered her house, she brushed her sandals against the front doormat to dislodge the sand. She hung her camera on the hook. The camera tapped twice against the wall before coming to rest. "That's it for noise," she thought. The silence was nothing new. The house had been a quiet one for quite some time, years before Glen died. "Do you have to do that here?" she asked him whenever she heard him watching a ballgame in the living room or strumming a series of chords on his guitar that didn't result in a song. "Do you have to do that here?" she asked him when he was snoring on the sofa. In time, he transferred himself and the accessories of his noise to the spare bedroom and the den at the far end of the house. "Thank God," she thought. "Finally some peace and quiet."

It was different now. She could no longer break up the peace and quiet of the house whenever she chose by merely calling out "Glen!" and waiting for the few seconds it would take for him to respond, either by him calling out "What is it?" or by her hearing the sound of his footsteps trudging down the hall to reach her and see what it was that she wanted this time. This new silence was different from the others; it was the silence of being alone. As soon as the camera settled against the wall, her heart started pounding, her skin felt clammy, she wanted to vomit. She ran to the kitchen sink and turned the hot and cold spigots to full force. The water temperature didn't matter. The sound of the gushing water was what mattered. Anything to drown out the new silence. She splashed water on her face. "There," she said to herself. "Better."

She walked down the hall and opened the doors to her late husband's domain. She knew he wouldn't be there. Still, she looked under the mattress and behind the entertainment unit. One never knew. He was capable of surprising her on occasion. Like the time the children flew in for her fiftieth birthday and hid in the coat closet until she returned with the groceries.

"Your father," she said to them. "He's something else."

"Yep," Aurora said. "We were so glad he was on board to have us fly in when Cal told him about our plan. Happy birthday, Mom!"

"Or the time he pulled into the driveway with a new car.

"Here," he said, holding out the keys. "For you."

"What's the occasion?" she asked.

"No occasion. Can't have you driving around in that piece of crap," he replied, pointing to the car she'd used for almost two decades.

"But Glen..."

"No buts. Look at the other driveways. Can't be slackers. Gotta keep up with the Joneses."

In the spare bedroom, she lifted the dust ruffle and didn't find him. Only dustballs. In the den, she dragged the entertainment unit away from the wall. More dustballs. "I'll vacuum tomorrow," she said to herself. "Something to do in the morning." She left the doors open behind her as she left to air them out. If Glen insisted on not being there, which was clearly the case, she didn't want to smell anything having to do with him either. It was enough that other signs of him were all over the house—the left side of the beige sectional sofa, whose removable armrest cover was blotched with the dark gray grime left by his arm and fingertips but that she never got around to tossing in the washer; the various sockets above baseboards that had the bodies of adapters plugged into them and wires trailing along the floor toward destinations never reached; the corner of the utility room, where his assorted outdoor footwear (rubber boots, flip-flops, sneakers, a pair of aquamarine flippers that still had the label fastening them together) were piled in the corner; and, oh, all the photos and vacation souvenirs on shelves and side tables everywhere. Making her way through the house, she took note of these objects, waiting for them to break the silence by evoking something, provoking something. Wasn't that the point of objects? she asked herself as she picked up a framed photo of her and Glen at the beach before the children were born, she in a strap bikini, he in a pair of white trunks cut well below the navel. They were smiling and looked happy. Glen had his arm around her shoulders, but there was a sliver of space along the length of their bodies separating them as if, even way back then, they'd started the gradual pulling away from each other. Where was that photo taken? Who took it? She couldn't recall. "Enough for tonight," she said to herself. She put the photo back on the shelf. "I'll vacuum the dust balls in the morning, call Goodwill later in the week."

The master bathroom was the only room in the house where there was no trace of him. He'd decamped from there long before he'd eased his way into one of the other bedrooms and claimed the den. "What are all these things you have here for?" he'd asked her one night when they were brushing their teeth at the same time.

"What things?"

He let his index finger sweep the surface of the double counter. "All this."

"Necessities," she replied.

"Would you mind keeping them on your side?" he asked, pushing the cord of her blow dryer away from the rim of his sink.

"There's an empty bathroom just down the hall."

"So there is." With one arm, he picked up the empty waste bin; with the other, he grazed the surface of his side of the countertop like a snow plow. The few toiletries he used fell into the bin. "There you go," he said. "The bathroom's all yours." With the bin swinging against his left calf, he faded into the darkness of the bedroom. "Do your magic, whatever it's worth."

She replaced the framed photo and went to the master bathroom. She couldn't remember the last time she found the toilet seat up or the bolt covers at the base of the bowl glazed in a pale yellow from his inability to aim. Not a trace of anything having to do with him. She switched on the vanity lights around the wall mirror, the beacons of truth. The double sinks were laden with beauty and anti-aging products that she'd tested once or twice and then abandoned after she couldn't see any difference: blushes, moisturizers, spot removers, exfoliating creams, lash extensions, silicone-based wrinkle smoothers, hair emoluments. She looked in the mirror. "Oh, dear. Not a pretty picture." She pressed her fingers into various pieces of excess flesh on her face—the folds on her upper eyelids, the sags at the rim of her jaw, the sacs below her cheekbones—and stretched them toward the back of her head until the topography of her face was smooth and taut. "Once upon a time, in a land far far away," she recited through overly stretched lips, and then laughed as she released her fingers and watched her flesh revert to droop. "Magic, indeed." She picked up her beauty items, one by one, studied their labels, and tossed them into the wastebin, leaving only her hairbrush, toothbrush, toothpaste and a plastic bottle of Lubriderm Daily Moisturizer with a spout at the top. She arranged the few remaining items on the left side of her sink. The rest of the counter—an immensity of white space—was bare, except for the film and the crusted shapes left by all of the items she'd just discarded. "I'll shine it up tomorrow," she said as she switched off the light. Her hand glided along the surface of the counter to guide her to the doorway to the bedroom. She could feel the grime accumulating on her fingertips. "So much to take care of tomorrow."

34

As the light pushed its way out of the darkness to announce the beginning of a new day, Honey set out to initiate the hugging. Up until this morning, they hugged in three sets of pairs, with Honey approaching one of the men, then the other, and then pulling back to let them complete the cycle; the odd one out would look out at the horizon line, seeking distance in order to allow the intimacies behind them to see themselves through unencumbered. This time, Honey and Hank were first; Hank and Seth were last.

From behind them, not far from the house, came high-pitched yowlings, brief and episodic, broken up by swift but furtive rustlings in the dunes before they started up again, like a violent choreography that could be heard but not seen.

"Bobcats," she said. "They'll mate soon. While they're getting down to business, it'll be quiet. Then it'll start up again afterward, when the male is still locked inside her and she wants him to pull out because, well, mission accomplished."

The three of them turned the upper half of their bodies away from the ocean and toward the vicinity of the house as soon as they heard the first yowl, which was too close for comfort.

"It sounds so awful," Hank said. "Like something in pain."

Seth struggled to hold back a smile that seemed perfectly natural to him but could cause either Honey or Hank, or both of them, to ask, "Why the smile?" Then he'd feel obliged to respond in some way, but the truth behind the smile seemed too private and risky to give words to. He couldn't imagine telling them that, when one thought about it, the bobcat's activity wasn't so different from that of homo sapiens; how the idea of sex or the promise of sex was enough to hold two people together for decades, forever even, no matter how mismatched or destructive their union might be; or how it could pull them apart before they got to know each other. No. Not the right time or place. Not yet the right people. He said nothing and remained motionless, head down. Had he lifted his head, he might have noticed that Honey was wearing the smile that he himself was holding back.

The bobcats copulated and detached soon enough. The quiet resumed. Hank and Seth turned back toward the sun, Honey toward the house. "Look at it," she said to them. "It's screaming too. For someone to restore it. Can't you feel it?"

Hank and Seth looked at the semi-dilapidated structure.

"It would make a great breakfast spot for beachgoers," Seth said.

"Wouldn't it though," she said. "All those people stopping by to grab a bite and then walking it off on the beach. Maybe too many people."

"I'm sure someone will buy it and make it nice," Hank said.

"I hope so," she said. "Maybe whoever buys it won't be so nice. Or maybe what the buyer turns it into won't be so nice. Or maybe both. Then where are we at?"

In unison, they returned their gaze to the horizon. The sun was bleaching away the secondary hues, as if to announce with its potent yellow, "I'm taking over the day."

"We can't risk it," she said. "No one comes here at this

hour except us. Your first time here, you guys could have turned left instead, toward the hotels, but you didn't. And you never have. You could sleep in from time to time, but you never have. You make sure to wake up early enough. You make sure to turn in the right direction. Toward here. So do I. Because we get this place. It deserves to belong to us."

Hank looked at her. "Nothing belongs to us. We don't possess anything."

Seth looked at her. "He's got a point."

She dug the toes of her left foot into the sand, creating a shallow crescent. "Gentlemen, I couldn't agree with you more, but there are certain things that we cling to anyway, as if our life depended on it. For me, it's this place. If this place has to change, I want to have a say."

Seth poked at her toes as they worked their way deeper into the sand. "And what would you say?"

She smoothed the pit she carved in the sand, which wasn't nearly deep enough to reach China, as she thought she could do when she was a child. "I'd say, 'Let's buy it.' That's what I'd say. I'd say it to you and to Hank."

"Is that what you'd say?"

"Yes."

"Is that what you are saying?"

They stopped their nattering. It was seven-eleven, the time the sun was scheduled to break through. Silence was in order. The silhouette of a sail could be seen in the distance. The fin of a dolphin (or was it a shark?) pierced the surface of the water. They noticed the two triangular piercings of the ocean's smooth surface as they focused on the sun.

"Did you see?" Hank asked. "Over there." He pointed vaguely outward and southward.

"There it is again!" Seth said. "Did you see it?" He pointed further southward just as a pelican was swooping down where the fin should have reappeared. The pterodactyl-like creature soared up again with a fish dangling from its beak. They watched as it headed inland toward the condos, its wings fully extended to harness enough of the breeze to avoid having to exert itself by flapping in order to stay well above everything that was below.

"Effortless flight. Majestic," Honey said as she wiped a tear from her cheek. "God how I envy them."

Hank walked to her and let his hands settle on her shoulders. "If I may. *Lord, how majestic is your name in all the earth! You have set your glory in the heavens....* *When I consider your heavens, the work of your fingers, the moon and the stars, which you have set in place, what is mankind that you are mindful of them, human beings that you care for them?*"

"I wonder what the house is worth," Seth said. Hank's intonation bypassed him, along with the pelican carrying a fish in its mouth and Hank's hands on Honey's shoulders. He was sealed inside himself, trying to not think about the impossibility of Daniel, or any future variation of a Daniel. Number-crunching was distracting and led to solid outcomes.

"Is that what you were thinking about?" Honey asked.

"Why not?" he said. "It can't hurt to know these things. You never know."

"You never know what?" She laughed. "I never know anything. I pretend to, but deep down I know that I don't. Mind you, 'deep down' isn't a place I get to often." She looked at him. "If the price were right, would you buy?" She waited for his eyes to meet hers and added, "Or are you just curious because it can't hurt to know these things?"

He lowered his head. "Does it matter?"

"I think so. Really. It way matters."

"Then I'll need to think on it more."

"And you? Hank? What do you think?"

Hank lowered his eyes and pulled the rim of his hat down for extra measure. "I'm sorry. I'm completely lost. Or maybe I just wasn't listening. The idea of those bobcats. It was disturbing."

They thought about the house without sharing their thoughts about it. Especially their thoughts about buying it. Too much. Too soon. Too pragmatic. Especially so early in the day.

"I need to go," Hank said. "I'll see you in the morning." He approached Seth first, arms extended for the embrace that needed to be gotten through. Then on to Honey, with whom he loosened up, since he could follow her lead, guru of hugs that she was. As he walked away from them, he didn't look back to see whether they too hugged each other before parting company or whether they stayed on to advance the conversation about the fin or the pelican or the house, or maybe to introduce another topic that he would miss altogether (but perhaps hear remnants of in the morning and be able to join in on). Retracing his footsteps along the sand toward his access point to the beach, he suspected that the audacious proposal (leave it to Honey to be audacious!, he thought) of the house being theirs was now embedded in each of them and would not be excised easily, much like the cilia-sized thorns of his cactus that found their way into his thumb if he wasn't careful as he walked by. The subject might be avoided the next time they met, and with some effort the time after that, but it couldn't be made to go away. It would accompany each of them in as a far-fetched but legitimate possibility that had surfaced with enough legitimacy to require serious consideration: the number of rooms that could be restored or recast to accommodate them as individuals and as a collective, plus any number of guests who might arrive and stay long enough to enjoy it and glean how and why such an unorthodox arrangement was ideal for the three of them; the financing arrangements for the purchase (joint title?) and day-to-day expenses (cookie jar on the kitchen counter?); the matter of dirty dishes, soiled clothes, grimy floors (who would clean what and when?)—an entirely unfamiliar and exotic menu to scan and choose from. They avoided the subject for a few months as they met each morning on the beach in the semi-darkness, an avoidance that was as direct as any discussion about the subject would have been. The skeleton of the house, jutting out like a monolith against the horizon and pleading for its bare bones to be transformed into a blood-and-flesh habitat for them to carry out their remaining days, made their connection strong and fearsome, despite the absence of words about the structure. The continual presence of the "For Sale" signs provided a grace period as they struggled to understand and accept the possibility of a surge of intimacy long after they'd resigned themselves to having nothing more to arrive at than a modest portion of wisdom-with-age mixed with a hefty dose of weariness.

35

The following morning, they walked to the house together. They didn't mean for it to happen that way. Like most other mornings, each of them ambled along the beach in their own company, feet grazing against the latest splash of ocean as it sank into the sand with little fanfare aside from the bubblings of the sand fleas below. Like most other mornings, they looked forward to converging in front of the house and stationing themselves there, sometimes two yards in front, other times twenty yards, depending on the tide. They'd look out toward the horizon, paying little attention to the sorry hovel behind them. On this morning, however, the sky was a pallet of ho-hum grays, and their habit of silence presented itself as an awkwardness. So they looked behind them, each in turn, away from the horizon and toward the distraction of the house, what with its splotches of yellow paint here and there. In some places, the yellow looked freshly applied; in others, it seemed to be a washed-out version of its original self, battered by years of brutal heat and light and the occasional hurricane; and still in others, it was peeling in thick curls like so much molting skin. None of them could tell whether these hues and textures of yellow seeping out of fallen beams, exposed pipes and sections of collapsed roof and walls were the result of having faded (as so many things did over the years, they reminded themselves), or whether the shades and textures had been the original and intended ones and had held fast in spite of the years.

"What a shame," Hank said. "Such decay."

"More like neglect," Seth added. "I don't get it. A place like this, on the beach. It's a sin."

"And all the yellows," Honey said. "My favorite color. So warm, so comfortable. A color to slip on and get through another day in. Let's go. Follow me." Like a scout master with her troops, she led them into the house.

In what was once the living room:

"Desiccated," Seth said. "Creepy."

"I can almost feel spirits," Hank said.

"What was Yoni like?" Honey asked Seth.

"Pretty wonderful. Smart, handsome, attentive, energetic, inquisitive. And aware of all his attributes."

"Why did you leave him?"

His shoulders and eyebrows arched upward. "Because the thought of staying with him made me unhappier than the thought of leaving him?"

They climbed the stairs to the second floor. "Watch your step," she said. "The floorboards are creaky."

In what was once the master bedroom:

"Great view," Hank said. "And there's a private balcony."

"It's yours," Honey said.

"What was Glen like?" Seth asked her.

"Once he was handsome and suave. Flirty and wanting to do things. Then the flicker went out in his eyes and he turned into a lump who liked to drink his beer."

"Why did you stay with him?"

"Because I knew what to expect. I was a coward."

Hank eased himself into the hallway.

"Wait for us," she called out.

"Okay," he replied. As they tread carefully down the hallway to visit the other bedrooms, he said to them, "Before it's my turn, I loved my wife. I always did. I always will. I miss her terribly."

They inspected the remaining rooms on the top floor and returned to the ground floor, where they went their separate ways to continue their walk-through until they reunited at the beach in front of the house.

"I say we buy it," she said.

She was met with stone silence. "Can we at least pretend we want to buy it? Inquire? Find out what they're asking?" she asked as she took a photograph of the realtors' signage with her cell phone. "I'll call them today and let you know what happens. Nothing to lose. Game on?"

"I'm game," Seth said.

Hank remained silent.

Honey glanced at Seth. "See that?" she said as she pointed to Hank's face. "The quiet one says it all with his eyes. Look at them. See the sparkle? And now I've made his cheeks turn red. Dear sweet Hank."

They met the real estate agent at four thirty the following afternoon. The sky hung low and gray. They expected the sun to burn it off by late morning, as it usually did this time of year. The damp, dreary celestial overhang persisted, at times releasing a drizzle, at others a short-lived downpour, but not enough to drain itself of the gray so that they could walk through the carcass and feel the effect of full light.

"Why don't you take a walk-through, then we can talk," Dawn said, sending them off with flicks of her wrist so dramatic that they couldn't help but notice the floral decals on the tips of long fingernails. She had no intention of accompanying them through the structure and its perils; she was wearing stiletto heels. She stationed herself on the sidewalk by the front yard, transacting with her cell phone. As soon as her potential clients receded into the house, she let her studied smile and wide eyes relax into the tired air she felt about the whole prospect. Her previous showings had been aborted soon after her clients pulled into the driveway and saw the deplorable condition of the house. Her standard expressions—"Look at the potential!" and "With just a bit of imagination!"—didn't convince any clients to get out of their car and at least show polite interest. She could no longer find it in her to fake enthusiasm about the listing. It was a hopeless dump.

They walked around again, at first exploring together but quickly branching off in order to privately appraise the things that mattered most to them: the mechanics (Hank); the aesthetics (Seth); the "feel" (Honey).

"What a disaster. A total remake, a tear-down," Hank thought.

"It's large and on the ocean. That's about it," Seth thought.

"A redo on the ocean. What more could we want?" Honey thought.

They found themselves regrouped in what was once probably the family room, or great room, or rec room; the space that was the largest and the central access point to the other rooms. They could feel a light mist settling on their heads and looked up toward the hole in the cathedral roof directly above them. They were being drizzled on.

"Yikes," she said.

"Can't argue that," Seth said.

"How can people let something so valuable go to seed?" Hank said.

Honey flipped the hood of her slicker on top of her head and brushed the mist from her brow with her sleeve. "So we're doing it."

"Doing what," Seth asked.

"Making an offer."

The two men forced a laugh, waiting for her to join in. She didn't. She was serious. It made them serious.

"An offer?" Hank asked.

"An offer. On this house. To save it."

"Save it?" he asked.

"Yes, save it."

"Save it," he repeated.

"You're right," she replied. "I stand corrected. To save us."

"We should go," Seth said. "Poor Dawn probably has wads of mascara running down her face from the rain."

They found Dawn pacing the driveway. Her cell phone was still against her ear. With her free hand, she ransacked her handbag and pulled out her business cards. "Here you are," she said to them. "Let me know if you're interested."

"She's not going to be a joy to work with," Honey said. "Clearly she doesn't believe in this place."

"Do you?" Seth asked.

"I do. Do you?"

"I think I could."

She turned to Hank. "And you?"

"I guess I think I could."

Her hair was in her eyes. She pushed it back. "We can let it go and chalk it up to folly. Or we can pursue it in the name of folly. Choose your folly."

Hank and Seth didn't respond.

"A or B?"

Silence.

"Dear God," she said. "And I thought I was stuck." She pulled out her camera. "Don't move," she said as adjusted the lens and snapped a few pictures.

"What are you taking pictures of?" Hank asked.

"The expressions on your faces. Deer caught in headlights."

Seth approached her. "Let me see."

She pulled back. "No. Not yet. Later. After we've settled in. Then I'll show them to you and you can have a good laugh."

"Did you get the house in the background?" Hank asked.

"Yep. Integral to the composition, the theme."

"The theme being?"

"Yep. Old neglected things standing in the sand day after day waiting for something to fall from the sky like a prayer answered."

"*Carpe diem*," Seth said. He turned around to face west. "Look at the sun."

Hank turned around. "It's getting late."

"In that case, you stand corrected," Honey said to Seth. "*Carpe noctem*." She extended her arms. "Hugs and good night."

Carpe noctem. Walking home, she called Dawn and made a lowball offer, which Dawn called her to accept two hours later while she was in the middle of watching "E.R." Honey called Seth first with the news.

"Maybe you should've offered less?"

"Maybe. But maybe it would've been rejected. Then we wouldn't have gotten this place."

"Maybe not," he said.

"But I didn't offer less. And we did get it."

Then she called Hank. "We got it."

"Goodness gracious!" he said.

"Yes," she replied. "You got that right. Goodness and grace."

She cut her conversation with them short. "Let's meet tomorrow morning," she told each of them before hanging up the phone. "The diner. Seven o'clock. My treat. We'll celebrate."

The daily specials were announced on a small chalkboard next to the hostess stand. "Banana walnut pancakes! Chicken-fried steak and eggs!" Exclamation marks framed the offerings, and the printing was almost calligraphic although that it veered slightly downward. They all noticed the downward slope, but Hank was the only one to then imagine how horizontal guidelines etched lightly onto the chalkboard with a T-bar would have prevented it.

They ordered simple fare: scrambled eggs for Honey; eggs over medium for Hank and Seth. Everyone ordered bacon, rye toast and coffee. No juice (the price was high for what was probably concentrate). As soon as the coffee was brought to the table by the server who introduced herself as Deedee, Honey reached for the pink packets of artificial sweetener; Hank and Seth shuffled through the packets and plucked out the granulated sugar. The sound of the three spoons clanging against the three mugs was asynchronous. Hank stirred counter-clockwise.

"What now?" Hank asked.

"We have to arrange for an inspection," she said.

"No. That's soon. I mean now. What now?"

"Oh. You mean like right now? How about you butter your toast so the butter soaks into the nooks and crannies? It tastes so much better that way. Is that what you mean?"

"You know what I mean," Hank said as he peeled the thin aluminum seal off one of the butter pats heaped on a saucer.

"Right. You mean something along the lines of 'Let's be practical.'"

"Yes."

Both of them looked toward Seth.

"I'm here. I'm listening."

She tore open the corner of her second sweetener and let its contents pour into her mug as she stirred clockwise. "Hank, a question for you. Do you want to be practical so you can decide whether to do this? Or do you want to be practical because you've already decided to not do this and you want to figure out how to make this not happen?"

"This is crazy."

"I agree. It is. But I also think it isn't."

Hank took a sip of coffee, waiting for her to continue.

"It'll undo everything that's come our way to give us the life that we've had up till now. That's for sure." She scooped a small, isolated mound of scrambled egg onto her fork. "But is the life we've had up till now the one we want to keep having?"

Seth swallowed a piece of bacon. "Forgive me, Honey, but are you really that unhappy?"

"Seth, please," Hank said.

"It's fine," she said, looking at Seth. "You could be right. Or maybe it has nothing to do with happiness. Hell if I know. But here I am, alive and breathing and having to listen to the same question that's inside every breath I take: 'Now what?' C'mon guys. You know the refrain. 'Now what?' I hear it a million times a day, like a radio ad for something that can't be good for you insisting that it's good for you."

Deedee rounded the corner, arm extended to the fullest to accommodate the three oval platters. Hank noticed a tattoo on her upper arm, between the second and third platter. It looked like an egret. The middle platter was in the way of what would have been the head of the winged creature, so he couldn't be sure. "Here you go," she said. "Top off your coffees?"

Before they could respond by word or gesture, Deedee put down their plates and pivoted away from them, scurrying to return with a pitcher of coffee, which she poured first into Honey's mug. None of them wanted to have their coffee topped off. They didn't want to make an issue out of it. It's what Deedee was trained to do. As she filled Seth's mug, he wondered how many times a day she asked the question, "Top off your coffees?"

"Can I get you anything else?" She pivoted again, figuring that at this point there wasn't anything they could ask for. The steaming platters were in front of them, their coffee mugs were full, and every condiment they could possibly need or desire was positioned on their table. She could forget about them for a while and move on.

"Tabasco?" Seth called out.

She turned. "Excuse me?"

"Tabasco please, Deedee," he repeated.

"Sure thing."

"What do you put Tabasco on?" Hank asked.

"Nothing, usually." Seth said. "She just seemed so programmed. I wanted to rattle her. Keep her on her toes. Test her sincerity. I can be difficult."

Hank salted his eggs. "Okay." He would have preferred his eggs to be less cooked. Seth thought they weren't cooked enough. Honey didn't judge. They ate heartily.

"My late husband's best friend has a brother who does home inspections," Honey said. "We're still in touch. I can call him."

"Sure," Seth said. "I'm the newcomer on the block. I leave it to you. What do I know about these things?" Stirring his coffee mug vigorously, he thought to himself "What do I know about most things, after all?" as he watched sweet and docile Hank, whose eyebrows didn't sink or arch to reveal anything underneath his gentle way of being. He kept his gaze on Hank, waiting to see how he'd respond. How could Hank manage to be honest and simple this time?

"Okay," Hank said.

Honey insisted on paying the check and they left. After the inspection revealed nothing serious beyond a need to update the electric in the kitchen area, they went to contract. All parties agreed to a closing three months out. No one was in a hurry. The seller was already settled elsewhere with no debts that required the sale of the house to pay them off; the three buyers preferred to take possession once the days became longer and warmer. Yes, a bit of time for them to ready themselves to put their initials and signatures to the many pages of the bill of sale that would certify their commitment to ending one way of getting through their days and embarking on a new way. In the interim, they yanked out choice hibiscus, firecracker and acacia from their respective properties (which they put on the market straight away) and transplanted them in the unarticulated mess of their new property, like buoys in a vast sea of sameness that they could cling to, catch their breath on, and proceed to dredge up the residual muck that had settled way down at the bottom of the layers of years they'd lived in order to discover some deposits of happiness.

After Honey paid the check, but before they left, Hank gathered up three of the red-and-white striped peppermint candies heaped in a dish by the cash register and extended his open hand toward them.

"You're a dear," Honey said. "I'm not much for peppermint. Love butterscotch, though."

"I can't eat candy in the morning," Seth said. "The sweet aftertaste goes on too long. Thanks anyway."

Hank squirreled them into the pocket of his shorts. He'd finish them by day's end. He had a weakness for hard candy, especially peppermint. In her later years, Marilyn was the one to do the squirreling. He could count on her to extract a hard candy from her purse at any time. She liked peppermint best too. In fact, he thought as he opened one of the three wrappers in his pocket, she was the one who got him in the habit of popping one into his mouth. "Have a peppermint, dear," she said to him, "You look so dour." She knew their power to take the edge off whatever it was that might be slicing into him. Pizza, on the other hand, was a self-professed weakness of his. Marilyn wasn't especially fond of it. "Too heavy. Gives me heartburn," she said. He came upon the idea of baking his own pizza after she died. When he slipped the pizza into the oven, he sometimes asked himself, "Am I taking revenge on her dying by doing one of the many silly things that we didn't meet eye to eye on?" At other times, "Am I proving to her that I'm a whole person in my own right, with or without her?" Most of the time, he was able to pull the pizza from the oven before the crust was burnt at the edges.

He fastened his seatbelt and popped a peppermint in his mouth. As its coolness spread through this mouth and hit the gumline above his molars, he considered inviting Honey and Hank over for a home-made pizza dinner before the time came for him to box up the contents of his kitchen for the move.

36

In this shared home, sharing was to be happenstance: passing each other in the hallway; settling down in the living room on whatever sofa or chair of theirs had found a spot there; sitting over a meal at the kitchen table; or mulling about in the back or front yard to examine a plant or check the mailbox. (Seth continued his subscription to the Washington Post, delivered to the driveway each morning; Hank received USA Today; Honey settled on the freebies—the local newsletters and coupon-laden circulars that arrived mid-week.) At night, when they felt the pull of slumber, they would safely pad off to their separate spaces to conduct their rituals of solitary intimacy—reflection, fantasy, hygiene—and their long-crafted ways of turning down the blanket and top sheet, of positioning the pillows and the body for a night of fitful or dream-saturated sleep, without the distractions of a person on the other side of the bed.

Their families thought they were crazy to live together. Not the kind of crazy to require a pow-wow and action plan of intervention, but crazy nonetheless.

"You're crazy," they said when the news of the move was announced.

"Maybe," their elders replied.

"Dad, don't you think you're jumping into this too fast?" Aurora asked.

"Is there a right speed?" Honey replied.

"Dad, how can you think about selling the house to do this?" Jonathan asked.

"Don't you think I thought about it a lot?" Hank replied.

"What on earth are you thinking about?" Yoni asked his ex.

"What right do you have to care anymore about what I think?" Seth replied.

For the most part, they were able to hold their own during these interrogations. Their ambivalence was at its most acute when it came to the fact of the sunrise and their no longer arriving at it on their own, at their own pace, anticipating with relish the break in the silence as they spotted the others in the distance and knew that an embrace was soon about to take place followed by the hum of their interaction and the feeling of a safety net having been spread beneath them as the sun's first rays stretched above them. No. Instead, they would be setting off together from their collective home to witness the spectacle of the sunrise, perhaps chatting along the few steps it would take them to reach the spot that they'd arrived at alone. The slow convergence would be eliminated. The journey would no longer carry the weight of their solitude and the reward of their coming together in a snug triangle. This new way of bearing witness to the sun rising might become too easy, almost irreverent, they thought, and the ease of it risked blunting the sharp edge of need that had brought them together in the first place.

Not one of the children could find it in them resort to the obvious alternative: "Come live with us." Not that Honey or Hank would have agreed to such a proposal. But the asking would have meant the world to them. Out of the mouth of babes. The proposal was never put forth, and it broke their hearts a little more. It also fortified their resolve.

They held firm. They visited the construction site each day to make sure that what was taking shape made sense. Sometimes they arrived at the same time, sometimes alone. They didn't schedule meetings. They felt comfortable in the arbitrariness of their individual and joint visits, however and whenever they took place. It gave them a fleeting sense of freedom to come and go and do as they pleased. It rained a lot. They looked for rainbows whenever the sun poked out. The area was known for rainbows, sometimes double ones. One had only to look skyward when a downpour was petering out to a drizzle with snatches of sunshine to behold a rainbow arc thrusting from some faraway piece of earth to the left, reaching its apex high in the sky, and cascading into some faraway chunk of earth to the right. Where did it end, they asked themselves. How did it end? Did it end?

They weren't bogged down by discussions over where to place the electrical outlets or what type of roofing or window treatment was best. They left these matters to the men they paid to show up, make an expert assessment, and execute the work. What was important to them was that they could bring into this new place a generous number of objects that carried their histories, regardless of how heavy, dark or downright ugly they were. So many of them would need to be relinquished to Goodwill or Craig's List., however large the windows may be, whatever tiles would be laid in the kitchen and living room, wherever the air handler and washer and dryer hook-ups would be located and hidden behind whatever kinds of doors. It was a question of determining how to select the ones that would make the cut and how to let go of all the others.

Day after day they went. With each visit, their sense of how unorthodox the enterprise was culled. After several weeks, the daily visits took on the aspect of just one more standard item to be dealt with in the course of a typical day: call cardiologist; water plants on front porch; pay water bill; defrost something to make for dinner; check progress of the new house. They functioned well with routines, and this particular task could be performed at any time that was convenient for them: in the early morning, during the mid-afternoon lull, or even late in the day. Gradually they began to converge toward sunset, when they could take stock of the day's progress together and perhaps nab a construction worker as he was respooling an extension cord or sweeping sawdust into a corner of what would be a room, in order to ask: "Is that where the microwave is going to go?," "How many stairs will there need to be?," "What is that hole for?" Simple questions with simple answers: "Yes, ma'am," "Ten or so," "To run the wiring." They didn't want to ask too many questions at dusk. The workers were calling it a day. They had families to go home to. Especially at this time of day, when darkness was slowly swallowing up the surfaces and objects that the workers had been laboring over for hours for the benefit of three people they didn't know. Once the workers were heading toward their pick-ups, they refrained from asking them anything. But they watched them nevertheless, refusing to turn away from them and toward each other, where they risked seeing a facial expression that might reveal a far more overriding question: "What in God's name are we doing?"

* * * *

Winter gave way to spring. The sweep of beach in front of the house widened as the cold winds and rain that caused the waves to eat away at it subsided. Sea grapes and sea grass along the dunes had begun to spread their branches and tendrils toward the ocean, creating a buffer zone of vegetation between the sand and the line of condos. The exterior walls of the house were completed. They agreed on a kiwi green. A new shingle roof and rain gutters were installed, the front and back yards seeded for new vegetation, the surviving clusters of trees and shrubs were encircled by scatterings of rust-colored mulch to indicate a work in progress. Any passerby would think that this was a house that was lived in, although inside its facade were the unending finishing touches to be given here and there and that enabled them to put off moving in and arranging their furniture, hanging their towels on towel racks, laying out their kitchen appliances on countertops. They didn't pressure the construction workers about the detail work. They grew used to watching the mess veer toward something habitable, but they were terrified of cohabiting it.

All of them had dining room tables, which made perfect sense, since each of their houses had a dining room, the room that was reserved for special occasions, so special that they didn't take place more than twice a year. They agreed to use Seth's table, which, like all three dining room tables, could seat six comfortably, eight in a pinch. Its frame was teak, its top an opaque glass that gave off an aquamarine hue. It didn't make a statement.

"I love my dining room table," Honey said. "It was my grandmother's. My mother inherited it from her, and it got passed on to me. It's on the ugly side, I know. Too dark and curly. But you know, you're supposed to find space for these things, even if they're ugly and clunky. Or you can also decide that the meaning they carry doesn't have to be as meaningful as you're trying to make it have, right? Your table is perfect, Seth."

"Your table will work well, Seth," Hank said. "Mine is too small. It used to have leaves, but they got warped from being stored in the garage most of the time. I don't even know if they work anymore. Let's go with yours."

The glass top of Seth's dining room table reflected the window that reflected the ocean, which the table seemed meant to do, even if it didn't do so in Seth's house, which wasn't close enough to the ocean. It made the new dining room seem liquid, and it made them hold tightly on to the solidity of their forks and knives when they sat at the table to eat a meal. (They opted for Hank's utensils, which were sturdy and nondescript.) They took turns cooking. They looked forward to the culinary offerings that each of the others prepared. Hank tried oysters for the first time, after Seth bought two dozen at a nearby seafood outlet that Hank didn't know existed, even though he liked seafood. Honey learned from Hank that rubbing raw egg whites on dinner rolls before baking them created that appealing glaze. Seth no longer derided a simple hamburger, after he watched Honey stir two teaspoons of minced onion, a sprig of freshly chopped rosemary and a dash of "Dr. Assburn" into the ground meat, transforming the burger into something more than comfort food to be scarfed down with only one objective in mind: to feel full. Most importantly, each of them thought, was the luxury of not having to think about preparing a meal every night—preparing it alone, eating it alone, and having no one to hand the dishes to stack them in the dishwasher. The new arrangement struck each of them as being some kind of divine and illicit pleasure, like going out for dinner without having to actually go out for it. The evening meal was looked forward to from day one. It guaranteed a snippet of company, at a time of day, sunset, when the ingredients of solitude had a nasty habit of combining to produce something thicker and heavier than they'd hoped for.

 The call to table—"Dinner's ready!"—would signal an end to solitude. A blessed call. Each time, once they were seated at the table, Hank delivered a simple but heartfelt prayer. Honey closed her eyes and listened as if a blessing over something as matter of fact as dinner was something she was experiencing for the first time. Seth allowed his eyes to flutter open during the prayer, unable to resist glancing at them to see if he was the only one incapable of being immersed in this a brief dialogue with God and his Son.

> *May the God of peace*
> *Bring peace to this house.*
> *May the Son of peace*
> *Bring peace to this house.*
> *May the Spirit of peace*
> *Bring peace to this house,*
> *This night and all night.*
> *Bless this house and those within,*
> *Bless our giving and receiving,*
> *Bless our words and conversation,*
> *Bless our hands and recreation,*
> *Bless our sowing and our growing,*
> *Bless our coming and our going,*
> *Bless all who enter and depart,*
> *Bless this house, your peace impart.*
> *Bless us, O Lord, and these Thy gifts, which we are*
>   *about the receive from Thy bounty. Through*
>   *Christ, our Lord. Amen.*

Seth opened his eyes fully to watch Honey and Hank make the sign of the cross. They performed the sequence of up-down-across with their hands automatically, as if it were little more than the reflex of those who sweep the shock of hair that continually falls over one eye. How to learn this language, how to become fluent in it, he thought. How many languages can I take on? One evening, he decided, he'd offer to share a Jewish prayer with them, bringing out the yarmulkas and Tanakh that were among the items he'd selected to bring to the new house with even if he couldn't remember the last time he'd used them.

* * * *

Peaches were his maiden offering to them when they all arrived at the house for their first day together in it. Seth chose them carefully at the supermarket from among the display of what were labeled as loose, tree-ripened Georgia peaches; most of them were hard as rocks. At the check-out, he placed them on the conveyor belt behind the canvas grocery bag that he brought with him whenever and wherever he went grocery shopping. He made sure to place his canvas bag first on the belt so that the cashier would see it coming and not have to ask him, "Is plastic okay?" He wondered what the alternatives would be if he were to respond, "Actually, it's not okay."

After the peaches, he placed a package of ground sirloin and a package of boneless chicken breasts on the belt. When they arrived at the scanner, the cashier asked him, "Would you like your meat in separate plastic?"

He knew that store regulations required the question to be asked when it came to meat. "But it's already wrapped in plastic." He pointed to the ground sirloin and the chicken breasts. "See?"

He arrived at the house in the late afternoon, in time to watch the last of the construction workers pack up and leave for their last scheduled day of work. They'd completed the items on the latest punch list. In time, he knew, the men would be called back to take care of minor glitches that would emerge, much like the skin rashes that had erupted on his arms and legs the first time he introduced his body to the eating of peanuts. Objects had the right to rebel against change too, he supposed; but even if that happened, their house was beyond a reasonable doubt ready to be relocated into and breathed inside of day in and day out, until the end of their days, despite whatever allergic reactions might come about.

He removed the peaches from the canvas bag and arranged them in the wicker basket he included among his belongings to be moved to the house. The basket had no sentimental value. In fact, he didn't remember where it came from or how or when it had been used. It held no particular aesthetic value either, at least not one that would be commented on by anyone who happened to notice it.

When the canvas bag was empty, he set the wicker basket dead center on the deep sill of the picture window in the dining room. There, he thought, stepping back to consider whether he should try to replicate the way the supermarket staff had arranged the fruit into a perfect pyramid. No. The asymmetry of the peaches in the basket made its own statement, much like the haphazard cascade of candies that Hank had poured into a dish as his first offering, bless his heart. Moreover, he realized, the delicate mounting of a pyramid of rounded fruit presented the risk of one or more of the peaches tumbling to the floor, ruining the composition and creating bruises on the fruit that would drip onto the spanking new tiles. He had no idea whether anyone had thought to bring paper towels or sponges to sop up such effluvia and, if they had, where they might have put them. Details. So many of them to be understood and made familiar.

Hank was moved by Seth's basket of peaches on the sill. What it cradled was so perishable, unlike the assortment of hard peppermint, butterscotch and lemon candies that he'd heaped in a cobalt-blue glass dish festooned with soft curves and curly-cues. He couldn't not bring the dish with him, after all the trouble he'd gone to take it from his grandparents' house (after his grandmother's open-casket wake was winding down) to the scrappy apartment he lived in during his bachelor days, and then to the house that he and Marilyn lived in. The dish wasn't used until Marilyn discovered it sitting on a shelf in the garage.

"What is this doing here?" she asked him.

"It was my grandmother's."

Marilyn brought it into the house like an abandoned puppy and set about filling it with an assortment of hard candies, which she placed in the dish one by one. Hank wondered whether his grandmother had to regularly replenish the dish or whether there was no need to since visitors didn't actually take a candy. They probably thought it would be such a shame it to ruin the arrangement and, besides, where would they discard the wrapper? Looking at the candy dish, which was now his candy dish to do with as he pleased, he understood how little he knew of his grandmother beyond her sweet, stooped and fatigued presence that deserved respect and forbearance. She was an elder. What did a candy dish matter? Who would notice it? Who would care? Here, in this new house, vying with fresh peaches for a respectable place, the candy dish seemed antiquated, uprooted from another time and style that no longer meant much of anything besides quaintness. He felt embarrassed as he placed the dish on the kitchen counter, hoping that its awkward presence would be understood by Honey and Seth, no youngsters themselves, and find its way to a permanent spot in the house, where he could count on it being his job to replenish it as part of a new routine that would confer responsibility upon him each day until it was time for bed.

As he placed the dish on the counter, he wondered where in the house it would end up and which flavor of candy would be the first to go. "Let me know if there are other kinds you like," he said to them. So many details. So much new routine to create and rely on to hold him together. To hold the three of them together in this new way of being.

"Butterscotch!" Honey cried, barely noticing the other candies scattered among the golden disks in their golden wrappers. "I hope you keep a good stash," she said, grabbing a candy, popping it into her mouth, and feeling the sticky residue as it made its way down her throat and repainted the places it had been stirred into or spread on top of when she was a child: butterscotch pudding, butterscotch sauce, butterscotch krimpets, butterscotch apples. How it quelled a small slice of her neediness and, as she thought about popping another one into her mouth, gave the adults a reprieve from that particular slice of her neediness. She had no idea what butterscotch was made from, but it was never in anything she didn't like and wanted more of, whatever it was made from.

On this, their first day together in the house, she didn't bring food. She enjoyed food and cooking. She was a woman, a wife, a mother, and understood the power that managing the kitchen conferred. She also understood the narrow confines of that kitchen power. It was a secondary power, a kind of consolation prize bestowed upon her as a woman, a wife and a mother by a man who worked hard all day and expected to kick back and have a good meal when the workday was over. She held sway in the kitchen throughout her marriage. The kitchen was the one room in the house where she had absolute domain. She set the rules there: what to prepare for a meal, how to place the dishes and silverware in the dishwasher, what needed replenishing on the shelves of pantry, refrigerator and freezer. In the first few years following their honeymoon in the Bahamas, Glen made a point of looking at her across the table during dinner to say, "This is delicious, honey. Just what the doctor ordered." He also made sure to accompany the praise with the sparkle in his eye that signaled a dose of love-making that night.

In the domain of the bedroom, she deferred to some of his needs. It was a shared space, after all. She chose the sheets and blankets; he ruled over what took place beneath them. She didn't mind so much. She enjoyed sex and the private connection it gave them without having to use words to pull them into intimacy. But after the first few post-Bahama years, he stopped turning his head to look at her intently after he'd rolled on his back to catch his breath when the sex was over. His need for relief had been satisfied and he wanted to drift away from her, possibly far far away. He seemed so distant once his heavy breathing leveled off. Just like in the kitchen, when he wiped his mouth after the last forkful of dessert, placed his crumpled napkin on the table, and rose to retreat into a room in the house that was away from her. She could feel it after each meal and sexual encounter, this turning away from her. The power and the prison of kitchen and bedroom.

"Men do this," she thought with a shrug of her shoulders and a cocking of her head each time she watched Glen withdraw from her with a sense of urgency, repugnance almost. She asked herself whether, if they'd both had a bit more patience and courage and trust in each other, he could have gotten into the swing of cooking from time to time, or of holding her close to him after the spasms of their sex had subsided and they'd burrowed back into themselves. She didn't push, and he didn't offer. He steered clear of the kitchen until he heard the clattering of plates and cutlery being laid out on the table. In the bedroom, he was the first to lie down on the mattress, and each night as she entered the bedroom from the hallway or from the en suite bathroom, she didn't know what position she would find him in: under or over the sheets, in pajamas or buff, turned on his side or splayed on his back, eyes open or shut. In whatever configuration she found him, she quickly understood what he wanted from her, what he expected from her. And she deferred to him.

Here, in the new house with these two men, she knew how easy it would be for her to claim the kitchen as her territory simply by virtue of being a woman. Her simple rearrangement of a potholder was probably all that would be needed for them to cede the kitchen to her. This time she didn't have to stake such a claim. These two men spent years living by themselves and feeding themselves. They were on intimate terms with kitchens. The kitchen—this kitchen—didn't need to delimit her powers this time. She could choose, and she was undecided. On this, their first day together, she opted against bringing a food offering. She needed more time to contemplate power, prisons, kitchens. She brought something else, which she left in the back seat of her car. She could bring it into the house later. It wasn't perishable.

"Anybody here?" she called as she entered the house.

"In the kitchen," a voice called out. She couldn't tell whether it was Seth or Hank. She entered the kitchen as Seth was positioning his basket of fruit and Hank his dish of candy.

"Be right back," she said to them after they'd stepped back from their home-warming contributions and appeared satisfied. She went to her car to fetch her offering: a framed and matted photograph of the sun rising over the ocean and silhouetting three human figures who might be them or might not be them, but was still about them, as three and as one. She set it on Seth's three-seater leather sofa that they agreed would be the sofa for the living room.

"Beautiful shot, Honey," Seth said. "Is it of us? Is that me in the middle?"

"I think that's me on the left," Hank said. "Look at the drooping shoulders. They're my shoulders for sure."

She considered revealing who was who. She considered challenging them too: if she was the photographer, how could she be the third silhouette that they'd shown complete indifference to? Or if she was the third silhouette, how could she have been the photographer? She didn't take up either challenge. "You guys can decide where to hang it," she said. It didn't matter. The larger matter of the kitchen had been resolved.

They set about hauling furniture and contents of unpacked boxes here and there, testing different locations as they bantered with each other and let their gazes linger on the faces of the others to discern any reactions that might signify impatience or irritation. It was too soon. For dinner, they ordered from a nearby Chinese restaurant that delivered. They were conservative in their selections, which they'd agreed to spread on the table for everyone to share: wonton soup, egg rolls, stir-fried chicken with vegetables, beef with broccoli, shrimp and lobster sauce. Included in their order were three fortune cookies in a wax paper bag at the top of the brown paper bag holding the meal, along with slender packets of soy, hot mustard and duck sauce. Seth offered to slice peaches for dessert while Honey and Hank unloaded the bag onto the table. He wanted a few minutes to privately guess which one of them might use the duck sauce for something and which one of them might actually know what duck sauce was. He hadn't a clue. He'd tried duck sauce twice, and there was nothing duck-like about it. Maybe one of them knew. He'd have to remember to ask.

By the time they arrived at the peaches, they were struggling to remain engaged in the meal, the conversation, the company. It had been a long day. They were tired. All they wanted to do was retreat to their beds, but they were apprehensive about the comfort that their beds could offer them in rooms that were unfamiliar to them. As they went about setting up the basics of the house earlier, they relished setting up their bedrooms, where they made a point of putting on sheets, pillowcases and blankets whose smells and consistencies had enveloped and soothed them for decades. They smoothed the linens out with sweeping motions of open palms, as they always did when they made up their bedroom. In these untried bedrooms, however, their fealty to the ritual of smoothing out linens offered little comfort, what with the strange hallway to navigate in order to arrive at their bedroom, the alien scent of the bedroom, and the pitch of the light coming in from windows that looked out on nightscapes whose darkness was altogether different from the darkness they'd gone to sleep under for so long so as to seem like a vast and permanent ally in their struggle to ward off the bogeymen, the monsters, the demons and all the other creepy voices that came to life at night to undermine the composure that had accrued during the day. Faced with a bowl of peaches or the prospect of confronting their bedrooms, they lingered at the table longer than they wanted to, each waiting for one of the others to ask to be excused or to just rise up and be brave enough to confront the new corridor and the private space it would confer to the left or to the right. As they spooned out the peaches, Honey was feeling the limits of her fatigue, the banter. One of them had to end. She considered excusing herself. Instead, she looked at Hank. So folded into himself, she thought.

"Do you miss your wife?"

"Yes. I do. Very much."

"What do you miss most?"

Hank closed his eyes as if in prayer. He didn't mind taking a moment or two to reflect. Silence in company didn't make him feel uncomfortable. Silence was as much a part of conversation as the words that interrupted it. Honey fixed her gaze on him, waiting for a reply. Seth slowly raised his glass and brought it to his mouth to take a sip of wine that he didn't want.

"Everything."

"What might you not miss all that much?"

As he was closing his eyes again, he said, "I'd say..." and here he paused. As he was opening them again, he added, "Nothing."

With someone else, she would have thought him evasive, cowardly, and probably would have egged him on. With him, she believed in his truth, his simplicity. Truth lies in simplicity, she reminded herself.

Seth put down his glass and looked at Honey. "And you? Do you miss Glen?"

"Of course I do," she said directly into his eyes, which were watching hers. Then she lowered her head toward her peaches, which she started stirring with a vigor that made a rasping sound as the teaspoon chafed the bottom of the bowl. "But in some respects I don't think so. Deep down."

"Yes and no. That's reasonable. In which proportions?"

She decelerated her stirring "I never thought about it in those terms. Too mathematical. I'm not good at math. I don't trust it."

"Maybe you don't trust it because you're not good at it." He wanted to kick himself in the teeth. "Sorry. What do I know about you and math?"

"I miss...the steady presence of another person in my life."

"You don't like being alone?"

"I don't mind. In fact, I like being alone as long as I know someone is there in the wings to stop it when I'm not liking it anymore."

"Like a pain killer."

"Maybe."

"And the 'I don't miss' part"?

She scooped two wedges of peach onto her spoon and brought them to her mouth. "Everything else, I guess." The peaches were sweet, but could have been sweeter, she thought.

"Wow. That's a lot to not miss."

"I guess."

"Sorry. I didn't mean to pry."

"Of course you did. Why else would you have asked? It's okay. We live here now. Together. Things are bound to come out. They should come out. It's good."

Seth dipped into the peaches. "I guess it's my turn. Goodness, I deserve it. Who wants to ask?"

Honey and Hank looked at each other.

"Hmmm. No takers. I'll consider the question to have been asked," Seth said. "Only fair." He put his spoon down onto his plate of peaches. "I miss a lot. I'm not sure whether what I miss is about who he was or whether it's about what I think we could have been. And then the long list of 'if only' kicks in. That's where I get lost."

Hank looked at him. "I don't understand."

"Wanna know something, Hank? I don't think I do, either. We expect too much from others because we want too much from them. Especially from the person who ends up being the special other. I'm a list-maker and I'm good at math. I keep a tab of my satisfactions and dissatisfactions on a mental scorecard. I know, it sounds so transactional. I can't help it. We can't help but be certain ways. Our ways of keeping track of things, taking stock of things, judging the progress of things, finding blame for shortcomings or downright failure of things. Don't tell me you don't have lists."

"I keep a grocery list," Honey said. "On the door of the refrigerator. A post-it stuck on the freezer door and a pencil attached to a string taped on the door."

"Chores for the day," Hank said. "I write them down the night before, after I've brushed my teeth." He put his elbow on the table and rested his chin on his fist. His eyes were cast downward.

"You look like Rodin's 'The Thinker,'" Seth said.

"What's that?"

"Not a 'what', a 'who.' Rodin is a, was a...Never mind. Sorry to interrupt. You were about to say something."

"No. I was finished." He finished his last peach wedge, deposited his spoon on his plate, and clasped his hands in prayer to mark the end of the meal. *"Lord, evermore give us that bread and wisdom to labor less for the meat which perisheth, and more for that which endures to everlasting life. The Lord give food to the hungry and send portions to them for* whom nothing is prepared. Let us be of those blessed ones that shall eat bread in the kingdom of God and shall eat of the hidden manna."

"Amen," Honey said.

"Not yet. There's more, but not much." He continued. "*O give thanks unto the Lord, for He is good; for His mercy endureth forever. He giveth food to all flesh; He giveth to the beast his food, and to the young ravens which cry. He delighteth not in the strength of the horse; He taketh not pleasure in the legs of a man. The Lord taketh pleasure in them that fear Him, in those that hope in His mercy. Amen.*"

"Amen," Honey said. She and Seth raised their goblets of wine, Hank his glass of water.

Seth was the first to rise. "I'm going to head off to my room." As he made his way down the first stretch of hallway, he turned to them. "I'm really tired. Long day, you know. Leave the dishes. I insist. I'll get them in the morning. And remind me to ask you something tomorrow too."

"What's that?" Honey asked.

"Just remember 'duck sauce.'"

"Duck sauce?"

"Duck sauce." He continued down the hall. "Good night."

"Good night," they said in unison.

As Honey cleared the table, Hank filled the kitchen sink with hot water and gave a hefty squeeze of the dish liquid bottle to create a sizeable bank of foam. He knew the foam wouldn't last until morning, but he believed in its power to cut grease and grime even after the bubbles had popped and disappeared. Honey released the plates into the water, where they glided in a zig-zag motion until they vanished under the surface of foam and landed at the bottom of the sink without making a noise. The utensils sank with a thud.

"I'll load them in the dishwasher," he said.

"Let's leave them until tomorrow."

Honey dried her hands on the dish towel draped over the oven handle. When she was done, she smoothed out its creases so that the towel would dry through and through, without leaving that musty smell. "I'm turning in too," she said. "Good night, Hank."

"Me too. Good night, Honey." When she was out of view, he loaded the dishes into the dishwasher.

* * * *

Inside the house on this first night, the typology of quiet is what they're used to, and they sleep deeply. Outside the house, only the faintest sound of waves penetrates the double-paned, hurricane-proof windows of their bedrooms, the immensity of water curling and crashing upon itself in a primal exhale before taking in the silent inhale it requires in order to gather up its momentum and repeat the timeless curl and crash along the shore. These undulations of sound and rhythm are the ones they've gone to sleep to for many years, however jarring they might be from time to time, especially during hurricane season. On this first night, they sleep deeply.

Outside the house, it's pitch black. The moon is new; cloud cover obscures the stars. Inside the house, the light is dim: four candle-shaped nightlights plugged into sockets directly above the floor molding; one in the hallway and one in each bathroom. They don't serve to awaken but merely to orient and comfort those who have already been roused by one of a medley of possible sleep disturbances—a dream fragment, a body part that needs to be rotated, a full bladder, residual anxiety—and remind them where they are. A safe place. Home.

Despite the newness of this house, their home, their bedrooms, they take easily to napping in the bright afternoon; and at night, they continue to wake up at their usual hour, well before morning has announced its arrival by a sign of the brightness to come. They are used to giving up on sleep in the still of the night. It ceased bothering them long ago. They've come to know and expect the private disturbances that jolt them to wakefulness when everything is still encased in darkness. Besides, they are retired and can nap midway through the day to take the edge off. They have no set schedule beyond the personal fixations and neuroses that demand a modicum of attention before nightfall. They look forward to their naps. Light doesn't mean safety. Darkness doesn't signal danger. They've lived through many restless days and sleepless nights and have come to understand this. When they wake up in darkness, they don't attempt to coax back sleep. They'll sleep later, when their body cries out for it.

There is something to be gained by getting up at this godforsaken hour between night and day, regardless of their private agitations: a walk along the beach, where they can bear witness to the sun as it blanches the darkness with a gentle fierceness that embodies humility, like a religion that needs not a single word, let alone a predication, to be listened to in order to be believed in.

Hank is the first to toss and turn and finally get out of bed. The larger window faces east, and he is used to cracking open an eye when he stirs and looking out a window facing west. Honey is second to get out of bed. The smell of her room is pleasant enough, but not familiar enough. Seth is last. His bladder is too full to ignore. At different intervals on this first night in the new house, they make their way to their new bathroom (is the sink to the left or the right?). At times, they hear what could be sounds caused by the presence of one of the others, but they pretend that what they are hearing are just the usual sounds of the night: a car, a siren, a soft rustling among palm fronds (opossum? racoon?), a distant crash of thunder. They don't want human contact. It is something to be avoided at this hour. It's too early in the morning, or too late at night, to find oneself brushing up against another person and having to engage. They've learned this, too, through their many years of being coupled and their many years of being alone. They've learned to cherish the absolute silence and darkness of this hour and its way of preparing them to cope with the light and the noisy enterprise and activity that will ensue, even if "activity" for a particular day may only consist of having to take a shirt to the dry cleaner and stick the receipt on the refrigerator door in order to remember to pick it up in two days. Blind and deaf at this hour. Alone and entirely within and unto themselves until shapes begin to make themselves out in the darkness, sounds begin to articulate themselves in the silence, and they say to themselves, "It's the beginning of another day. Already?"

Hank slips on the clothes for the day that he set on a chair before going to bed. A decades-old habit, this need to select his attire for the next day and lay it out on the chair after he has listened to the weather forecast before switching off the television to go to bed. He likes to be in some degree of readiness when he rises to greet the onset of another day. The weather forecast gives him a sense of preparedness for things out of his control; and his choice of clothing gives him a sense of control. For years he has laid out his clothes on a Shaker chair that belonged to his in-laws. The chair is too large for the new bedroom, but he has positioned it at a diagonal in the corner, where it works.

Before leaving the house, he grabs his pocket New Testament and nestles it into the side pocket of his jacket, where it juts out because of the layers of Kleenex that he keeps in the same pocket and that eventually settle to the bottom. He goes out the side door. It gives onto a narrow path that the construction workers created with white pebbles. The path leads to the driveway; the driveway to the main road. He crosses the main road and walks in the direction of the house he lived in before the move, the same house he lived in with his wife and, once upon a time, with his wife and their two boys. He's not sure whether he'll walk by it, but he wants to be tempted to. "I'm such a sentimental fool," he thinks to himself. He cries easily. It bothers him and it doesn't. Crying is a good thing, a healthy thing, he believes, and when he is sentimental the tears flow without censure, which must be a very healthy thing, he believes. It does feel uncomfortable, though. And embarrassing sometimes.

He pulls out his pocket Bible and pages through it until he finds the psalm he is looking for: 127. *"Unless the Lord builds the house, its builders labor uselessly. Unless the Lord guards the city, its security forces keep watch uselessly."* That's enough, he decides. I won't go there. I don't live there. He turns left at the intersection and continues walking along a residential street that is parallel to the beach. He has walked this street before, but not often, and never in the dark. In the dark, nothing there presents itself as something he's familiar with.

Honey is second. From her bathroom, she hears stirrings down the hall as she studies herself in the mirror to see if the lighting she has selected is flattering. Not particularly, she thinks, but who am I kidding? Look at me! By the time she has bent over, splashed warm water on her face and turned off the spigot, the hallway stirrings have stopped. They don't alarm her, but she doesn't know what they are. One thing she knows they aren't: Glen waking up one of the two or three times in the night to pee. That ritual of sound is over and done with, she reminds herself as she dries her face on the bath towel and realizes she has to navigate the hallway with its unfamiliar stirrings. "I can't stay in the bathroom all night," she says to herself. She holds tight until an interval of silence passes that is long enough to convince her that she's safe to leave the bathroom and go down the hallway to the back door. She grabs her small camera, tucks it inside her blouse, steps into the darkness and takes a gulp of night air. "Whew. I made it!"

The beach is in front of her, but she turns away from it abruptly, as if in an act of rebellion, and walks down the driveway toward the road. Unlike Hank, she takes a right and heads toward the main drag, where the shops and restaurants will have closed long ago but where the street is brightly lit twenty-four-seven. It should be relatively safe there for a woman walking at night, she hopes. Oh, to be a big burly man, she thinks. I could go wherever I like whenever I like. But she wouldn't want to be a man, she realizes. Burly or otherwise. It would mean giving up pregnancy, being colonized by another human being, giving birth to it, loosening the grip as it transformed into the adult, and then letting go. Like with her children. Accomplished adults. Adults she admired. And so much her doing, although she strived for humility. No, she wouldn't give it up for anything, even if it meant feeling safe to walk around at night wherever and whenever she liked, even in a place as small as an unfamiliar hallway in an unfamiliar place that she'll have to learn to think of as her home.

She's not taken many photos at night. She prefers the sun and the way it fiddles with defined surfaces of objects: a person, a building, a bird, a shell, a tree. At this hour, there is little in the way of definition, and she feels in the mood to see what that can inspire. "Dare I?", she asks herself as she turns away from the beach and heads toward the bustling and peopled stretch of town, even if it will be empty at this hour.

Seth is third. He leaves by the front door. Winston is by his side as he turns the doorknob gently in order to ward off any creakings it might make during its rotation. "I don't know this doorknob," he tells himself. "I don't want to wake the others." The dog cocks his head. "I know, buddy. This is new. This is different. We're going for a walk at this hour. We're being stealthy." The dog cocks his head again. "I know, buddy. You don't get it." He fastens the leash to Winston's collar. "I don't either." Winston forges ahead to the Bismarck palm in the front yard, where he lifts his leg to mark his turf. He looks up at his master contented. Seth cocks his head. How can contentment arrive so simply?

"Which way?" he asks himself. "Does it matter?" He lets Winston make the decision. At the end of the driveway, the dog turns right. He is resolute about it, as if he possesses an extra-sensory perception that can't be bothered with the torment of reflection. Seth is envious. Not that he knows what the dog is thinking. Perhaps nothing at all. In his wildest imaginings, he can't imagine what it's like to think nothing, although he suspects that thinking nothing is probably the best way to go about thinking. The absence of thought. Pure being. Something like that. In the few moments it takes for him to arrive at the end of the driveway and feel Winston pull him toward the right, the darkness has already lined up its usual cast of potential characters—from bad (cash-strapped thugs lurking behind bushes or dumpsters), to neutral (unpopulated stretches ahead) to good (sex-craving men loitering around bushes or dumpsters, although he wouldn't dare approach them, but still). If it wasn't for Winston, he wouldn't know which way to turn.

He bends over to pass his hand back and forth along Winston's back as a reward for his decisiveness and to see whether, as he bends over, the ache in his lower vertebrae has eased up. He's been careful not to bend over lately. It usually does the trick. There is no pain and Winston takes in the stroking with a look of utter bliss. How long would Winston stand there delighting in the back rub? Probably forever, he thought.

Turning right at the end of the driveway, he recalls the brief interval of time (in New York, before Yoni, but just as exotic although in a different way) that he spent with Newell DeValpine and her husband Rolf. Their names alone emitted the stench of breeding, of pedigree, of wealth. And wealth they had, so much of it that the concept of money was an abstraction for them. They spent three hours every Saturday in Central Park, each of them clutching a copy of the Oxford Concise English Dictionary until they arrived at a shady spot and could sit down, place their copy on their lap, and choose words at random by closing their eyes while their index finger grazed against the entries on a page. When they opened their eyes, they would stop their grazing, look at the word their finger had landed on, and announce it out loud, waiting to see which one of them would be the first to define the word. He spent his Saturday mornings at the laundromat stuffing enough soiled clothes into available machines to ensure that he wouldn't need to return there until the following Saturday. "Recherché," "atavistic," "senescence". They shared their word landings with him on their Sunday meetings with him over brunch or an afternoon cocktail—"Delightful to see you again," they told him for each Sunday encounter—which was brief because the DeValpines always had another engagement to scurry off to. He wondered what words they didn't share with him. Surely their fingers must have landed on blander items: "the," "brick," "do." He lost touch with them decades ago and discovered that both died recently. He doesn't remember how he found out or how they died, only that Newell died a few months after Rolf did. It must have been difficult for her to lose such a companion. He couldn't imagine an intimacy so deep that dictionary outings could be as routine as grocery shopping. But then again, he supposed, they were rich enough to do whatever they wanted and whenever they wanted. Even so, they ended up being dead in their sixties. So much for wealth, breeding and pedigree. He feels a twinge of comeuppance as his sweet simple dog tugs on the leash, eager to continue exploring new terrain at an hour when he is usually nuzzled against the side of his master in bed. Seth follows his lead. He wants away from the new house, even at this hour. Not that he isn't satisfied with the new arrangement of his life. "It feels right," he thinks, but there are certain details that make him pause. Some of them are new, like the handrails in the showers. They are chrome and have a sleek satin finish, which he chose himself; nevertheless, the showers now have handrails on three of the four walls. Handrails! And then there are many objects that aren't new, the ones they've brought with them and positioned here and there to prevent them from being unfastened entirely from the long stretch of life lived so far.

Winston is pulling on the leash, bent on quickening the pace. As Seth accelerates, he is aware of the flesh under his biceps, buttocks and knees. It no longer retains its tautness when he walks briskly. He can feel his skin flapping and wonders whether this walk in the dark is just some last-ditch attempt to win a round over Time? He continues to let Winston lead him farther away from the house, from Hank and Honey with their gray filmy hair and loose bodies, from his own age and ageing. He is sixty-four. No getting around that number. Winston circles a patch of grass next to an electrical pole and arches his back. Seth pulls out a plastic bag. A poop is about to happen. He knows the dance.

Their walk is long enough to pass through the gradual shift of darkness to light. All the while, Seth takes note of the countless times that Winston has lifted a hind leg to release a drop or two of pee on a tree, a pole, a blade of grass, after each object has been painstakingly sniffed out. He pauses while Winston deliberates, keeping the leash slack. Why pull it? Toward where? There is no destination, not at this hour or on this walk. Instead, he pauses and watches Winston scope out the new geography and asks himself what Winston is seeking to establish or declare by releasing a drop or two of liquid from deep inside onto these seemingly random bits outside him. A sense of propriety? Dominance? Permanence? In these moments, he wants to return to the house and get the down to the business of establishing a routine with Honey and Hank. They have a long road to travel. He wonders whether they are as dumbstruck as he is by the quantum leap they've made, especially at their age.

He gives a tenuous tug on the leash. "C'mon, boy. Let's go."

Winston cocks his head.

"Home."

* * * *

Long after the sun has risen and its rays have seared away the dreamy state of the early morning hours, Honey, Hank and Seth are still ambling along the streets. The beach has been forgotten this morning. The harsher light has announced that the time for ambling is over, that the demands of the day need to be attended to and checked off their respective to-do lists. They go about their errands: a trip to the hardware store, the produce market, the seafood outlet (all within walking distance, they've discovered). They take care of their lists but they take their time about it. Eventually they wend their way back home with their bags of purchases and enter slowly, hoping to find no one else in the house as they each make a beeline to the kitchen counter, where they slip the handles of the bags off their shoulders and take in that moment of delicious levitation they experience whenever they unburden themselves from the weight of their acquisitions. Quietly and efficiently they put their bounty away—personal items go in their bedroom and bathroom, communal items in the common drawers and shelves. They fear that their placement of the communal items may not be agreeable to the others. For them, it makes sense, even if the putting away of items in this place feels so odd. Throughout their enterprise of unloading items in the new house, they hear no stirrings from the others, just as they'd hoped. When they finish, they step onto the front patio, open its new screen door and go to the beach. It would be foolish not to. People work fifty-one weeks a year to be able to spend the one week remaining at a beach leading to an ocean. And here it is, in front of them, every day, the stuff of the rich and famous. They are neither, but they have it, this place where they can remind themselves of things larger and more significant than themselves, where they stand an excellent chance of bringing humility back into a life driven by self-concern. Especially at their age, and so late in the day. Or so they say to themselves as they realize that no place has been designated for storing the empty grocery bags.

 One by one, they go to the beach by the most direct route—through the screen door on the front porch. Hank is the only one to notice the squeaking sound of the door as it glides back to its frame. "I'll take care of it tomorrow," he thinks to himself, relieved that a sense of purpose, however minor, has already begun to announce itself. Honey is focused on the slate path that leads from the front porch to the dunes and the overgrowth of sand-daisy tendrils and sea-grape saplings that she'll need to prune before they take over. Seth is peering beyond their property line toward the "Y" to see if they are there (he is undecided about whether he wants to spot them there) and above the "Y" toward the residual light in the sky at this hour. Unlike the morning light, this light is on the wane and makes the beach feel entirely different, still wise and with important secrets, but weary after the day's travails. Morning is long gone. It is late in the day.

 One by one they arrive at the "Y." They can't help but end up there. Old habits die hard, they think to themselves, hoping the others are thinking the same thing. They form their triangle, as three points on any surface have no choice but to do. And they are glad for the company.

"Here we are," Honey says.

Hank looks out toward the horizon line with its blues and pinks and yellows that have little in common with their morning counterparts. These hues, he thinks, are paler. They're relinquishing some kind of power or intensity. "Yes," he says to Honey, "Here we are."

"Yes," says Seth, turning his head, first toward Hank, then toward Honey, then toward the sun sinking into the horizon behind his back in the west. He notices the paler colors too. They are as glorious as the display of color that the three of them have witnessed in silence so many mornings in the east. But at this hour, the sun is behind them. Will they too turn their heads around to make sure it's still there? He turns back to them. "Yes," he says again. "We're here. We are, aren't we?"

Honey opens her arms. "Yes, we are."

ABOUT ATMOSPHERE PRESS

Atmosphere Press is an independent, full-service publisher for excellent books in all genres and for all audiences. Learn more about what we do at atmospherepress.com.

We encourage you to check out some of Atmosphere's latest releases, which are available at Amazon.com and via order from your local bookstore:

Dancing with David, a novel by Siegfried Johnson
The Friendship Quilts, a novel by June Calender
My Significant Nobody, a novel by Stevie D. Parker
Nine Days, a novel by Judy Lannon
Shining New Testament: The Cloning of Jay Christ, a novel by Cliff Williamson
Shadows of Robyst, a novel by K. E. Maroudas
Home Within a Landscape, a novel by Alexey L. Kovalev
Motherhood, a novel by Siamak Vakili
Death, The Pharmacist, a novel by D. Ike Horst
Mystery of the Lost Years, a novel by Bobby J. Bixler
Bone Deep Bonds, a novel by B. G. Arnold
Terriers in the Jungle, a novel by Georja Umano
Into the Emerald Dream, a novel by Autumn Allen
His Name Was Ellis, a novel by Joseph Libonati
The Cup, a novel by D. P. Hardwick
The Empathy Academy, a novel by Dustin Grinnell
Tholocco's Wake, a novel by W. W. VanOverbeke
Dying to Live, a novel by Barbara Macpherson Reyelts
Looking for Lawson, a novel by Mark Kirby

ABOUT THE AUTHOR

Brett Shapiro is an American writer and the author the *Those Around Him,* a novel published in 2019. His best-selling memoir *L'Intruso* was published in Italy, where he lived for 25 years, and later became an award-winning film and theatrical production. He is the author of two children's books, one of which was the recipient of Austria's National Book Award. His short stories have been performed in theatres throughout Italy. He is a veteran writer for the United Nations and currently lives by the beach in Florida.

CPSIA information can be obtained
at www.ICGtesting.com
Printed in the USA
BVHW051200031122
651062BV00003B/132